The Fatah-Hamas Rift

The Fatah-Hamas Rift

An Analysis of Failed Negotiations

GADI HITMAN

Published by State University of New York Press, Albany

Printed in the United States of America

For information, contact State University of New York Press, Albany, NY
www.sunypress.edu

Library of Congress Cataloging-in-Publication Data

Name: Hitman, Gadi, author.
Title: The Fatah-Hamas rift : an analysis of failed negotiations / by Gadi Hitman.
Description: Albany : State University of New York Press, [2022] | Includes bibliographical references and index.
Identifiers: ISBN 9781438487038 (hardcover : alk. paper) | ISBN 9781438487052 (ebook)
Further information is available at the Library of Congress.

10 9 8 7 6 5 4 3 2 1

To my beloved parents, Miriam and Yoske,
March 2021

Contents

Introduction

In August 2020, during a global health epidemic, Israel and the United Arab Emirates announced cooperation, attempting to find a vaccine against the deadly virus. A few days later the two countries announced that they would sign a peace agreement between them. It was a visible move in the direction of trying to shape a new reality in the Middle East. The "Abraham agreement" was signed on September 14, 2020, between the two states at the White House, under the United States auspices.

The Israeli-Emirati political move provoked strong protest in the Palestinian system, with accusations against the Emirates of treason because the Palestinians had not yet fulfilled their vision of establishing an independent state. For the first time since 2013, representatives of all Palestinian organizations met and agreed to work together against the new agreement. This decision might have sounded like the beginning of a new friendship or at least a renewal of such a friendship, but it raised questions and doubts about the ability of the Palestinians to act together. This is mainly because there has been a political rift between the Palestinian Authority and Hamas since 2007, not to mention ideological disagreements that have been going on for decades.

The Israeli-Arab conflict, and within it the Israeli-Palestinian conflict, has been a constant topic of research writing for several decades. Despite significant changes in Israeli-Arab relations, the most notable of which are peace agreements with Egypt (1979) and Jordan (1994), and normative relations with other Arab states without signed agreements, the Palestinian question has not yet been resolved. For years, a leading perception among all those following developments in the Palestinian arena is that Israel is the most influential factor in this arena. It has exercised military rule in Judea and Samaria, also known as the West Bank, continuously since June 1967; it has established in these regions a broad settlement of half a million Jews; and it has overseen virtually uninterrupted security and settlement in these areas since June 1967. This was also the reality in the Gaza Strip before August 2005, when Israel unilaterally disengaged from that area and evacuated twenty-one settlements where some eight thousand Jews lived. Since then, Israeli influence on the Gaza Strip has continued through control of the crossing points between Gaza and Israel.

Even if we accept this description as historical fact, it cannot explain the geopolitical situation that has existed in the Palestinian arena since June 2007, when Hamas forcibly took control of the Gaza Strip. Since then, Palestinian society, which has common historical, legal, religious, and traditional roots, as well as a shared ethnic character, has been divided—geographically, politically, and ideologically. Despite having a common national ethos, consisting of a dream of liberating Palestine (which is dominated by foreign rule, that is, by Israel), returning refugees to their homes, commemorating the martyrs, and freeing prisoners, the Palestinian system is split. The Palestinian Authority (hereinafter PA) controls the West Bank and Hamas is the dominant political power in the Gaza Strip.

This book asks why: Why has the Palestinian leadership and the central, major political forces failed to solve the ongoing rift between them? Why did nine rounds of negotiations from 2007 to 2017—most with assistance from Arab mediators—not end with an accord accepted by both sides? In order to answer these questions, a comprehensive study requires examination of elements such as: theories about negotiations; negotiation as it is known in an Arab-Muslim culture; an examination of the Palestinian national ethos; and an analysis of the negotiation process between the parties, namely the Palestinian Authority (based on Fatah elements) and Hamas.

This book is mostly about the negotiations between the Palestinian Authority and Hamas from 2007 to 2017. Previous studies in the Palestinian arena did not discuss this issue, which has a significant impact on Palestinians. My main argument is that personal, sometimes also organizational, interests and a constant mutual lack of trust between the parties on national interests prevailed and negatively influenced the outcome of the negotiations. Moreover, I claim that both parties share a common national ethos, based on common history, language, customs, linkage to territory, Nakba memories, and feelings of victimhood; but over the years, the PA (dominated by the Fatah organization) and Hamas have developed different visions regarding the future of the Palestinian society.

The first chapter of the book focuses on theories relating to negotiation. The general assumption is that negotiations between rivals with different cultures are difficult, and that similar negotiations between rivals from the same culture are less complicated. Can people belonging to the same culture, with the same national ethos, more easily bridge gaps between them—or is it precisely because of this cultural closeness that they can see the other side of the dialogue as a rival, despite sharing the same culture, making the possibility of agreement less likely? Are leaders from both parties really interested in reaching an agreement or do they lack the readiness and maturity to put personal interests aside, as well as ideological concepts of their movements' interests? Since both parties are Muslim, I find it useful to discuss principles of dialogue within Islam alongside Western theories on negotiation. Basically, Western scholars suggest seven different variables in negotiation, and Islamic tradition adds five more components. The full list includes: (1) alternatives, (2) interests, (3) options, (4) legitimacy, (5) commitment, (6) communications, and (7) relationships. Muslim scholarship, which goes back to the days of Imam 'Ali, the fourth caliph in early Islam of the mid-seventh century (656–661), adds five more attributes: (1) knowledge, (2) leadership and responsibility, (3) variables, (4) patience and consistency, and (5) justice.

The second chapter discusses elements of the Palestinian ethos, shared by both sides. Following that, the question is how the secular and religious streams fail to bridge the gaps between them and unite forces to maintain the ethos. Following this, I argue that the geopolitical split that has existed in the Palestinian system since 2007 has created two Palestinian communities that differ in terms of vision and identity. This split has sharpened both parties' understanding that having political control within the Palestinian system is a prerequisite for resolving the Palestinian question (each side advocates a different solution). This necessity remains as a constant shadow in all rounds of negotiations between the Palestinian Authority and Hamas from February 2007 to October 2017. In fact, as of the completion of this book, it still prevents the two sides from resolving the rift between them—despite their shared Palestinian national ethos, which was developing throughout the twentieth century.

The rest of the book (chapter 4 onward) analyzes the negotiations between the parties from February 2007 to October 2017, based on the relevant theories on interactions between two rival parties. Usually, when two rival parties are in conflict, the expectation is to find a solution acceptable to both sides. Moreover, one may expect that both sides seek the best alternative to a negotiated agreement (BATNA)—which is the leading approach to analyzing negotiations.[1]

Looking closely into the Palestinian society, the evolution of political powers started during the era of the British Mandate in Palestine, or the Land of Israel (Eretz Israel). The major emergence of significant power was in the 1950s, when young, educated people such as Yasser Arafat, Khalil Al-Wazir (Abu-Jihad), Mahmood Abbas (Abu Mazen), and others founded the Palestinian Liberation Movement (Fatah) in 1959. These founders had three goals: to offer new, young, and authentic Palestinian leadership to refugees scattered in Arab countries after the 1948 war; to establish a military force capable of fighting for the return of Palestine to its rightful people; and to create a unique national identity for the Palestinians.[2] It is important at this point to mention Fatah's development over the years as an instrumental organization that has learned to change policies and procedures in order to maximize its interests. This was the case, for example, in the mid-1970s, when the Fatah leadership proved that it could pursue a policy that takes into consideration a political constraint. A prominent example was Fatah's decision to stop carrying out terrorist acts abroad, and the unofficial agreement between Israel and Fatah in the summer of 1981 on a ceasefire in southern Lebanon. Another example was Arafat's decision to turn to a political channel, in parallel with terrorism, as early as the October 1973 war, which culminated in the Oslo Accords (1993).[3] Following Fatah's foundation, the Palestinian Liberation Organization (PLO) was established in 1964, and after June 1967 it became the umbrella organization of seventeen different Palestinian military (some also political) groups that have been established to liberate Palestine. The PLO is an essentially secular organization. Over time, the organization has become the sole and exclusive representative of the Palestinian people.

The second stage of that political evolution occurred in December 1987, when Sheikh Ahmed Yassin founded Hamas, an Arabic acronym for Islamic resistance movement (Harakat al-Muqawama al-Islamiyya). This followed a long period of preparation, in which Yassin established a large-scale organizational and social infrastructure in the Gaza Strip that provided education, health, and welfare services to the public, and sought to establish a society based on Islamic law (*shari'a*). The religious framework also had a military wing (such as the PLO member organizations) that carried out terrorist attacks against Israel. Since its establishment, Hamas has challenged the PLO's political hegemony, which has created tension between the parties up to the present.

The PLO and Hamas have become the major political forces within the Palestinian arena. They shared, at least until 1993, a common vision of liberating Palestine from the Jews but are split over how to do so. They also have different views regarding the nature of the regime and the character of Palestinian society. In 1996, a serious rift developed between the parties after Arafat, who was head of the PLO and the Palestinian Authority that was founded in 1994 on the basis of the Oslo agreement signed with Israel, ordered his security forces to act violently against Hamas activists who carried out attacks against Israelis. Hamas activists were arrested, tortured, and humiliated, publicly. Hamas's response came in 2007, when the movement seized control of the Gaza Strip and engaged in severe retaliation against the Palestinian Authority security forces and Fatah members.

After the 1996 conflict, the two sides maintained respectable relations, but Hamas never recognized the Oslo Accords and continued to be an ideological and political opposition to the PA. It formed a party whose representatives served on the Palestinian Legislative Council and represented Hamas's religious ideology. Throughout the second Palestinian uprising (intifada), the Palestinian Authority was ineffective in preventing Hamas's terror attacks against Israel. The death of Yasser Arafat in November 2004, who was praised by Hamas as a Palestinian national symbol and a member of a religious family, enabled Hamas to start challenging the PA's hegemony in the Palestinian political arena.

Since June 2007, the Palestinian arena has, in fact, contained two separate entities: the West Bank and the Gaza Strip. Abu Mazen is the elected Palestinian president (the last elections were in 2005), who has control of the West Bank, and Hamas is the dominant political power in Gaza. Ever since June 2007, there has been a geopolitical crisis between the parties. As a result, the two sides have had nine rounds of negotiations, trying to reach a reconciliation agreement that would allow them to achieve national goals. In three cases the mediator was Egypt, and in other rounds, mediation has been divided between Saudi Arabia, Qatar, Syria, and Yemen.

Finally, the Middle East region has witnessed turmoil starting in December 2010. These upheavals focused academic research on phenomena such as the struggle between Sunni and Shia, the development of the Islamic State, and the fate of the millions who became refugees due to civil wars. These events have led to a dearth of studies on the Palestinian issue. Studies have been published on various topics related to the Palestinian system. For instance, Leech and Simanovsky discuss, separately, Salam Fayyad's plan to build the Palestinian Authority's institutions, Kanfani checks the Palestinian economy, while others analyze what led to the failure of the political process between Israel and the Palestinians.[4] As for Hamas, Nüsse offers her perspective on Hamas's ideology, and Gleis and Berti compare Hamas and Hezbollah. Others explore Israel-Hamas interactions during military clashes (Operation Cast Lead, 2008–2009; Pillar of Clouds, 2012; and Operation Protective Edge, 2014) and the ramifications of these collisions on the population.[5] None has analyzed the political rift between the Palestinian Authority and Hamas, as this book seeks to do.

Chapter 1

Theoretical Framework for Negotiation

Negotiation is a daily habit. It is a social process of decision-making in which parties are mutually dependent on each other. While formal definitions of negotiation vary, theorists do accept certain basic tenets. Foremost among them is the assumption that parties who negotiate agree in at least one fundamental respect: they share a belief that their respective purposes will be better served by entering into negotiation with the other party. If they do not agree on that basic perception, why bother to discuss matters in the first place?

The process of negotiation has two different, however inseparable, aspects, that are important to introduce at the beginning of the discussion: strategy and tactic. Strategy is "a careful plan or method, especially for achieving an end." Whereas the use of tactics refers to "the skill of using available means" to reach that end. The term strategy has almost always been defined as a deliberate, conscious set of guidelines that determines decisions into the future. In military or negotiation theory, strategy is "the utilization during both peace and war, of all of the nation's forces, through large-scale, long range planning and development, to ensure security and victory."[1]

Everybody negotiates in different cycles whether at home, work, shopping, the business world, or diplomacy. People have three reasons to negotiate: they want to acquire something from someone; they want to create something that they cannot create alone and therefore must ask for assistance from other people; they want to solve a conflict. When it comes to politics, Iklé and Leites suggest that "to construct a model of negotiations between two countries (or between two opposing alliances) we initially make the following simplifying assumption: the negotiations deal with an agreement where the two sides have a conflict of interest in only one set of mutually exclusive alternatives, A, B, C, . . . N; and one side always prefers A to B, B to C, . . . (N–1) to N, while the preferences of the other side are in reverse order."[2] This assumption can provide a theoretical platform for analyzing the Palestinian Authority and Hamas's interests through the nine rounds of negotiation. In this respect, it is critical to check whether the mutual Palestinian national ethos can serve as a basis for bridging the Fatah and Hamas stance gaps to create political unity for the national cause. It is also important to explore to what extent the two parties are ready to make concessions, meaning to drop topics that the other side will never agree to compromise on.

In their seminal study *Getting to Yes* Fisher, Ury, and Patton supply a theoretical basis for negotiation between two parties who are not necessarily rivals. They offer four different variables involved in negotiation:[3]

1. People. People act and behave, automatically, based on a combination of emotions and rationality. They embrace their behavior and positions with respect to different issues according to a worldview that is shaped by life experience, accumulated experiences, values, beliefs, norms, and visions of the future. Naturally, they have different positions, goals, or interests. When they enter negotiations, they always have an opening position aimed at maximizing all the interests of the public on their way to realizing the vision. People reach most decisions through negotiation. If there is an agreed-upon accord and it fits with the parties' opening stances, it increases their chances to maximize their interests. People have two ways to negotiate: soft or hard. The soft negotiator seeks to avoid personal conflict and looks for an agreement. The hard negotiator perceives the dialogue process as a contest; therefore, the situation becomes a "zero-sum game," where the winner takes all. People can take approaches that are in between soft and hard: a negotiator can look for mutual gains if that is possible, and at the same time adopt an uncompromising position when it conflicts with his or her interests. Finally,

it is recommended to distinguish between people and problems, a separation that is not easy in a negotiation such as the internal Palestinian one.

2. Interest is the aspiration of a social entity (individual, institution, or social group) to achieve a specific goal, for which it is ready to act. We all have different sorts of interests that can be divided into short- and long-term interests. Moreover, we can classify interests as follows:

    a. Mutual interest—an interest shared by two parties striving to achieve the same goal, such as two people becoming business partners.

    b. Complementary interests—interests of two people seeking to achieve different goals, which can only be done through an agreement after negotiation. A good example is a negotiation between an asset lessor and an asset lessee.

    c. Conflict interests—interests associated with a political negotiation that takes place after the parties realize that they cannot satisfy their interests by themselves.

    d. Overt interests—visible interests that each negotiating party presents to the other.

    e. Covert interests—interests that one party or both parties in the negotiations conceal during the talks.

When people enter a negotiation, it is important for them to concentrate on achieving their interests. As Fisher, Ury, and Patton explain, "Your position is something you have decided upon. Your interests are what caused you to so decide."[4] Once negotiation starts it is important to identify the interests of the other party. It is reasonable to assume that each party has several interests with different priorities underlying their position through the negotiation process. As the negotiations get longer, it must be considered that interests can change and that their prioritization will be different, due to, inter alia, proposals from the other party.

3. Options. In negotiations, options are possible solutions to a problem shared by two or more parties. Often, when

people negotiate, they tend to stick to their first plan in order to maximize their profit. This pattern of behavior makes them blind to, and unable to think of, different options that might have enabled them to break the deadlock and reach the solution they seek, perhaps even to increase their profits. It is important to generate a variety of options before entering into dialogue. A process of brainstorming, where people are allowed to suggest ideas, may be beneficial. Naturally, every negotiator wants to achieve as many interests as possible during the talks, but at the same time it is right to prepare second or even third options in case the negotiator needs them. This can be beneficial for a number of reasons: first, to initiate a move the other party did not think of; second, to respond to the other party's proposal with a counteroffer; and third, to prove to the other party that one is a willing to be flexible in order to reach an agreement that is a victory for both parties (win-win situation). A softer style and a willingness to compromise should not be automatically seen as weaknesses, but as advantages over barricading oneself and demonstrating a stubborn stance that does not allow progress and reaching an agreement through negotiation aimed at achieving reconciliation.

4. Criteria. Objective criteria are independent standards used in negotiation that are factual and therefore fair to both sides. Since negotiation is in fact an arena of battle among different wills, objective criteria support the three requirements for successful negotiation: First, fairness. Objective criteria relying on precedent, scientific merit, and community practices strengthen the agreement—it is less vulnerable to attack, and both sides are more likely to ensure smooth implementation. Second, efficiency. The negotiation process is more efficient and less adversarial when the two sides focus on standards and solutions, rather than on forcing their position on the other side. Third, a better working relationship; having avoided a battle for dominance, the two sides are more likely to work cooperatively in the future.

Being mindful of these variables, each side asks to enter negotiation from a powerful position. Power in negotiation can be defined as the probability that a negotiator will influence a negotiation in the direction of his or her ideal outcome. The search for power relies on the assumption that it helps to achieve maximum interests. Power in negotiation derives from four different sources: alternatives, information, status, and social capital.[5]

Alternatives are related to the BATNA (best alternative to a negotiated agreement) model, which is the most advantageous alternative course of action a party can take if negotiations fail and an agreement cannot be reached. The exact opposite of this option is the WATNA (worst alternative to a negotiated agreement). Negotiators have greater power when they have more, and more valuable, alternatives. A valuable outside offer allows a negotiator to put pressure on the opponent, for example, by threatening to leave the bargaining table if the value of one's BATNA is not met. Power can come from multiple alternatives because it is an advantage for one party when the other side has only one option. This creates an unequal equation around the discussion table and forces the other side to recalculate because the first party has more than one alternative for successfully concluding the negotiations.

Gathering information early, especially about the other side's interests, vision, preferences, and reservations, can be important for achieving one's goals. It gives time to prepare in advance of the start of talks. Such information allows one party to open the dialogue with more than one alternative, so that the other side may find itself in an inferior and disadvantageous position, perhaps even on the defensive. Negotiators can gain information in three ways. First, they can do their homework and search for information prior to the negotiation. Second, they can ask the other side for information during the talks. Third, they can try guessing what the other party's position is. Focusing on the case study of the Palestinian Authority and Hamas interactions since 2007, each side has tried to have as much information as possible about the other side's position before negotiations opened, as we will see.

Status is the extent to which a negotiator is respected by the other side.[6] If one side in the negotiations dismisses the other, it will not take the other's positions seriously in dialogue. If one side goes in the opposite direction, by overestimating the other, it will be overly respectful of the other's positions and may compromise when it is not necessary. The more the parties respect each other, the more balanced the discussion will be.

Social capital as a source of power is being used by scholars in relation to subjects such as finding jobs, market information, or the business world.[7] The concept is simple: the more people are connected to others—directly or indirectly—the greater their chances to have relevant information for achieving their interest growth. But social capital can also be relevant to political negotiations, mainly during preparation time before the dialogues begin. Negotiators can acquire ideas from as many people as possible before they formulate the alternatives and their opening position in the negotiations. Not only that, but by gathering information from social media, leaders and negotiators can get an indication of the public's interests.

Obviously, all of these are relevant to the nine rounds of negotiations that took place between Fatah (or the Fatah-dominated Palestinian Authority) and Hamas from February 2007 to October 2017, trying to end the political crisis between the parties. But are all of these parameters, offered by Western scholars, for analyzing two rivals in the Islamic world, valid or are there other important aspects to consider, such as cultural characteristics, the dimension of time, the effects of negotiations and their consequences not only on participants but also on the groups they represent? And what about the style during calls between parties? Should they be managed in soft or firm tones? With condescension or consideration? Or is it more appropriate and relevant to use these elements interchangeably during and after the dialogue?

Moreover, if we accept Fisher, Kopelman, and Schneider's theory, negotiation also requires good communication between the parties, which means not only presenting your side but also similarly listening to the other.[8] Fisher, a professor of law, and his colleague assumed that both parties wished to maintain their connection after reaching an agreement.

In discussing cooperation, Robert Axelrod suggests that there is no need to assume trust between the two parties, because the use of reciprocity can be enough to work together. He also argues that no central authority is needed: Cooperation based on reciprocity can be self-policing. This theory works regarding Western cultures but is not applicable to negotiation in Muslim society, as I will discuss later.[9]

This hypothesis needs rethinking while exploring the Palestinian Authority and Hamas interaction, especially when the two parties have de facto sovereignty in different territories. The purpose of the study is to analyze the talks between the parties, to explore which of the four variables had an influence on the participants, and to try to answer these questions: What stands between the parties and a successful agreement? Is it difference of ideology, a lack of trust between the parties, a political fight over hegemony in the Palestinian society, or another reason?

At this point a significant perceptual angle to the subject of the book should be pointed out: In general, ever since Western research on the Middle East began, various scholars have tried to offer explanations for trends and phenomena occurring in the region based on terms used in the West, such as nationalism, pluralism, or democracy.[10] In the Middle East, all of these terms take on a different meaning and it appears, therefore, that Western theories cannot explain social or political developments in other regions, such as the Middle East. This concern, seeing the Middle East through Western glasses, also applies to the issue of negotiation. But here, there is a significant difference. Negotiation, as a phenomenon, also existed in ancient Islam. Both the Palestinian Authority and Hamas are mainly Muslim; therefore, it is required to review the subject of negotiation in Islam, and to identify if there are any impacts of the Muslim heritage of Islam on the internal Palestinian dialogue. 'Ali bin abu Taleb, the fourth caliph in early Islam (656–661) and the prophet Muhammad's cousin, is considered the founder of negotiation in Islam and the person who wrote the Khodibiya contract in 628. 'Ali explained that the first verse Gabriel revealed to Muhammad was, "Recite in the name of your Lord who created man from a clinging substance. Recite and your Lord is the most Generous, who taught by the pen, taught man that which he knew not."[11]

Saeb Erekat, a political scientist and senior Palestinian statesman who negotiated with Israel on the Oslo Accords (1993), analyzed the negotiations that the prophet Muhammad had with the people of the Quraish tribe, following his divine revelation and receipt of the Qur'an. Three different delegations of the tribe offered him respect, status of influence, and assets that would normally make him the most important man in the tribe. They also explained to him how severe a step he took when he proposed a new religion that split the tribes in two. For his part, he explained that he was not looking for assets. He was committed to divine revelation. In other words, they offered to give up what was important to them and not what was important to him; therefore, this negotiation was doomed to failure. Regarding mutual respect between subjects and other people, it is worth mentioning that during the signing of the Khodibiya agreement, the prophet Muhammad did not object to removing the words "the messenger of God" and was willing to call himself Muhammad bin Abdullah, expressing that it was the content of the agreement rather than honor that was important to him. Recognizing that he was the weaker side at the time, the Khodibiya pact was agreed upon. Muhammad's interest was to spread—as far as possible—a new divine religion. Therefore, his goal was to live peacefully with the Quraish people. This is a historical example that accurately illustrates the theoretical model presented earlier: focus on the interests and problem solving rather than on the people.[12]

'Ali followed the Prophet when he suggested that interest in Islam is an outcome of Islamic law (*shari'a*). According to Imam 'Ali, opportunities to reach a good agreement lie in identifying the interests for both parties concerned—that is, interest based on certainty, which comes only if people subordinate to God (Allah). If people believe in Allah and do good deeds based on that belief, then satisfying one's interest is attainable, perhaps even assured, since the foundation is the Islamic law. Every person needs to identify when an interest is possible to attain (in this situation not to hesitate) and when that is not possible (then it is better to wait). One question that this study investigates is whether Fatah or Hamas introduced basic sharia interests during the discussions.

A similar question can be asked about the relationship between Fatah and Hamas. According to Islamic tradition, which began in 'Ali's era, the recipe for good relationships is as follows: "Mix with people in a manner that if you pass away they will cry for you and if you live they will show you sympathy."[13] All rounds of talks between the parties—in Cairo, Doha, or elsewhere—opened with mutual greetings but ended with agreements that neither side could fulfill or without an agreement at all. Other components that Western scholars suggest for a successful negotiation, such as alternatives (options), legitimacy, communication, and commitment were well known to ancestors of today's Islamic leaders. 'Ali added five more elements than are found in Western thought that may be very useful to negotiators. Their relevancy for this study is high because it deals with inter-Muslim negotiation:

1. Knowledge. The holy bible of Islam, the Qur'an, says: "Allah will raise those who have believed among you and those who were given knowledge, by degree."[14] 'Ali believed that no negotiation will be a full one if people do not know how to link the process with the final results. The right way to do it is only by connecting with the

other side, mutual listening, and seeking solutions. In other words, knowledge is a gift from God, and people should train their minds and seek facts. Therefore, a comprehensive negotiation requires knowledge, which is metaphorical, and means God's presence around the table. If possible, it is better to get information about the other side's preferences, meaning that knowledge is power during the time of negotiation.

2. Leadership and responsibility. Modern literature distinguishes between two types of leader: transformational and transactional. In short, the former focuses on people and striving to be a mentor to them. The latter centers on targets or goals.[15] For Imam 'Ali, back in the seventh century, leadership included responsibility and the ability to be able at the same time to organize the work, to be patient, to show mercy, to forgive, and to make decisions. Careful preparation prevents both chaos and confusion within the community, as well as confusion and embarrassment during negotiation. 'Ali's thought was that leadership and organization are considered the main foundations of negotiation. Moreover, people need to agree on one accepted leader, because the worst situation in which people can live is to have multiple emirs or authorities. 'Ali's perspective is relevant for Hamas and Fatah, because in ancient times the community was divided between those who joined the messenger of God and those who opposed him.[16] Just as there was a split in the seventh century within the Islamic world, so was there a split in the Palestinian arena; therefore, the principles established by the Imam regarding negotiation are also relevant to the analysis of dialogue between two Muslim sides in modern times, regardless of their level of religiosity. Clearly, if people elect their leader, as in the case of Abu Mazen for Palestinian president in 2005 and Ismail Haniyeh, Hamas's prime minister in the 2006 elections, both leaders enjoy legitimacy while negotiating with each other.

3. Variables. Erekat used the term variables to describe two behavioral patterns of people: first, to acknowledge that

the world is changing, and accordingly, to respond to environmental change. Second, to recognize that it is right to do good deeds for others.[17] It seems that the term elasticity is more appropriate for these behaviors and is also relevant to negotiating, with the understanding that the parties' positions can change, and in principle, an agreement must be reached between the communities that both parties represent. Also, 'Ali was aware that the term good is subjective and that what is good for one side is not necessarily good for the other. In a discussion of two-party negotiations that do not lead to a win-win situation, this is an important point that requires consideration and analysis of the interests of both parties.

4. Patience and consistency. 'Ali learned about the virtues of patience and perseverance from the prophet Muhammad, who said, "Victory is brought about by patience." 'Ali reiterates the same concept saying, "Patience is of two kinds: patience over what pains you, and patience against what you covet."[18] Both virtues derive, according to 'Ali, from faith in Allah, and that faith has four columns—endurance, conviction, justice, and jihad. Endurance itself, however, is a virtue that has four attributes: eagerness, fear, piety, and anticipation. If you have this full basket of virtues before entering a negotiation, you increase the chance of achieving maximum interests. The central message of Imam 'Ali's legacy is that patience and consistency are necessary for victory. In the case of Fatah and Hamas, victory can be a win-win agreement for both parties. 'Ali made a direct linkage between patience and consistency, and knowledge and wisdom, arguing that if a person has these characteristics, one then has supremacy over other people. This situation provides this person an advantage during negotiation. It allows one to negotiate persistently and tolerantly, utilizing knowledge and wisdom to achieve the required interests. However, make sure that perseverance does not become unnecessary insistence, which does not allow for as much flexibility of mind as is required to reach the desired agreement. To conclude this point,

for 'Ali, patience is resistance to calamities, and fear is an adversity—therefore patience is good, and fear is bad and ugly.

5. Justice is the optimal termination of any negotiation, when both parties feel they have reached a just agreement. If one side feels an outcome is unjust, dissatisfaction can lead to protests and violence to the point of bloodshed. Imam 'Ali was aware of all this when he wrote, "Use justice and beware of tyranny and injustice. Injustice causes bitterness, and tyranny leads to the sword [war]. Injustice is the cause of division, wars, and conflicts. It cannot last forever no matter how strong those who exercise it are."[19] Fourteen centuries later it seems that this description reflects the Fatah-Hamas interaction, considering the fact that nine rounds of discussions did not lead to a just accord. In 'Ali's interpretation, justice has four aspects: depth of understanding, profoundness of knowledge, fairness of judgment, and clearness of mind. He made a direct linkage between justice and faith, claiming, "Who exaggerates enmity commits an act of injustice, and whoever undermines it is oppressed. Those living in conflict and enmity cannot worship Allah."[20] This statement of 'Ali is also relevant to the subject of the study not only because both sides are Muslim, but also because one side, that of Hamas, is characterized by religious piety. This situation leads, almost automatically, to the question of whether Hamas is prepared to sign an unjust agreement in its view, because signing such an agreement would in fact be heretical. 'Ali's statement may suggest that a just agreement requires patience and perseverance from both sides.

To conclude theoretical aspects of required virtues, attributes, and skills for a successful negotiator, these are the characteristics:

1. Loyalty and integrity. A negotiator must be a person with loyalty and integrity vis-à-vis three elements—his or her—constituencies, him or herself, and the other side. If

negotiators turn their backs on the truth, they will betray themselves, the trust of their constituents, and the trust of the other party with whom they negotiate. The issue of trust in negotiation situations is a key factor in the success of the whole process, because if there is no trust between the parties, the chance of success is small. There are those who argue that trust should not necessarily be considered in situations involving morality; but in the case of the PA-Hamas dialogue, as we shall see later, the two sides judged the level of morality of the other side, especially in all that pertained to the relationship between them. The heavy weight given to the morality of the other side influenced the outcome of the negotiations.[21]

2. Commitment. Simply carry out the obligations that you, as negotiator and decision maker, have promised. If not, you lose credibility and trust.

3. Courage. If the negotiator is also the decision maker and the leader, he or she must be brave to implement a signed accord. If the negotiator is not the decision maker, he or she must have enough bravery to tell the decision maker what is needed for a successful negotiation before the dialogue begins, during the discussions, and of course after signing an agreement.

4. Focusing on the interests of people means to think with the head and not with the heart. Determine your interests before opening negotiations, rank them in order of importance, present them eloquently during conversations, and avoid as much as possible discussions on topics that you have not prepared or do not understand, so as not to commit to things that cannot be realized in the future.

5. Based on facts. In any negotiation avoid presenting arguments that have different interpretations. If the negotiation is between two Muslim rivals, be aware of quoting from the Qur'an, because this holy book for Muslims is subject to dissimilar understandings.

6. Wisdom is a term that embodies discretion, thoughtfulness, patience, perseverance, and tolerance. The aforementioned

> are acquired traits that a smart personality can develop through experience, and thus avoid mistakes. Since negotiation processes are dynamic and have changing situations, wisdom is required to identify threats and opportunities in order to maximize profits. While highlighting positive skills, wisdom is also beneficial for hiding negative ones. A negotiator who stays calm, not angry or frustrated, and who treats his or her colleagues and rivals without superiority, has wisdom. Imam 'Ali relied on God's (Allah's), words, according to the Qur'an, which were: "Invite to the way of your Lord with wisdom and good instruction and argue with them in a way that is best." According to 'Ali, the prophet Muhammad negotiated with his opponents according to the divine commandment and acted wisely, because at the end of the process he achieved his goals.[22]

Alon and Brett's research focuses on the perception of time during negotiations in the Arabic-speaking Islamic world.[23] The purpose of their study, as they put it, is to "encourage negotiators from the West to be more knowledgeable about the way they, as well as negotiators from Arabic-speaking Islamic cultures, use time in negotiations. Time influences bargaining, trust, and negotiation tactics, including stall-and-delay tactics, the use of the past as an objective standard, and limits on negotiating the future."[24] They conclude that conceptualization of time is culture dependent, and the conceptualization of time in Arabic-speaking Islamic culture varies in important ways from the conceptualization of time in Western culture. However, their conclusions are based on comparative research between Western culture (Western Europe and North America) and Middle Eastern countries, where Islam is the main religion and the language is Arabic.

In Islam, the heavenly domain dominates the earthly domain: believers must act with the knowledge that they will stand trial on Judgment Day.[25] This belief meets the criteria of knowledge, suggested back in the seventh century by Imam 'Ali. Knowledge combines with patience to form a preference for event time over clock time. Social time, in contrast to clock time, is described as "the patterns and orientations that relate to social processes and to the conceptualization of the ordering of social life."[26] Arabic-speaking Islamic culture is more event-time oriented and less clock-time oriented. As early as in 1963, Pierre Bourdieu described event time in the Arab world as follows: "There are not precise hours for meals; they are eaten whenever the preparation is complete, and eating is leisurely. The notion of an exact appointment is unknown; they agree only to meet 'at the next market.'"[27] The PA-Hamas negotiations were characterized by long intervals between one round of negotiation to another.

In Arabic-speaking Islamic culture, bargaining is regarded in a more favorable light. It is not viewed as inefficient, but rather as a trust-building mechanism, whose essence is its lengthiness.[28] A Syrian proverb encourages bargaining and yet emphasizes trust: "Haggle as smartly as you wish, but do not cheat on the scales!" In the previous article I cited, Fuad Khuri suggests a rule that the duration of negotiation should be proportional to the value of the goods. Therefore, in the Arab and Muslim world negotiators do not enter immediately into dialogue. They start with small talk to learn about each other, perhaps collecting pieces of information to expand their knowledge—an important stage according to Imam 'Ali—before talking business. Patience, or *sabr* in Arabic, is recommended because time works for and not against the believer. This tradition has been promoted by ethics, norms, and values since the early days of Islam.

In the case before us, based on measures of spirit, persistence, and value of goods in political terms, it can be argued that both sides—the Palestinian Authority and Hamas—are leisurely taking their time out of awareness of what the political goods on the discussion table are worth. That means that no matter how long negotiation takes, a Muslim true believer who has wisdom and patience will not sign an accord that does not match his interests. For the agreement to be signed, both parties must build a high enough degree of trust and be assured that the other party is not trying to mislead or harm them by reaching an agreement. The long mutual history of the Palestinian national (and religious) movements, including direct and indirect dialogue with various actors in the Middle East, teaches both sides to respect and to suspect their potential rivals. When the two political streams—the secular and the religious—became rivals, it appears that they will not rush to sign an agreement.

Tanya Alfredson and Azeta Cungu mapped five different types of negotiations between people and parties:[29]

1. Structural approach. This approach considers negotiated outcomes to be a function of the characteristics or structural features that define each particular negotiation. These

characteristics may include features such as the number of parties and issues involved in the negotiation and their composition. It argues that this approach is stressing the "explanations of outcomes in patterns of relationships between parties or their goals." In structural approaches to negotiation theory, analysts tend to define negotiations as conflict scenarios between opponents who maintain incompatible goals. This was the case between Catholics and Protestants in Northern Ireland. This approach, though not alone, could fit with the analysis of the PA-Hamas negotiations from 2007 to 2017. It can map a two-player structure in direct negotiations or three-player negotiations if mediation is involved. It is also relevant because the goals of the parties are different, and they themselves refer to the negotiations as a competition arena where the winner takes all. But this is only what I define as the technical aspect of the negotiation between the Palestinian political forces. The reason for my claim is not only because the stronger side does not always win. Even if we agree to this argument and accept that the structural approach highlights power as the major component defining the parties' odds of maximizing their interests, it still ignores the influence of other variables, such as the history of previous dialogue between people/parties, the personal behavior of people during discussions, attributes such as patience and tolerance, time as strategic element, and justice. All these virtues have already been suggested by Imam 'Ali for a successful Muslim dialogue.

2. Strategic approach. This approach considers strategy as "a plan, method, or series of maneuvers for obtaining a specific goal or result."[30] It has roots in mathematics, decision theory, and rational choice theory; it benefits from major contributions in the areas of economics, biology, and conflict analysis; and it focuses on final results, meaning the ends. This focus is rational because negotiators concentrate on interests and not on people. Mostly, such a negotiator calculates the cost-benefits of the options he or she has before deciding—rationally—which option maximizes profits. Seemingly, the choice of this approach seems informed and

logical. However, it ignores aspects of past participation and mutual suspicion between parties, such as in the case of the Palestinian Authority and Hamas. It also does not consider the various personality traits of actors, including those that focus on themselves and not the public they represent.

3. Behavioral approach. This approach originated from psychological and experimental traditions, but also from centuries-old diplomatic treaties. These traditions share the perspective that negotiations—whether between nations, employers and unions, or neighbors—are ultimately about the individuals involved. Naturally, it concentrates on the role of personalities—human tendencies, emotions and skills, in this case, those of the negotiators on both sides. It stresses the interactions between the negotiating parties (shopkeeper and customers, for instance) and classifies negotiators as hard liners or soft liners.

In 1958, Deutsch had already articulated three different types of personalities in negotiations: the first one was the cooperative type who "was led to feel that the welfare of the other person as well as his own welfare was of concern to him and that the other person felt the same way." The second was the individualistic type, who "felt that his only interest was in doing as well for himself as he could without regard to how well the other person did and to the other person feeling the same way." The third one was the competitive type, who "felt that he wanted to do as well as he could for himself and that he also wanted to do better than the other person and that the other person felt the same way."[31]

Some scholars argue that a tough negotiator and a hard liner are likely to gain more of their demands in a negotiated solution. The tradeoff is that in adopting this stance, they are less likely to conclude an agreement at all. My suggested contribution at this point is that any negotiator can be a hard/soft liner at the same time in every negotiation. That simply means that a negotiator can adopt a rigid stance on one issue discussed between the parties and in the same negotiation take a softer stance on another issue. In addition, the fact that negotiations last for a long time can also affect the negotiator's positions, meaning that he or she can change position from hard to soft and vice versa. In sum, soft of hard position is basically a question of flexibility in respect to interests.

Other researchers from the behavioral school have emphasized factors such as relationships, culture, norms, attitudes, expectations, and trust. This approach seems relevant and helpful for analyzing the rounds of negotiation between the Palestinian Authority and Hamas. It embodies attributes such as communication, patience, consistency, and responsibility, which Imam 'Ali believed a negotiator needs for a successful outcome. It also enables us to explore what types of personality the PA and Hamas representatives have, and how the personality component has affected the outcome of the negotiations between the parties.

4. Processual approach. This approach looks at negotiation "as a learning process in which parties react to each other's concession behavior."[32] We can take this description a step further. Negotiation between two (or more) parties needs time, which means it is a process. Metaphorically, it is a tango, as the parties progress one step forward and two steps back, until agreements or negotiations reach a deadlock. Each side tries to learn the other's behavior (not only possible concessions) and when necessary, they take a break to reassess their positions. At this point in the dialogue process, they can stick to their primary stance or they can change it—if they conclude that it does not serve their vision, interests, or goals. Leadership, courage, responsibility, and commitment to the public are recommended attributes during this process of reevaluation of the negotiator's positions. The greater the flexibility of the mind, which allows it to soften or harden positions in its own interest or in that of the public it represents, the more likely it is that the negotiation process will achieve a good outcome. Moreover, according to Imam 'Ali, this pattern of behavior increases the negotiator's legitimacy within his or her community to be their representative. The negotiation process between Israel and the Palestinians (1991, Madrid Conference; 1993, Oslo Accord) included ten rounds of talks in Washington is a good example of the processual approach.

5. Integrative approach. This approach sees negotiation as the frame for a win-win situation, in which the dialogue is a tool to maximize interests for both parties. In contrast to the zero-sum perspective, the integrative view looks to

> expand the profits, so that there is more to share between parties as a result of negotiation. This approach has objective criteria such as mutual gain, cooperation, exchange of information, mutual identification of problems and solutions, and decision-making. The integrative approach identifies three different phases of negotiation: the first is the diagnostic phase, which focuses on mapping the problems and looking for optional solutions. This phase precedes the opening point of the negotiations and can also be defined as the stage of dialogue preparation. The second stage is the formula phase, which concentrates on delineating a basis for mutually agreed on principles for signing an accord. The chance of reaching a successful formula increases if parties are willing to share information openly, considering the perspective of the other side, and if they have an interest in building upon commonly shared principles or values. The last stage is the details phase, where both parties translate the principles into specific details and practical steps. The more both sides understand each other, the less confidence-building measures are needed. However, it is important to notice that in practice, the three phases do not necessarily fall in this sequence, and often negotiators move back and forth between phases. This pattern of dialogue—moving forward and back—is one of the characteristics of the PA-Hamas negotiations.

Table 1.1 summarizes the main points of the various approaches. Based on these theories, I am suggesting an approach or combined approaches apply to the case study of the Palestinian Authority and Hamas interactions from 2007 to 2017.

The basic premise of this study is that a three-pronged approach is needed to analyze the PA and Hamas negotiation rounds from 2007 to 2017. The structural, behavioral, and intersectional approaches can be a theoretical basis for this, plus one component of the strategic approach: rationality in decision-making. The structural approach provides the framework for identifying the participants within the dialogue: PA and Hamas representatives and the different mediators. The processual approach allows monitoring of the progress of the negotiations, the will-

Table 1.1. Negotiation Approaches and Their Suitability to PA-Hamas Dialogue

Approach	Basic features	Assumptions	Limitations	Relevancy
Structural	Focus on means, positions, and power	Win-Lose	Being locked into positions might lead to lost opportunity for mutually beneficial agreement; overemphasis on power	Positive, although not by itself
Strategic	Focus on ends, rationality, positions	Win-Lose, existence of optimal solutions and rationality of players	Excludes use of power, players undifferentiated (apart from differences in the quality of options open to each)	Negative
Behavioral	Focus on personality traits	Win-Lose, role of perceptions and expectations	Emphasis on positions	Positive, although not by itself
Processual	Focus on concession-making behavior, positions	Win-Lose, moves as learned (reactive) responses	Emphasis on positions; lack of predictiveness	Positive, although not by itself
Integrative	Focus on problem solving, creating value, communicating, win-win solutions	Win-Win potential	Parties should still recognize and be prepared for encounters with nonintegrative; time-consuming for bargainers	Negative

ingness of players to compromise or consolidate their positions on the timeline, and to identify turnarounds if these are present in the talks. The behavioral approach supplies the tools for analyzing each side's declaration relating to the topics in discussions, the attitude toward the other side, and to evaluate their decision. For this purpose, the main argument is that each side's decisions were made from a rational stance, which is a component of the strategic approach. Rationalism here refers to both parties' understanding that an agreed-upon accord would harm their current political power. There we can demarcate the theoretical basis of the study as shown in the chart 1.1.

Structural + Behavioral + Processual + Rational	PA-Hamas Negotiations from 2007 to 2017

Chart 1.1. Theoretical Basis of the Study

The questions this study will focus on will be: What was the character of the dialogue between the actors prior to, during, and after the "peak" of the conflict/crisis? To what extent has the dialogue been successful? What determines whether a dialogue can succeed or not? What theory or theories can explain the nature of the PA-Hamas negotiations?

Chapter 2

The National Palestinian Ethos

National Ethos—Theoretical Aspects

The word ethos has its origins in Greek. It means morality or showing a moral character. Aristotle was among the first to discuss it, writing that the virtues of mankind are divisible into two kinds: intellectual and moral. The former is inherent in a person from birth. The latter needs time and experience to acquire. Ethos is in fact the habit (or set of habits) that determine everyone's beliefs, values, and behavior. The more who believe in the same values, the greater the odds for creating a collective ethos. In ancient Greece, Aristotle linked "good ethos" with law and justice.[1] We can then define ethos as the stories that a given group tells itself about itself. It is the shared history, values, memories, beliefs and legacy of a collective community.

The national ethos of a political entity derives from the array of shared particularistic values and traditions that form a people's visions of its future and past. The ethos integrates the community into feeling a common mutual destiny and forms the foundations of its unique identity as a distinctive social, as well as political, group. The integrative ethos also constitutes the moral source for the national community's informal social controls. It enforces commitments upon society and drives its members into a largely voluntary social order. Ethos is widely defined as the configuration of central societal beliefs that provide a unique orientation to a society. It combines dominant societal beliefs into a structure and forms conditions necessary for social systems to function, acting as lenses through which each member perceives and comprehends the spirit of his social group. Thus, the ethos of a collective group of people who strive to be a nation is, in fact, one of the most important key factors in a people's ability to unite into a cohesive society.[2] National ethos is composed of three basic constituents: a sense of collective victimhood, a feeling of victory, and a belief in the group's collective morality.

Collective Victimhood

The political theory of victimhood that pertains to the Palestinian case study distinguishes between victimization as an act of harm perpetrated against a person or group and victimhood as a form of collective identity based on that harm.[3] Whereas collective victimization refers to the objective infliction of harm by one group on another, collective victimhood refers to the psychological experience and consequences of such harm. These consequences affect cognitions and behaviors that shape collective identity. Most instances of collective victimhood are preceded by some form of victimization, whereas not every act of victimization result in a state of victimhood.[4]

Although collective victimhood can be identified in nonviolent conflicts, such as the intergroup relations in Belgium between French and Dutch speakers, groups tend to maintain a sense of collective victimhood as a result of various traumatic experiences—such as past colonial occupation, widespread harm and damage, wars, prolonged exploitation and discrimination, or genocide. Many of these events fall within the framework of vicious and violent conflicts, as in such cases as the Kurds in Iraq, Arab-Palestinian society in mandatory Palestine, Indigenous peoples in America, and the Finnish civil war.[5]

This definition or description fits the Palestinian national collective identity, which was developed in the twentieth century, particularly after the 1948 War. The Arabic word Nakba has become a common and systematic currency in Palestinian society, and in fact in the entire Arab world since this war. The sense of victimization among Palestinians has intensified, not only because they have become refugees but also because they lost their status and property in the aftermath of the war, and because most of the Arab states that absorbed them instituted a rigid, exclusionary, and hostile policy toward them.[6] Palestinian leaders from Fatah and Hamas have repeatedly claimed that the Palestinians are the victims of the 1948 War (and of the June 1967 War).[7]

Collective victimhood is defined as a mindset that is shared by group members following perceived intentional harm with severe and lasting consequences inflicted on the members of the group by others. Collective victimhood experiences are complex, multilayered, and are among some of the most impactful experiences that individuals and groups can have. The harm caused to group members is viewed as undeserved, unjust, immoral, and unavoidable. It is noteworthy that collective victimhood can develop within a society even if the harm has not been experienced personally but only by other members of the group. Furthermore, it could also develop if the event did not occur in one's lifetime but happened decades or centuries ago, as was the case with Catalunya, the Armenian people, and the Palestinians. Ervin Staub and Daniel Bar-Tal phrase it accurately: "Groups encode important experiences, especially extensive suffering, in their collective memory, which can maintain a sense of woundedness and past injustice through generations."[8]

Thus, a victim is not necessarily just someone who suffered one catastrophe (the meaning of Nakba in Arabic) or another. Victimhood is a perception, and it has to do with one's definition of oneself—whether one person or a given community. The group's definition, in this case study the Palestinian collective memory and identity, is an outcome of a chain of historical events. A collective self-definition as a victim requires five conditions: (1) the people were harmed; (2) they were not responsible for the occurrence of the harmful act; (3) they could not prevent the harm; (4) they are morally right and suffering from injustice done to them; (5) they deserve sympathy. The Palestinian victim identity meets all five of these conditions, as their literature, poetry, theater, arts, and graffiti have shown since 1948.[9]

Collective victimhood in the past becomes a prism through which current events are viewed, and these events are seen as a continuation of historical victimization. At this point, as part of the national ethos, Maurice Halbwachs's argument seems relevant: the memory does not belong to someone within the community. The memory, the shapes, the present, and the vision are collective and lean on recollections of all members.[10] There are various representations of collective victimhood; three major ones will be mentioned here: siege mentality, perpetual victimization, and competitive victimhood. *Siege mentality* entails the belief that the group is surrounded by enemies and therefore must always defend itself.[11] *Perpetual victimization* is the belief that the group has been victimized in the past and continues to be under threat.[12] *Competitive victimhood* focuses on the uniqueness of the group's victimization and establishes the belief that the group has suffered more than any other group—particularly more than groups who are in competition with it.[13] These three components—siege mentality, perpetual victimization, and a strong sense of having been victimized more than the other side—exist in the Palestinian ethos. In this case, it is the sense of victimization by the Israeli side, especially after the 1948 War, that forms one of the basic components of Palestinian collective victimhood.

In order to maintain the sense of victimhood, social agents and institutions are either recruited to adopt this mindset or do so on their own initiative, due to the strength of the ethos, and participate in all the channels of communication. Leaders maintain victimhood in their public speeches, often using it as a source of power. A major role is played by the educational system in inserting the proper beliefs into textbooks, educational programs, and ceremonies—and above all, through the explicit and implicit messages of teachers. In the cultural sphere, memorial days, religious and national holidays, and the ceremonies that accompany them serve as annual routines to remind group members of their victimization. Additionally, cultural products such as books, films, art exhibitions, and theater convey the sense of collective victimhood to consumers of these cultural products. Textbooks in the PA's educational system include many references to the elements of the Palestinian ethos, such as the Nakba, the sense of sacrifice and victimization, and their confidence that they will win the struggle, as well as the fact that they are right and the other side (Israel) is wrong.[14]

Victory

On May 13, 1940, Sir Winston Churchill addressed the House of Commons, stating, "What is our aim? Victory, victory at all costs, victory in spite of all terror; victory, however long and hard the road may be; for without victory, there is no survival."[15] Six decades later, Tommy Franks, a retired general of the US Army, who participated in the US military campaign against Iraq, responded to the question, what is victory? Does victory mean the accomplishment of objectives and goals that we had in mind when we initially became involved in a conflict? How do we understand victory? In some cases, Franks argues, victory has been defined as the removal of a particular threat, either to us or to our friends. Perhaps it is more accurate to define victory when the conflict is over and a treaty, or pact, or alliance, or an accord is achieved and security is guaranteed. Franks analyzed this theoretical and conceptual issue by discussing secondary objectives. Maybe the victory is political, as in the returning of a state to the community of nations, as was the case of Germany and Japan after World War II.[16]

Feelings of victory and patriotism are directly affiliated with historical collective memories of the national community, since every nation needs to proclaim its people's achievements in every aspect of daily life, from politics to the economy, science, and sports.[17] The accurate context of victory depends on how the goals of the campaign are defined. A successful military campaign, for example, is not a sufficient condition for victory, nor is it always a necessary one. Political, economic, and civic forces may all shape the longer-term outcome of the war, so as to render it an overall success or failure.[18]

The military, civilian, and political dimensions of war and victory have always been inextricably intertwined. However, they have become even more entangled in contemporary wars. Whereas the classic form of victory is a phenomenon that is presented only on battlefields, twenty-first-century warfare can no longer be reduced to just a military campaign, and there are ongoing attempts to formulate victory using longer-term, more abstract, and more complex criteria. Wars have become about long-term change, requiring not only aggression but also a measure of compassion, particularly regarding individual targets; consequently, the political and civilian dimensions of victory have outgrown the military one. Hence, in post–World War II reality, victory has become more difficult to identify, define, and evaluate.

In the Palestinian ethos, victory is a return to Palestine. Between 1948 and 1993, the year when the Oslo Accords were signed, the Palestinian way of doing this was through armed struggle. The Palestine National Charter of 1968 verified it.[19] Hamas, founded on religious ideology in 1987, also adopted violent struggle, namely the use of terror, to try to free Palestine. In this respect, the desire to return to Palestine is a central pillar of the national ethos not only shared by the secular (Fatah/PLO/Palestinian Authority) and religious (Hamas) streams. It is also tangible insurance for defining victory—military, political, historical.

My premise, which will be explored later, is that the secular stream has changed its perception in respect to the term ethos and strives to implement the Palestinian vision in peaceful ways. The ethos's elements of the secular stream and the religious stream (Hamas) remain the same, but the former is willing to settle for partial victory, that is, establishing an independent state in parts of Palestine rather than in the entire territory. In contrast, Hamas's ideology remains unchanged, requiring Islamic rule over all of Palestine. When this happens, it will be the ultimate victory, one that results in the destruction of the ideological and moral values of the nation's rival society and in reestablishing the foundations of the enemy state. Both sides, the PA and Hamas, use the ethos to claim to be the just side of the conflict.

Collective Morality

National ethos is a source of deep belief in the justness of the group's goals and the collective positive self-image—as opposed to an affirmation of the wickedness of the opponents' goals and characteristics. Focusing on the injustices, atrocities, harm, and evil committed by the group's enemies leads society members to present themselves as the source of human morality. All the responsibility for the ongoing conflict lies with the group's opponents. These opponents will always be portrayed as the repository of evil, where violence, atrocities, cruelty, lack of concern for human life, and viciousness rule. The more the other side is inhuman and brutal, the more one's group is pure and honorable. Defeating the wicked party is not merely a victory over rivals but a triumph of the loftiest universal values, since the perception was in the first place that the conflict was imposed by an adversary who fought for unjust goals and used violent and immoral means.[20]

In order to understand the role that morality plays within the framework of the national ethos, Émile Durkheim's theory may be useful. For Durkheim, morality has its basis in social engagement. The construction of morality is fully sociological, since it depends on collective experiences that shape both the emotions and thoughts of human agents.[21] Durkheim views moral rules as emotionally grounded products of society. He associates moral rules with social facts—that is, facts that are perceived as such because they arise through collective sentiments and come to hold a compelling and coercive power over the individual's consciousness. In Durkheim's work, "moral" is often synonymous with "social," and accordingly, "individual" stands for immoral qualities, articulating one's egoistic passions.[22]

The Palestinian National Ethos

THE SECULAR STREAM (FATAH, PLO, PA)

In 1949, Musa Alami (1897–1984), member of a Palestinian noble family from Jerusalem, published an article entitled "The Lesson of Palestine." He explained how the Arab-Palestinian side happened to lose territory in the battle against the Jews in the 1947–1949 wars in Palestine (which became the State of Israel). His explanation suggested two factors: first, Britain, which promised the Jews a national home and fulfilled its obligation; second, the Arab leadership that failed to understand the political and military situation, underestimated the Zionist opponent, and failed to produce a national common denominator for Arabs in Palestine under the British mandate (1918–1948).[23]

As strange as this may be, there is no research literature defining the Palestinian ethos, the spirit of the people (*rooh sh'abi*). Existing literature, written by scholars active in the Israeli-Palestinian conflict or others, touches on various aspects of group memory and mobilization for the national struggle. From those studies, it is possible to identify various elements that produce a mosaic of a Palestinian national ethos, at least as people who define themselves as Palestinians perceive it. Although this book is mostly about the negotiations between the Palestinian Authority and Hamas, it first seeks to discuss the elements of the Palestinian ethos, shared by both sides, and to ask how, despite a shared ethos, the secular and religious streams fail to bridge the gaps between them and unite forces to realize the ethos.[24]

The dominant national narrative of the Palestinian community concerning the struggle with Israel is embedded in the concept of identifying the establishment of the State of Israel as a catastrophe (Nakba). The term Nakba encompasses the Palestinian loss of lands and their transformation to refugees in neighboring territory, unable to return to their homes. The Palestinian narrative of the Nakba puts full responsibility on the Zionist movement and presents the Palestinians as eternal victims. This narrative has been repeated time and again in Palestinian poetry, plays, and scholarly works.[25]

For decades, the Palestinian vision has been to return to the homeland, Palestine. Thus, the land and the right of return have become inseparable parts of the national ethos. Rashid Hamid, for example, as far back as 1974, described the disaster not only as Palestinians becoming refugees who lost their homes, assets, and political-social-economic status in Palestine under the British Mandate. It was also catastrophic because of the Arab host states' policy regarding refugees. They all monitored the political and social situation in refugee camps and suppressed any attempt to start political activity. At the same time, young Palestinians, among them Yasser Arafat, realized, particularly after Egypt's defeat in the 1956 War and the breakup of the United Arab Republic (Egypt-Syria-Iraq) in 1961, that Arab unity is not possible and if Palestinians want to fulfill their national ethos, they must lead, perhaps without tangible Arab support, this complicated mission.[26] They founded a newspaper under the title *Our Palestine* (*Filastinuna*), hoping to recruit as many of the Palestinians who fled from Israel in 1948 as possible and to establish an armed organization. They also changed the slogan from "Arab unity is the way to liberate Palestine" to "the liberation of Palestine is the way to Arab unity."[27]

This was the era of building up the national spirit of the Palestinian people. In November 1959, Fatah's newspaper wrote: "The youth of the catastrophe (Nakba) are dispersed. The youth of the catastrophe are dispersed. . . . To die for our beloved Fatherland is better and more honorable than life, which forces us to eat our daily bread in humiliation or to receive it as charity at the cost of our honor. We, the sons of the catastrophe, are no longer willing to live this dirty, despicable life, this life that has destroyed our cultural, moral, and political existence and destroyed our human dignity."[28] This had become a continual message of Fatah's newspaper. The July 1960 issue "called for carrying the flag of freedom for their Fatherland. They are called to arms, in order to declare revolution with the goal to do away once and for all with the illegal Jewish robbery of our Fatherland."[29]

Self-esteem, dignity, longing for the homeland, and a preference for death rather than diaspora among the poor and miserable have become the basis for the Palestinian national ethos. It is important to mention briefly that the concept of armed struggle is the third component of the Palestinian national ethos. The new organization of Fatah engraved the concept of armed struggle as the only way to liberate Palestine. This pattern of thought was not unique to Fatah back in the 1950s. In 1952, the Arab National Movement, headed by George Habash and Wadi'a Nasser, already embraced the armed struggle concept.[30] They asked to do it with the Arab states' assistance. Fatah founders felt that the odds for gaining that assistance were low, and they focused instead on uniquely Palestinian national feelings.

Two significant events took place in 1967 and 1968 that shaped the Palestinian national ethos. First, after the war in June 1967, and following Nasser's death in 1970, the Palestinians realized that Arab unity was not an option anymore, especially after the Arabs lost three times to Israel (1948, 1956, and 1967), the breakup of the UAR in 1961, and Egypt's military involvement in Yemen (1962–1965). Following the Israeli victory, the West Bank, which had been under Jordanian sovereignty since 1948, and the Gaza Strip (under Egypt's control) were controlled by Israel. This led to nearly 250,000 Palestinians abandoning their homes and moving to Jordan and Egypt. In early 1969, the Israeli commander of the Gaza Strip Mordecai Goor described the political situation in Gaza as "a total embarrassment among the public. They have no idea what their future situation will be." Based on his talks and those of other government officials with local dignitaries, the Israelis felt that the Gaza Strip's tendency toward becoming a Palestinian entity was resolved "without knowing exactly what it was." The flags raised at the demonstrations were PLO flags.[31] These demonstrations were exactly the reality that Fatah (which after the 1967 War became the dominant political force within the PLO) wished to see. The spirit of the people, their ethos, had already been expressed by Gazans in 1969 in their aspirations for a free Palestine.

The second event was the Karameh Battle. On March 21, 1968, an IDF force released three armored companies, four paratrooper battalions, engineering forces, and an auxiliary air force to raid the Jordanian village of Karameh. The purpose of the action was to strike Palestinian organizations and prevent them from operating in Israeli territory. Between June 1967 and March 1968, recognition grew among Palestinians that the weaker Arab states could not help them liberate Palestine. As part of the ethos of returning to the homeland, the heads of Palestinian organizations decided to turn to guerrilla war against Israel and terrorize it until it surrendered to their demands. Young Palestinians were recruited and trained in military camps in Algeria, China, and Syria. More than 150 Palestinians were killed in the battle of Karameh, but Fatah leaders saw this as an important achievement in that they conducted a campaign against the IDF and caused damage to it. They compared their success to the failure of Arab states in the June 1967 War. Jordanian government officials, civilians, and military personnel attended the funerals of those killed in the Karameh Battle. Within a few days, five thousand people applied to enlist in the ranks of Fatah, which was perceived as a winner in Karameh due to its steadfast standing. Fatah was not prepared to receive such a high number of recruits, and after careful screening, recruited nine hundred of them.[32] This military campaign intensified Fatah's role as an important organization; photographs of their fighters roused Arab streets in 1968. For Arafat and his colleagues this activity sharpened the national ethos.

The military campaign of Karameh village demonstrated the armed struggle aspect of the PLO. This was expressed, also, in the 1968 Palestinian National Convention, which compared to 1964 convention, put more focus on armed struggle (*kifah mussalah*) as a salient feature of the national Palestinian ethos. The components of the Palestinian ethos—refugees, right of return, and an independent Palestinian state—are all in the Palestine National Charter of 1968. The Palestinian covenant has thirty-three articles and their analysis easily proves to reflect the elements of the national ethos. Section 1 defines Palestine as "the homeland of the Arab Palestinian people," a definition that determines Palestinian identity on a territorial basis. Section 2 sees Palestine "with the boundaries it had during the British Mandate as an indivisible territorial unit." This perception strengthened the territorial dimension as well as the link between the West Bank and the Gaza Strip, which should constitute an integral national unit but as of 2007 turned into two separate geopolitical units.

Section 4 of the covenant deals with the refugees' part of the national ethos: "The Palestinian identity is a genuine, essential, and inherent characteristic. It is transmitted from parents to children. . . . The dispersal of the Palestinian Arab people, through the disasters that befell them, do not make them lose their Palestinian identity and their membership in the Palestinian community." This is the national legacy of the ethos: the direct and inseparable linkage between the human being and the land. This connection never ends. It goes from generation to generation. Palestinian scholars repeat the element of refugee return as central to the Palestinian ethos and rely on leaders' statements as well as the National Charter.[33]

Sections 8 and 9 emphasize the armed struggle as the only way to liberate the homeland, Palestine: "This phase in their history, through which the Palestinian people are now [July 1968] living, is that of a national (*watani*—in the sense of homeland) struggle for Palestine. Armed struggle is the only way to liberate Palestine. This is overall strategy, not merely a tactical phase."[34] In order to achieve this vision, section 11 of the covenant determines that the Palestinian people aspire to adhere to three slogans, which are part of the national ethos: national unity, national recruitment, and liberation. This national covenant is still valid; therefore, it almost immediately raises the question of how the PA, a political entity that is an outcome of the Oslo Accords, and Hamas failed to cooperate in turning the vision and the ethos into reality.

The Palestine National Charter refers to universal justice, which is one of the three baselines of the ethos. Sections 18 and 19 clarify that the "liberation of Palestine is a defensive act, and therefore the Palestinian people must have contact with all the nations and look for support from freedom-loving and peace-loving states in order to restore their legitimate (and just) rights." Section 23 repeats that message and sees the Zionist movement in Israel as an illegal movement, meaning that everything that is an outcome of Zionism is wrong. The last section of the covenant, section 33, determines that changes to the text can be made if two-thirds of the Palestinian National Council (PNC) support it. In 1996, following Israel's demand that PLO chairman and PA president Yasser Arafat delete from the covenant the sections that call for Israel's extermination, 504 of 669 of PNC members assembled in the Gaza Strip. They discussed the issue but voting on the requested changes never took place.

Since the mid-1950s, the Palestinian ethos has also been shaped by embracing radical perceptions of armed struggle and by social acceptance of readiness to sacrifice lives as martyrs, as the National Liberation Front (Front de Libération Nationale, FLN) did in Algeria. Over one decade (1968–1978), the PLO carried out ninety-one terror attacks against Israeli targets within Israel and overseas. Forty-five of them were executed by Fatah (under Arafat's instructions) and the Popular Front for Liberation of Palestine (PFLP, under George Habash). The political goals of these attacks were: (1) placing the Palestinian issue on the agenda in every international political forum; (2) disruption of air and maritime traffic from Israel; (3) sowing fear and embarrassment in Israeli offices and institutions and among Jews around the world; and (4) damage to tourism, the Israeli economy, and Israel's image as a strong and victorious country after the June 1967 War.[35]

The spirit of the Palestinian people, the national ethos, was the basis for the first popular uprising (intifada) in 1987 and the second armed intifada of 2000. Suicide bombings, self-sacrifice attacks, and the use of firearms became daily happenings in the West Bank and the Gaza Strip. Various symbols of the Palestinian national ethos were employed during this period, including enhancement of the image of the victim vis-à-vis the Israeli occupier and glorification of the martyrs. Allen defines it as "surviving during the intifada" and turning the abstract ethos into a tangible one by describing the daily routine of West Bank residents.[36]

During the second intifada (2000–2005), commemorating the martyrs became social convention at funerals, restaurants, schools, shops, and homes. Children wore shirts with T-shirts with images of martyrs. Pictures of terrorists who sacrificed themselves for the homeland were pasted on textbooks and cars. Those who joined the military cells of Fatah, Hamas, or the Palestinian Islamic Jihad (PIJ) were motivated by, among other factors, this national ethos. As Moghadam puts it:

> Videotapes of suicide bombers, as well as statements of volunteers, living martyrs, or families of suicide bombers clearly suggest that many Palestinians perceive a deep injustice done to them by a "Zionist entity" that deprived Palestinians of their land and continues to deny them a worthy existence on what they regard to be Palestinian soil. Most suicide bombers express a willingness to avoid the repetition of the 1948 *Nakba*.[37]

Recent studies argue that the martyrs have become Palestinian icons, in fact, part of the ethos.[38] The official website of the Palestinian news agency has an electronic archive, with more than one hundred thousand news reports that appeared in the Palestinian daily newspapers from the day the intifada broke out to the end of 2005. The three daily newspapers were: *Al-Quds*, *Al-Ayyam*, and *Al-Hayat Al-Jadeeda*.[39] The headlines showed that an average of ten reports related to the intifada appeared on average every day. The reports dealt with incidents in which Palestinians were killed or injured, attacks in which Israelis were killed or injured, friction between settlers and Palestinians, collective punishment by Israel, damage to the Palestinian economy because of the conflict, statements about the willingness to struggle until victory, and calls to the international community to save the Palestinians from Israeli aggression. These reports are a manifestation of the various elements of the Palestinian ethos and have a bearing on deepening the

Palestinian consciousness, the characteristics of which are the sense of sacrifice vis-à-vis the Israeli occupier, willingness to fight until victory, and achieving a just solution for the Palestinians, which is essentially the victory of universal justice.

During the second intifada, the Palestinian media reported, on a daily basis, on Arafat's activity relating to the security escalation. From October 2000 to November 2004 (Arafat died on November 11, 2004), he made more than 2,700 public statements, as table 2.1 shows. There are various examples of the sense of collective victimhood in Arafat's speeches. On October 1, 2000, the Palestinian representation in France warned that Israel was responsible for the escalation, and on the next day Chairman Arafat declared that the Palestinians were ready for any possibility that may arise.[40] Three weeks later, a summit of Arab countries convened in Sharm el-Sheikh, Egypt, at the request of the Palestinians. Arafat addressed the summit, accusing Israel of committing crimes against the Palestinians, meaning that the Palestinians were the victims. He added that the Israeli threats against holy mosques in Jerusalem were indeed threats against the entire Islamic and Arab world. "This summit must end the Palestinian suffering and agony."[41]

Various expressions of Palestinian victimhood were published day after day. *Al-Quds* (October 11, 2000) reported attacks by settlers against Arabs in East Jerusalem—breaking windows, vandalizing cars, and damaging property, and two weeks later the Arab Front Liberation[42] began to distribute assistance to families of victims who were killed. As the escalation continued, Arafat appealed to the US administration, asking them not to stop international protection of the Palestinians, and Bassam

Table 2.1. Yasser Arafat's Speeches Included in the Analysis

Year	Victim	Victory	Moral	Total Number of Speeches
2000	8	6	4	120
2001	16	9	14	293
2002	21	8	18	477
2003	10	9	10	764
2004	11	7	10	1,081

Based on reporting in *Al-Quds*, *Al-Ayyam*, and *Al-Hayat Al-Jadeeda*, three daily newspapers in the Palestinian Authority between 2000 and November 11, 2004, the day of Arafat's death.

Abu Sharif, a senior Palestinian official, explained that such protection was necessary because the Palestinians were victims of Israeli aggression.[43]

When Israel decided to launch the Defensive Shield operation (March–May 2002), the Palestinians, once again, intensified their grievances about being victims. Arafat, replying to CNN's Christiane Amanpour who asked him about Palestinian terrorism, grew angry and asked her: "You ask me why I am under siege. The question is not worthy of a serious journalist." It was an expression of Arafat's sense of victimization that made Arafat vilify the destruction of the presidential compound in Ramallah "using American weapons." Moreover, Arafat found himself in a very embarrassing, not to say humiliating, situation for a man who was educated in the lap of Muslim and Arab culture when he had to publicly explain to a woman, a journalist from the West, his inferior status as a result of Israel's actions.[44]

As Israel's military operation continued, so did the Palestinians' outcry that highlighted their weakness and their seeing themselves as victims of brutal Israeli activity. Bassam Al-Sharif, a senior Palestinian, confirmed the arrival of two hundred bodies to hospitals in the West Bank,[45] and on the very same day it was reported that Arafat was besieged in the presidential compound (*muqata'a*) in Ramallah, unable to visit his people. Recognizing the balance of power at the time, the Palestinians appealed to international authorities for help to remove the siege.[46] Arafat himself used holy religious sites to accuse Israel of perpetrating terror by putting him under siege and firing at the Nativity Church in Bethlehem: "How can the world remain silent when Israel fires at the Church as it fired at the Al-Aqsa Mosque in 1969?"[47]

The feeling of victory was a dominant theme in the Palestinian narrative throughout their years of struggle; they have never ceased to declare their willingness to fight until victory. Triumph, according to Palestinian officials, can be achieved through implementing UN resolutions or by steadfastness (*sumud*), another important element of the national ethos and a quality that was enhanced after 1948. Senior Palestinians like Yasser Abd Rabo, for instance, said that the popular resistance against the Israeli occupation would continue until the national vision was realized. Marwan Bargouthi clarified that the intifada would not stop until the settlements were dismantled.[48] A week later Arafat decided to convene the Central Committee of Fatah to announce the establishment of an independent state, and in mid-November 2000 he stressed that the Palestinian people were determined to continue their holy war (jihad) all the way to victory.[49]

After Ariel Sharon won the 2001 elections, Arafat called for the Palestinians to stand firm against Israeli aggression. On January 21, 2001, *Al-Ayyam* reported that the Palestinian economy had lost one billion dollars since the intifada began, which is a tangible expression of victimhood, and on February 11, 2001, the Grand Mufti of Jerusalem warned that if Israeli violence continued, the gates of hell would open. Arafat himself called on the Palestinian people to be patient until victory came.[50] The more Israel intensified its military activity, the more Arafat emphasized that the intifada would never end, or in other words, until victory is achieved.[51]

On January 3, 2002, when Israel took control of the *Karine A* ship, which carried weapons to the Palestinian Authority, Arafat denied any connection with the ship. He convened the Central Committee of Fatah and repeated his position on the continuation of the struggle until all goals were achieved, including the right of return and the preservation of Palestinian blood.[52] Amid Operation Defensive Shield, Arafat made a point of declaring every few days that the spirit of the Palestinians would never surrender on the path to victory and that they would rebuild everything that Israel destroyed. He also declared that Jenin would be renamed Jenin-*grad* to symbolize the Palestinian steadfastness (*sumud*) as did the people of Stalingrad under the siege they experienced in World War II.[53]

In mid-2002, a political and public debate began in Israel regarding the possibility that Arafat would be expelled from the territory. This led to a wave of support in Palestinian society for Arafat's leadership as a personification of the ethos of the revolution and the realization of the Palestinian vision. Arafat himself rarely addressed the issue, but his two statements illustrate his adherence to the path he chose. In May 2003 he made it clear that Palestine was the homeland, and that lying and deceit would not defeat the Palestinians until they were victorious.[54] A few months later, he announced that he would be ready to defend the country with his own weapon and that the entire Palestinian people were struggling for their independence, again, a clear instance of the ethos.[55]

The third theme, a belief in the group's collective morality, was also typical of the way Arafat portrayed Palestinian history and the national ethos. The suffering of Palestinian victims was almost always interwoven with their claim that they were the just side in the struggle against Israel. Statements made by Arafat and other Palestinian leaders calling on Israel to comply with international resolutions (e.g., Resolutions 181, 194, and 242) and to give the Palestinians their rights—and thus establish world moral justice—were commonplace. At the beginning of November 2000, Arafat requested that Gerhard Schröder, then German chancellor, keep the peace process alive; simultaneously, he asked the US administration not to prevent international protection of Palestinians.[56] In between, Al-Tayeb abd Al-Rahim, the general secretary of the Palestinian Authority, stated that peace in the region would not be achieved until the Palestinians had their legitimate rights.[57] Arafat made it clear that the Palestinian vision was not for sale.[58]

Arafat used the Arab summit of May 22, 2004, in Tunisia to remind the participants that the Palestinians were on the right and just side of the conflict. He accused Israel of committing crimes violating basic human international ethics. The Palestinians, according to Arafat, were ready to resume peace in order to achieve their independence, but Israel refused to do so and its brutal violence against his people eliminated any chance for a real peace.[59]

To sum up, there is direct linkage between the three constituents of the ethos: victimhood, exemplified by remembering the 1948 defeat as the event that transformed British Mandate Arabs into refugees; victory, in the form of the *sumud* principle, which was developed after 1948, meaning clinging to the land at any price, along with a willingness to sacrifice one's life to preserve the homeland; and universal moral measures, represented by Palestinian longing for a just peace.

The Religious Stream (Hamas)

From a historical perspective, the emergence of Hamas consisted of four phases: the first, the social phase, started in the early 1970s when Sheikh Ahmed Yassin established a wide array of educational, welfare, health, and religious institutions throughout the Gaza Strip. Based on theories of social movement analysis (mainly, constructivism) the sheikh's goal was to correct the flaws in Palestinian society by returning to religion and observance, as taught in the Qur'an.[60] Yassin, who joined the Muslim Brotherhood while studying in Egypt, returned to the Gaza Strip after the war in June 1967 and sought to incorporate the religious world into the population. Through the social institutions he established, Yassin made a name for himself in the Gaza Strip during the 1970s.

In the early 1980s, when he and his supporters felt strong, they moved on to the second stage, which is the phase of the exercise of power and the transition to terrorism. The sheikh was arrested, for the first time, in 1984 by Israeli authorities. He was convicted, after numerous weapons were found in his home, of membership in an unlawful association, a terrorist operation, and of intending to eliminate the State of Israel. He was sentenced to thirteen years in prison but was released a year later as part of a deal to exchange prisoners between Israel and Palestinian organizations.[61]

After his release from prison in 1985, Sheikh Yassin deepened his activities in the social and military fields. In the mid-eighties Hamas already formed a military wing, calling it the Izz al-Din al-Qassam Brigades (from 1991). The sheikh became not only the spiritual leader of Hamas but the man who dictated the policy of the attacks. In December 1987, the first intifada broke out, and in response Yassin decided, after a series of consultations, to establish the Islamic Resistance Movement (Harakat al-Mukawama al-Islamiyya), abbreviated as Hamas.[62]

Before introducing the third and the fourth phases, it is important to discuss the Hamas Covenant. In August 1988, twenty years after the PLO manifested the Palestine National Charter, Hamas published its own ideological perceptions. Hamas's covenant has an introduction and thirty-six articles, all of which are affiliated with the Palestinian national ethos. Comparing Hamas's covenant to that of the PLO, the former includes religious ideology around Palestine, so Hamas is a national-religious movement. Since Hamas published its covenant, the movement has changed neither its covenant nor its ideology. For Hamas, the conflict over Palestine has a religious aspect and the struggle is between Islam and heretic Jews. The territory of Palestine is a holy land (*waqf*), therefore any thought of compromising with the infidels or making any concessions is forbidden.

This national-religious amalgamation is reflected in Hamas's ideological manifest. The covenant reveals similarities to the PLO's covenant regarding the national ethos. Its introduction distinguishes between Muslims, the righteous camp of mankind, and the "people of the book," a nickname for Christians and Jews, the sinners, as the Qur'an describes them.[63] As its opening section continues, the charter explains that the conditions for establishing a movement in which Hamas would join hands with jihad fighters for the liberation of Palestine have matured, a mixture of national vision and divine imperative (holy war). This perception is directly linked to the martyrs (*shuhada'*), an integral part of the ethos. The term jihad in the national (and religious) context is repeated time and again through the covenant—for example, in section 7 where Hamas explains that the movement is "a chain of the holy war against the Zionist invasion of Palestine." The martyr (*shaeed*) Izz al-Din al-Qassam, who fought against Zionism (and the British Mandate) already in the 1930s, has a place of honor in the treaty and is mentioned as a way of glorifying the freedom fighters.

Hamas's path defined as "the Islamic Resistance Movement, is the path of Islam, from which it draws its principles, concepts, terms, and worldview about life and man. It turns to [Islam] when religious rulings are required and asks [Islam] for inspiration to guide its steps."[64] Section 6 makes the necessary link between religion, nation, and territory: "The Islamic Resistance Movement is uniquely Palestinian. It has faith in Allah and adopts Islam as its way of life. It acts to fly the banner of Allah over all of Palestine."[65] Later, in section 11, the land of Palestine is described as sacred "until the resurrection, according to Islamic Law (*shari'a*)." According to Hamas, the justification for this view is simple: Palestine, a holy land, was conquered by the enemy, so it is a religious (and national) duty to fight for the homeland (*watan*).

On this ideological national-religious platform, Khaled Masha'al, who headed Hamas from 2004 for almost a decade, explained that Hamas carried out terror attacks after Yasser Arafat signed the Oslo Accords:

> It is not true that Hamas sought to destroy the peace process during the 1990s. Hamas was against the Oslo Accords, which we considered an unjust agreement that would not lead to a state or to independence or to restoration of the rights of our people. But the operations we carried out were for other reasons, not to target the political process, because we were convinced that it contained the seeds of its own destruction and had no future. This was our belief and stance from the outset of the Oslo process in 1993.[66]

Hamas's contribution to the national Palestinian ethos has been suicide terror attacks. The martyrs' attacks against Israelis started in 1993, and in 1996 Khaled Masha'al, as Hamas's leader, justified them, claiming that they were a response to brutal Israeli attacks against Palestinians, and he specifically mentioned Yahya Ayyash's assassination by Israel. For him, it is only natural to resist an occupier in any circumstances, meaning the Palestinians are the victims. Victimhood connects to justice, Masha'al continues, because Hamas started to hit Israeli civilians after Israel did so against the Palestinian population.[67] Suicide attacks became a common occurrence during the second intifada. Between 2000 and 2005, 147 suicide attacks were recorded, 40 percent of which were committed by Hamas personnel. In these attacks, 525 people were killed and 3,350 injured.[68]

Section 27 of the Hamas covenant illustrates the joint ethos of secular and religious Palestinians. It defines the PLO as "closest to the Islamic Resistance Movement and it is [considered] father, brother, relative, [and] friend. Can any Muslim shun his father or brother or relative or friend? After all, our homeland is one, our catastrophe one, our fate one, and we have a common enemy." If this is the case, how have both sides failed since 2007 to find the formula that will allow them to end a geopolitical crisis that is hurting the effort to realize the common national vision? The first answer to this question is in the same article 27. Hamas explains that the PLO arose at a time when there was conceptual confusion in the Arab world that led the organization to adopt the concept of a secular independent state. To Hamas, this view goes against the religious view. Therefore, it is not possible to replace Palestine's Muslimness, because Islam and Palestine are bound together.

This is also the reason why Hamas sees—differently from the PLO—the role of the Arab and Muslim world regarding the Palestine question. Article 14 of the Hamas convention designates a role in the liberation of Palestine and in the fight against Zionism to all three cycles: Palestinians, Arabs, and Muslims. This position is derived from the fact that Palestine is an Islamic land. Hamas has held this position steadily since it was founded. This position was the basis for the third phase of the movement's development, the political phase, that began after Arafat decided to accept negotiations with Israel as a path to end the historical conflict. Since the signing of the Oslo Accords, Hamas has turned out to be the major opposition to the PA, which was established, mostly, by Fatah members.

Sheikh Yassin, the founder of Hamas, clarified his perspective toward Palestine: no one has the right to give up or sell a holy land (*waqf*), and holy war (*jihad*) is the way to liberate Palestine. From this stance, the sheikh refused to accept any compromise with the enemy, as was the case with the Oslo Accords in 1993.[69] My argument here is that the rift between the Palestinian Authority and Hamas began immediately after the Oslo Accords on the basis of different worldviews regarding the resolution of the conflict with Israel (the enemy) through dialogue. During the first decade of the twenty-first century, disagreements developed into an ongoing political crisis that also included a struggle for hegemony within the Palestinian system. Both parties practice a zero-sum game (based on a personal, structural, and behavioral approach)—hence the inability to reach a consensus.

Since the establishment of the PA in 1994, the relationship between the secular, the dominant political power, and the religious has known its ups and downs. The parties have the national ethos in common, but a dispute has emerged between them about the course of action to be taken to achieve the national goals. The secular stream led by Arafat agreed to enter a political process with Israel. The religious stream ruled it out. This disagreement would eventually lead not only to political crisis, but to different visions.

Previous research has indicated that Arafat was not ready—politically and psychologically—to get past the barriers to signing a lasting peace agreement with Israel. Although he was the first president of the PA, he continued to be involved in terror activity carried out by Fatah members and other organizations against Israel.[70] This fact, as well as Arafat's origins in a religious family and his close relationship with Sheikh Yassin, led to a relationship of mutual respect between the Palestinian Authority and Hamas, despite ideological disagreements over the renunciation of parts of Palestine. Arafat, who symbolized the Palestinian national ethos, as a revolutionist, freedom fighter, and man of steadfastness, refused to accept Bill Clinton's offer of a lasting peace between Palestinians and Israelis, during a meeting in Washington, on December 19, 2000—a time when the second Palestinian uprising had already begun.[71] This stance garnered him appreciation, respect, and credit among Hamas, because he stood against the pressure to make any concessions over the holy land.

The capture of the Gaza Strip in June 2007 opened the fourth phase, which was the state sovereignty phase. For the first time, the religious-national movement had de facto responsibility for the Gaza population. This responsibility, plus the movement's political aspiration to end the dominance of the secular camp, controlled its decisions from that moment. All this was at the root of the rift, which dated to the mid-1990s and culminated in the ongoing crisis beginning in 2007, as the coming chapters will analyze.

In conclusion, the Palestinian national ethos is based on history, tradition, memories, experiences, language, struggle against the enemy, the principle of standing firm, and a willingness to act in any conceivable way, including violence, for the homeland (*al-watan*). It was also built by statements by leaders, at least one of whom, Arafat, also became a national symbol. It is expressed in the PLO and Hamas covenants and is common to all people who define themselves as Palestinians.

However, it does not necessarily produce a unified vision for all Palestinian people, nor is it reflected in all Palestinian political ideas and organizations, as I will explain later. This is because the Palestinian system has become divided between two political streams, one secular and the other religious.

Chapter 3

The Political-Security Escalation within the Palestinian Authority

This chapter outlines the complicated relationship between the Palestinian Authority and Hamas from the establishment of the PA (1994) until Hamas took control of the Gaza Strip in mid-June 2007. It was the peak of more than a decade of internal tension and conflict within Palestinian society between the PA and Hamas. In August 1994, just after Yasser Arafat returned to Gaza from a long exile, he had already ordered Palestinian security forces to arrest Hamas activists. The official explanation was their resistance to the new PA, which was a new political entity following the Oslo Accords between the PLO and Israel. On August 14, hundreds of security personnel of the PA launched a campaign that targeted and arrested about one hundred Palestinian youths in Gaza who were suspected of sympathizing with Resistance factions.[1]

This picture of arrests among Hamas (and other opposition organizations) in the Gaza Strip and the West Bank became a common phenomenon in those years. These organizations, headed by Hamas, perpetrated attacks against Israelis whenever they sought to oppose a political settlement with Israel, which would mean giving up parts of Palestine—a sanctified land their view. Following these attacks, Israel pressured Arafat to launch his security forces against the terrorist squads. Hamas activists (and members of other organizations) were arrested, questioned, released on warning, and returned to their homes. Some also returned to the cycle of terror. A severe security escalation occurred during the first months of 1996. Fifty-nine Israelis were killed in four suicide attacks—two in Jerusalem, one in Tel Aviv, and one in Ashkelon (southern Israel), carried out by Hamas terror cells during February and March. Following Israeli pressure, Arafat used an even heavier hand against Hamas, and more than a thousand Hamas members were arrested by mid-April. Mohammad Dahlan, then the head of the thwarting security apparatus in the Gaza Strip, said that "it was the largest arrest campaign that Gaza had seen since 1967."[2] At least three senior members of Hamas within Gaza were arrested then: Mahmood al-Zahar, Sayyid abu Msamah, and Ahmad Bahr. All of them had participated in previous dialogue with PA representatives trying to alleviate the tension between the parties. Journalists, lawyers, and academics were among the detainees, not only in the Gaza Strip but also in the West Bank.[3] Some of them were beaten and tortured, others had their beards forcibly shaved and were then publicly presented without their beards, a tactic designed to humiliate. Over the years, Palestinian journalists and bloggers expressed their grievances with the PA's security policy, accusing it of serving Israel's and the United States' agenda and violating human rights. People who called to implement the right of return upon Security Council 194 resolution, and return to Jaffa and Haifa, two cities in Israel, also were arrested.[4] The consequences of this policy, especially public arrests of opposition activists, were engraved in the memories of Hamas's people and undermined their confidence in the PA. Moreover, this distrust and failure to regulate relations between the Palestinian Authority and opposition organizations has been the backdrop to the nine rounds of negotiations since February 2007, as will be analyzed later.

The second intifada that started on September 29, 2000, exacerbated the tension between the PA and the opposition organizations, headed by Hamas. The failure of the "Camp David Summit 2" (July 2000) to reach a political agreement between the PLO and Israel drove Arafat, again, to choose terror and popular resistance.[5] Yasser Arafat strived for an outbreak of violence. This time, the violence against Israel was agreed on by all Palestinian factions and brought the PA and Hamas closer.[6] Armed youths carried out various types of terror attacks, parades took place very frequently, and Palestinian media reported extensively on security escalation.[7] Fatah/*tanzim* activists (a Fatah street cadre that received a license to carry weapons from the PA) and Hamas members joined to conduct terror operations against Israeli military and civil targets. Hammami and Tamri argue that during the second uprising, Fatah-armed groups were the dominant power against Israel, while Hamas remained relatively silent. Regardless of whether they were right, Fatah's involvement in an armed struggle against Israel was viewed positively by Hamas members and created a common denominator for action based on the elements of the Palestinian ethos: liberating Palestine and willingness to sacrifice (martyrs or imprisonment in Israeli prisons)—plus the belief that Palestinian victory would eventually come. The discourse on uncompromising struggle until victory quickly became the main discourse in Palestinian society. In this reality, the PA's strict security policy against Hamas eased, although Hamas members recalled the humiliations they suffered in the 1990s. They waited for revenge that came in 2006 and 2007.

Consequences of Arafat's Death: General Election and Increasing Violence

Yasser Arafat died on November 11, 2004. His death started a new era in Palestinian society. For the Palestinian, Arafat, as Dennis Ross describes him, was "an icon . . . a symbol of a cause and a father figure."[8] Mahmood Abbas (Abu Mazen) was elected as the new president. In February 2005, during the Sharem al-Shikh summit, he announced that the second Palestinian uprising had ended and from now on, the PA and Israel would resume talks in order to reach a peaceful agreement.[9] Unlike Arafat, Abu Mazen has never been a symbol of the Palestinian national struggle. He was not a fighter, traditionally opposed armed struggle, and was seen as a man who did more for his home and family than for the Palestinian people. As a person who disliked power, Mahmoud Abbas refrained from running a harsh and strict policy against the opposition. So, as Israel cooperated with Abu Mazen, Hamas opposition elements challenged him in two key ways: they launched high-trajectory rockets from the Gaza Strip toward Israel during the summer of 2005, and at the same time pressured him to hold elections for the Palestinian Legislative Council. The previous elections had been held in 1996.

In July 2005, the Palestinian law dealing with elections to the legislative council was amended, and the number of seats in the House increased to 132.[10] At this point, Hamas increased the pressure to hold elections as soon as possible in view of its assessment that its chances of winning were high. This was thanks to an orderly organization that included branches, charities, welfare institutions, education, and health care, which provided assistance to many Palestinians. Fatah, on the other hand, wanted to postpone the elections as much as possible. Ahmad

Qurie (Abu 'Ala'a) recommended that Abu Mazen not hold elections, because the ranks of the organization had many differences of opinion that caused rivalries among the members, including the senior officials.

For Hamas, which lost earlier in 2004 Sheikh Ahmad Yassin, the founder of the movement, and 'Abd al-Aziz al-Rantisi, a prominent leader, Arafat's removal was the opening shot to try changing the political roles and balance of power within the Palestinian arena. Various representatives of the movement accused PA seniors of corruption. Moreover, Israel's unilateral decision to withdraw from the Gaza Strip (August 2005) was a new opportunity for Hamas to demonstrate its power. The PA and Hamas disagreed about the question "Who will have power after the Israeli withdrawal?" Fatah seniors suspected that Hamas would try to resist and to challenge the PA, which was the dominant political power.[11]

Hamas took the general elections seriously. It was the first time that the movement decided to test its political strength within Palestinian society. The elections were the peak of its third phase, the political one (after the social and military phases). The first political move was toward Israel: Hamas suggested a truce (*hudnah*—temporary ceasefire). From a historical perspective it was a state-sovereignty tactic, even before the movement won the elections. Mahmood al-Zahar, a senior leader of Hamas explained:

> Participation in this election has become a necessity for several reasons . . . because of the level of corruption we [Palestinians] have reached, the level of economic and political anarchy, the great anarchy in security, the lives that are being lost in trivial feuds between clans . . . this security anarchy, which is being exploited for political purposes . . . [and] the political anarchy and the corruption have reached a point where we ourselves [Palestinians are] building settlements, and supplying them [Israelis] with cement. Today, we no longer know where the resources and money of the Palestinian people go. We want one Palestinian authority, but right now the only authority is Israel.[12]

That was the clear stance of Hamas, striving to change the balance of power in the Palestinian political system, and a thick hint for its political aspirations.

Hamas's next move was the founding of a new political framework, the "change and reform party," which offered the voters a clear manifesto. Hamas focused on the Palestinians' concerns and daily life issues, as well as on corruption, unemployment, and security. It also suggested a comprehensive plan to reform the Palestinian administration. The goal was clear: winning the election. Hamas stopped concentrating on terror and started emphasizing civil affairs. Nashat Aqtash was appointed as a political campaign director: "We have established a campaign office in every town, with a strategist, a fundraiser and a support coordinator."[13] Focusing on the fight against corruption, promoting the situation of the residents, and the development of Palestinian society were clear signals that Hamas was actually aiming to rule. The election in the legislative council was the beginning of Hamas's transition from phase three to phase four, which is to become the overriding political power in Palestine.

Hamas won in a sweeping election victory (January 2006). Its campaign turned out to be very successful. In addition, the election results revealed a major internal crisis within Fatah's ranks and a lack of leadership to unite the organization's operatives. This failure of Abu Mazen has continued throughout his years as president of the Palestinian Authority. The victory gave Hamas a significant boost to claim the status of influencer in the Palestinian political arena. Mahmoud Abbas was forced to appoint Ismail Haniyeh, Hamas's senior member in the Gaza Strip, to the new prime minister position after the January 2006 legislative elections. For Hamas it was a change of discourse, because from then on, under Haniyeh's government, the movement had to take care of all the Palestinians, regardless of their political affiliation. The political phase and the state-sovereignty phase overlapped in 2006.

The period from February 2006 to June 2007 changed the rules of the political game within the Palestinian system. Dominance of the secular stream, which had continued for more than four decades, had ended. Abu Mazen and Fatah's disgraceful failure and the success of Hamas in the elections created a different reality. Hamas officials, especially in the Gaza Strip, realized that they had a mandate from the Palestinian public to change.[14] Fatah officially acknowledged the results of the elections. In practice, Abu Mazen acted to harm Hamas and its government through security mechanisms, which in fact continued to be subject to Fatah. Shortly after the establishment of the Hamas government, the movements were subject to ongoing conflict over a series of issues: control of security mechanisms, power struggles between the presidency (controlled by Fatah) and the government (controlled by Hamas), nonpayment of salaries to PA employees (most of whom identified at this time with Fatah), and the relationship between the Authority and external parties. Political debates began to gradually deteriorate into clashes between the movement's activists on the ground, gradually leading to a series of moves that each party took to gain a greater share of the government. During this period, the most notable move was the establishment of a Hamas operative force—an independent security apparatus loyal to the ranks of the movement, which disbanded after the Hamas takeover of the Gaza Strip in June 2007. The first fatalities in the clash between the movements were in May 2006 in an attempt to assassinate Tarek Abu Rajeb, one of the thwarted security commanders in the Gaza Strip at that time. Tawfik Tirawi, the deputy head of the intelligence apparatus, accused Hamas of trying to assassinate Abu Rajeb.[15] Dozens of Palestinians were killed between May and June 2006 during massive armed clashes and demonstrations within the Gaza Strip.[16]

During the summer of 2006, the tension between the Palestinian Authority and Hamas diminished considerably. This was the result of a direct military confrontation between Hamas and Israel following the kidnapping of an Israeli soldier (June 25, 2006). However, in September, intra-Palestinian clashes resumed more intensively than before. The presidential palace (Fatah) and the government (Hamas) were battling each other for power, to the benefit of Abu Mazen. Trade unions—doctors, engineers, workers, traders, and others—ruled at that time by Fatah's sabotage to pressure the Hamas government, led by Haniyeh, to allow Abu Mazen to rule. An attempt to establish a unity government was made for the first time in autumn 2006, without success.

In December 2006, a new wave of violence surged among PA and Fatah members toward Hamas activists. A Hamas military group opened fire on the car of Baha Ba'alusha, a senior official of the intelligence apparatus in Gaza, killing his three children.[17] During the same period, a series of assassinations of senior officials on both sides was recorded, including failed attempts to kill Abu Mazen and Ismail Haniyeh. On one occasion, Hamas activists kidnapped Sufyan abu Zaida, a senior member of Fatah. He was released after several hours. At the beginning of 2007, security personnel of the PA entered the Islamic University in Gaza looking for weapons. The mutual clashes continued and took the lives of at least fifty people. Throughout this period, representatives of the other Palestinian organizations (Popular Front, Palestinian Islamic Jihad) tried to reconcile the parties and end the tension, without success.[18] The Palestinian Islamic Jihad, for instance, warned that the internal conflict was far more dangerous than external threats and emphasized the need for all Palestinians to rally around the common ground of the national ethos in order to address the various challenges, most notably the Israeli threat to the Palestinian arena.[19] Direct contacts between the parties, such as occurred in May 2006 at Prime Minister Haniyeh's office, when they agreed to set up a joint coordination committee to calm tensions in the area, collapsed, because in reality the two sides continued to hurt each other.[20]

Hamas's victory in the legislative council led to a deepening of the political rift in the Palestinian arena, culminating in Hamas's takeover of the Gaza Strip in June 2007. Over a period of eighteen months, a relationship of hostility, mutual suspicion, and mistrust between the Palestinian Authority and Hamas personnel developed. The violent daily clashes, the high death toll on both sides, and disagreement over the unity government all contributed to the conditions that formed the basis of the Mecca agreement of February 2007.

This chapter reviewed the complex relationship between the Palestinian Authority since its inception in 1994 and Hamas—the main opposition force in the Palestinian arena—until Hamas took control of the Gaza Strip in June 2007. Each side was highly suspicious of and acted violently against the other. Yasser Arafat's decision to reach a political settlement with Israel was, in effect, the beginning of a practical, not only ideological, split between the parties regarding their visions—not their shared ethos. Arafat's death sharpened tensions between them until the violent confrontation in mid-2007. Realities of the Palestinian system have formed the fragile basis for rounds of negotiations between the Palestinian Authority and Hamas.

Chapter 4

Mecca Agreement, February 2007

The Road to Mecca

This chapter opens the analysis of the negotiations between the PA and Hamas, starting at Mecca, February 2007. The road to the Mecca agreement, the first agreement between the parties, followed two tracks: the first was the continued violent clashes between the Palestinian Authority and Hamas elements, mainly in the Gaza Strip during 2006 and the first half of 2007. The second track was increasing pressure from Arab leaders on both sides to manage a dialogue at the same period.

The deterioration of security was reflected not only in the deaths of Palestinians but also in a growing sense of personal insecurity in the face of multiple shootings. The last quarter of 2006 and the beginning of 2007, as mentioned in the closing paragraphs of chapter 3, were marked by significant, even dramatic, events. The situation on the ground was complicated by a multitude of factors involved in the clashes. On one side were Palestinian security forces (preventive security members and the Presidential Guard) and Abu Musa Brigades, whose members were also members of Fatah. On the other side of the barricade were members of the Izz al-Din al-Qassam, the military wing of Hamas and a special support force set up by the movement. In the middle were the Popular Resistance Committees, which were divided between the two parties according to alliances and degrees of trust determined by family and relations among neighbors.[1] Attempts at mutual harm, which involved senior officials from both organizations, attested to quickly deteriorating relations between the parties. On December 13, a few days after the three children of Baha Ba'alusha were killed, Fatah operatives executed a Hamas military commander in Khan Yunis. The boldness required to mark and hit senior targets was a clear expression of the intent to deter the other side and to prove who the stronger side was. Such a situation is certainly not optimal for opening negotiations aimed at bringing about order and finding a solution to the bloodshed.

The first incident occurred in mid-December. As a rule, Israel, despite its crucial impact on the Palestinians since 1967, was not involved in the internal clashes between the Palestinian factions. The official policy of Jerusalem was simple: the "good" side was the PA and the "bad" side was Hamas. Therefore, when Israel had a chance to intervene, it took the PA's side. Such was the case on December 14, 2006: Following the assassination of the Hamas commander in Khan Yunis, Hamas's prime minister Ismail Haniyeh cut short his visit to Sudan. While he was trying to cross the Rafah checkpoint, Israel closed the border, suspecting that Haniyeh would smuggle thirty-five million dollars. In response, military activists of Hamas opened fire on the terminal, where the Presidential Guard personnel were. Haniyeh finally entered the Gaza Strip after mediation by Egypt—without the money. Fatah militants opened fire at his car. One Hamas member was killed and thirty-five were injured, among them Haniyeh's son. The prime minister himself stated: "We know the party that opened fire and we know how to deal with it."[2] This incident almost immediately affected other places within the PA. Conflicts between Fatah and Hamas quickly spread across Gaza and to Jenin and Ramallah, until a ceasefire finally took hold only ten days after the Rafah crossing clash.

The second occasion was at the beginning of 2007. In the Gaza Strip and all over the West Bank (Al-Bireh, Hebron, Jenin, Tul Karem), the two sides harmed each other. On January 8, 2007, Mohammad Dahlan, the strongest Fatah figure and the head of Preventive Security apparatus, addressed a Fatah rally to mark the forty-second anniversary, calling Hamas "a group of gangs. We are going to leave this venue with a new policy. If anyone from Fatah is attacked, we will hit back twice as hard."[3]

The third event began on January 23, when some Hamas militants raided a vacant beach resort in Gaza controlled by Dahlan and blew up a reception hall, causing no injuries. This led to several days of local clashes between Hamas and Fatah. On one occasion, Hamas activated an Abu Musa Brigade in response to kidnappings involving nine Hamas members and five Fatah members. Two days later, the internal conflict surfaced, striking diplomatic delegates, as gunmen fired at Canadian, German, and Chinese delegations. The situation on the ground deteriorated rapidly and by the end of January, the Gaza Strip had shut down, with civilians shutting themselves into their homes for safety.

The second track was the political effort to end the continuing crisis. Abu Mazen and Haniyeh failed to reach an understanding regarding the division of power. During the last quarter of 2006, the Palestinian president damaged the negotiations after choosing to include in his speech at the United Nation General Assembly points of disagreement between the rival parties. Outwardly, he continued to have contact with Prime Minister Haniyeh, without any intention of decentralizing governmental powers. According to Imam 'Ali, such a move indicated distrust on the part of one side of the other, a situation that made it very difficult to reach an agreement. Beyond that, it was Abu Mazen's personal behavior, even before his arrival to the negotiation in Mecca, that demonstrated his opposition to decentralization. Presenting the controversies publicly, at an international event, also indirectly called for outside parties to intervene in an internal Palestinian crisis. On the other side, Hamas maintained interior and finance ministries posts in the new government (the former controls security forces; the latter oversees the budget).

Ismail Haniyeh was aware of Abu Mazen's superior position as an executive president. Therefore, he took three steps that broadcast business as usual for him: (1) He offered to continue his negotiations with Abu Mazen in order to calm the situation on the ground; (2) he embarked on a journey in Middle Eastern countries (Egypt, Iran, Jordan, Kuwait, Lebanon, Qatar, Saudi Arabia, Syria, and Sudan) in an effort to raise funding for the functioning of the Palestinian government; (3) he drafted a document entitled "Proposal for Creating Suitable Conditions for Ending the Conflict," suggesting, inter alia, a five-year ceasefire with Israel.[4]

At the beginning of 2007 Arab leaders started to put pressure on both sides, particularly on Abu Mazen, to stop the internal conflict. In mid-January, the Syrian president, Bashar al-Assad, invited him to Damascus to meet Khaled Masha'al, the leader of Hamas. Abu Mazen's refusal to accept the invitation reflected his lack of trust, if he ever had any, in this dialogue. Eventually, he arrived at the Syrian capital after heavy pressure from the Syrians. The meeting between the two Palestinian rivals on January 21 was the first—after more than six months of mutual hostility, violence, and bloodshed. Before heading to Damascus, Abu Mazen insisted on a unity government, without Ismail Haniyeh as prime minister.[5] This precondition of the Palestinians, before entering into negotiations, fits the theoretical model suggested here: structural, processual, rational, and behavioral. Abu Mazen accepted a trilateral dialogue, meaning through an Arab mediator. His consent came after a process that included pressure from various parties; his rationale was to leave the government powers in control and to keep his main rival out of power; and finally, his behavior before entering into negotiations reflected an inflexible attitude toward the prime minister, who represented Hamas, the movement that won the election in January 2006. As for Hamas, Masha'al realized that his movement had the legal power after winning the legislative council elections. Consequently, he called for an open and direct dialogue between the parties, in order to put an end to the violence and to reach an agreement on a government that would benefit the Palestinian people.[6]

Following their meeting, both leaders stated that they made "substantial progress," but this was only for the press. Masha'al gave an interview that left no room for doubt: "There will remain a state called Israel. The problem is not that there is an entity called Israel. The problem is that the Palestinian state is non-existent."[7] It was a clear message not only for Israel. It was for Abu Mazen, in order to validate what the Palestinian president already knew: Hamas recognized neither Israel nor the PA, because the existing Palestinian entity was the result of an unacceptable, wrong accord, which was signed in 1993.

The meeting in Damascus failed to deescalate the situation. At the end of January 2007, the mutual clashes renewed, including heavy fighting. At this point, King Abdallah of Saudi Arabia invited PA and Hamas leaders to Mecca. The rapid deteriorating of the clashes to high-scale violence urged them to accept the invitation. Both sides arrived at Mecca with low expectations after failing to implement a ceasefire mediated by Egypt. Hamas also issued a statement announcing that its West Bank members were being threatened and attacked by Palestinian Authority officials.[8]

The Agreement

On February 8, 2007, both sides announced, publicly, that they reached an agreement under the auspices of Saudi Arabia's King Abdallah. The signing ceremony was attended by Abu Mazen, the president of the Palestinian Authority, and Khaled Masha'al, chairman of Hamas's political bureau. The purpose of the agreement was to stop the collision between the parties following Hamas's victory in the 2006 general elections. It is the only agreement that the parties reached before Hamas forcibly controlled the Gaza Strip in June 2007.

At first glance, one may argue the PA and Hamas chose the integrative approach by accepting the format of unity government. But focusing on Abu Mazen's speech at the opening meeting reveals his interest, which was not in Hamas's interest. The Palestinian president strived to reactivate the PLO's institutions, the only legitimate representative of the Palestinian people.[9] In addition, one of his salient interests was lifting the sanctions imposed by the International Quartet (US, Russia, UN, European Union) on the PA. This could be done only if the new government, under Hamas's control, accepted their early conditions: recognition of Israel, the renouncing of violence, and the acceptance of past agreements signed between both parties, namely, the Oslo Accords.[10]

Unlike Abu Mazem, Khaled Masha'al did not forget to mention any piece of the Palestinian ethos in his opening speech: "We came here, to Mecca, a holy place, for Palestine, for Jerusalem, for our people who paid 'homeland tax' (*'daribat el-Watan*), for those who are injured, for the prisoners within the Israeli jails, for the refugees and finally for Palestinian unity."[11] This was a clear statement of Hamas's priorities, because unity was the last issue mentioned. In contrast, Palestine, all of Palestine, according to Hamas's vision, was the first topic. He also did what was expected at the opening of the negotiations: He thanked the mediator and expressed his hope to come out of Mecca with an agreement that would end violence between the parties and allow them to cooperate on external challenges. At this point, he naturally offered no concessions to Abu Mazen.

Both parties entered into negotiations while not equipped with everything required for negotiations to lead to an agreement serving both of them. Of the twelve required attributes, as Imam 'Ali and Western scholars suggest, five can be labeled as guiding both parties during the discussions, which resulted in a fairly general agreement that left substantial gaps between them. First, each had different interests that dictated their positions. Second, they chose the negotiating alternative over continued bloodshed, but in fact that was the only alternative that they really considered. The disagreements that remained between them after the signing indicated that the only thing that was important to both sides was to please the host (the Saudi king), who also donated a billion dollars to the Palestinians, no more than that. This was an interest that the Palestinian Authority and Hamas had in common, although it did not bring the parties to an agreement that would be a win-win situation.

Third, they both saw themselves as having the legitimacy of representing the Palestinian people. Abu Mazen drew his legitimacy from being the PLO chairman, the traditional representative of the people, and from being the presidential candidate in January 2005. Hamas based its legitimacy on its victory in the legislative council in January 2006. The legitimacy of the negotiations did not amount to representation either—that is, to the authority to make decisions regarding agreements with the other party. Finally, both parties did not seek comprehensive justice for the Palestinian people. Each was focused on its own interests, believing it was on the right side of the conflict.

The Mecca agreement contained four short sections.[12] The opening section reads as follows:

> To stress banning the shedding of Palestinian blood and to take all measures and arrangements to prevent the shedding of Palestinian blood, to stress the importance of national unity as the basis for national steadfastness and confronting the occupation, and to achieve the legitimate national goals of the Palestinian people and adopt the language of dialogue as the sole basis for solving the political disagreements on the Palestinian arena. Within this context, we offer gratitude to the brothers in Egypt and the Egyptian security delegation in Gaza who exerted tremendous efforts to calm the conditions in the Gaza Strip in the past period.[13]

This section embodied the elements of the ethos agreed upon by the two sides: a stop to violent acts that shed Palestinian blood in vain, and a firm and united stance against the Israeli occupation in order to return to Palestine.

Section 2 confirmed a final agreement to form a Palestinian national unity government according to a detailed agreement ratified by both sides, and to start on an urgent basis to take the constitutional measures to form this government. The new government would be formed in five weeks. In practice, the new Palestinian government that was eventually sworn in on March 17 was an expression of the deep controversy between the parties over the division of powers. Hamas had nine seats in the new cabinet, Fatah had six: five seats for the independent factions and another four for smaller parties. However, the parties failed to agree on controversial portfolios such as finance, interior, foreign affairs, social affairs, and information. The temporary compromise was to give these portfolios to independent technocrats or smaller parties. The rationale was not only political but also diplomatic—to encourage the international community to lift the boycott, so that the PA could receive assistance.

Analyzing this section reveals, in fact, a deep political disagreement between the parties, which explains why eventually, despite reaching an agreement, it fell apart. Both sides sought political power by controlling: (1) resource allocation (Ministry of Finance); (2) security forces (Ministry of the Interior); (3) information, in order to control the contents of the public agenda on the Palestinian street; (4) welfare—to ensure support for those in need in the population. All of this leads to the realization that, despite the common ethos, each party sought to realize its own vision through political control. Both sides barricaded themselves in their positions despite the signing of a strike agreement. These positions were allocated in the next rounds of talks after Hamas took over the Gaza Strip in June 2007.

Section 2 enabled Hamas to nominate three of the independent ministers, while Fatah is permitted to appoint two. Abu Mazen had right to veto Hamas nominations, but Hamas did not have the right to veto Fatah nominees. He also insisted on maintaining control over most of the security forces. These two issues—the veto right and the direct linkage to security apparatuses—reflected Abu Mazen's distrust of Hamas. On the other hand, Hamas asserted that the agreement did not require it to recognize Israel, a political position derived from a rigid ideology whereby all of Palestine should be liberated. This position was different from Abu Mazen's, despite the shared ethos.

Sections 3 and 4 of the agreement dealt with political measures that should be taken to stimulate reform within the PLO and the PA. Basically, Hamas was interested in being part of the PLO, the legitimate source of the PA. This interest served the political vision of the movement to become the dominant power in the Palestinian political system. Obviously, Abu Mazen could not afford for Hamas to have a foothold in the secular organization under his leadership. As for the PA, section 4 highlighted the principle of political partnership based on the effective laws of the PA and according to political pluralism.

Both clauses were formulated in the agreement in general without specific measures being taken by the parties. As I mentioned earlier, the new government got under way by mid-March 2007. During the period leading up to that, quite a few disagreements emerged between the parties, which again reflected the choice of behavioral attitude over the integrative approach. In other words, neither party that signed the Mecca agreement did so wholeheartedly, and both believed the chance of successfully implementing it to be faint to impossible.

Abu Mazen's speech at the end of the discussions was brief and almost entirely dedicated to expressing gratitude to the Saudi host. In his final paragraph he wished Ismail Haniyeh and the new Palestinian government success in its challenges.[14] This was a general statement, which included neither his commitment to help the government nor any willingness to give up his positions. In this sense, Abu Mazen lacks key attributes that negotiators require, such as leadership, responsibility, commitment, and good relations with the other party.

Reinforcement of Abu Mazen's position came two months later. In May 2007, the Palestinian president made a speech marking fifty-nine years since the Nakba. In his speech, he included all the elements of the shared Palestinian ethos, both the secular and religious streams: the Nakba; the vision of establishing an independent state with Jerusalem as the capital; the suffering of refugees, prisoners, and martyrs; and finally, Arafat, the commander and symbol of the Palestinian struggle. In that speech, he briefly noted the existence of the national unity government and chose to focus on article 3 of the Mecca agreement: the need to maintain the PLO, the only legal representative of the Palestinian people, and the source of authority for the unity government led by Hamas. Abu Mazen chose to mention that the PA is committed to all the agreements it has signed, thus effectively distinguishing between the two movements: a shared ethos, yes, but two different ways of fulfilling the vision—one negotiating with Israel and the other liberating Palestine through armed struggle.[15]

The basic disagreement between the parties, specifically over the control of the security apparatuses, continued, almost automatically, after the PA and Hamas delegations returned from Mecca to the territories. On February 14, Abu Mazen already announced that he was canceling his planned speech on the unity government because "there are disputes with Hamas over the implementation of the Mecca accord." Haniyeh, on his part, submitted to Abu Mazen a list of demands, the most important of which were: (1) that Fatah and Hamas agree on who would fill the posts of interior minister and deputy to the prime minister (in fact, Hamas had proposed two names for interior minister, but Abbas had vetoed both); (2) that Abbas guarantee that the Executive Security Force of Hamas be allowed to continue to operate as a separate unit from the other Abbas-controlled security forces. Haniyeh resigned officially on February 15, a week after the Mecca accord was signed, and accepted the mandate to form a new government according to Mecca agreement.

Developments in the field, in the internal Palestinian arena, and at that time between the Palestinian factions and Israel presented significant obstacles to Ismail Haniyeh:

1. Al-Aqsa Martyr Brigades (AMB), a nickname for Fatah armed groups and Islamic Jihad activists, carried out a suicide bombing in the southern city of Eilat (January 29, 2007). The message was sent to both PA and Hamas leaders: There was no place for a unity government that agrees to any concessions to Israel.[16]

2. The Israel Antiquities Authority began (February 6, 2007) carrying out salvage excavations in the archaeological park to place permanent, raised pillars—to be built for the welfare of visitors and for their safety. The new structure would replace the temporary wooden bridge erected following the collapse of the old upland.[17] This led to protests in the Palestinian territories. In the West Bank, the IDF stepped up its activity, which included arrest raids, house searches, home demolitions, and restrictions on Palestinian travel. At the same period settlers' violence against Palestinians escalated.

3. In the Gaza Strip, Palestinians continued to launch high-trajectory weapons at Israel. From mid-January to mid-February, the Palestinians fired more than seventy rockets at Israel, and the Israeli Defense Forces (IDF) retaliated, killing four Palestinians. The Israeli Air Force launched missiles at launching sites of Hamas and other terror organizations all over the Gaza Strip, homes of militants, and smugglers' tunnels.

The security escalation on the ground and the mutual violence between the Palestinians and Israelis diverted Abu Mazen's attention from the internal political situation. He invested his time in directly and indirectly asking (through the United States) Israel to end the round of violence. All this significantly delayed the negotiations between him and Haniyeh on the formation of the new government. It was only at the beginning of March 2007 that he renewed contact with Hamas. The parties announced on March 14 their agreement on a new government, which was sworn in three days later.[18] Prime Minister Haniyeh of Hamas said the coalition wanted to set up a Palestinian state in the lands that Israel occupied in the 1967 Mideast War. He said the Palestinians affirmed the right to resist occupation but would also seek to expand a truce with Israel. His speech ignored the Quartet demand to accept their conditions, and it was a clear message that the prime minister's national interests in Palestine did not agree with Abu Mazen's.

Despite the new government, PA-Hamas interactions deteriorated quickly during the first half of 2007. Abu Mazen, again, clung to his own interests (the behavioral approach) and took action to consolidate power, especially in the security sphere, with the assistance of the US. This was perceived by Hamas as a cynical maneuver, particularly when Abu Mazen refused to approve a plan drawn up by the interior minister (Hani Qawasmeh, Independent) designed to integrate the Executive Security Force (ESF) of Hamas, which acted like police, into security mechanisms. The interior minister sought to increase security forces in the field. The Palestinian president saw this as a threat to the homogeneity of the security forces, which consisted of Fatah members. At that time, he was interested in strengthening his security forces through assistance that he received from the United States. Moreover, heads of security apparatuses informed the minister that they intended to report directly to the Palestinian president. In early April 2007, Mohammad Dahlan, the head of Preventive Security Forces, completed the first step of forming a new Fatah special force (1,400 members). Their main task was to be an intervention force if clashes with Hamas were to resume. He even asked Israel to allow them to receive large shipments of arms and ammunition from Arab countries, including Egypt, in order to fight against Hamas.[19]

Abu Mazen backed Dahlan and even appointed him as a national security adviser. The move led to the resignation of Hani Qawasmeh, the interior minister (April 23), on the grounds that he could not perform his role in front of the security forces. Ismail Haniyeh rejected the resignation. Two weeks later Abu Mazen decided, unilaterally, to deploy three thousand PA security personnel in central and northern Gaza as part of a new crackdown to "improve law and order."

Following the presidential decision, Fatah members and security forces started setting up roadblocks, stopping cars for random security checks, and conducting high-profile patrols across Gaza. They refused to coordinate efforts with the interior minister or with the ESF of Hamas. On May 14, 2007, Qawasmeh resigned, explaining that "he had not been given authority to direct the security forces that were supposed to be under his control."[20] By the time Qawasmeh left his office, twenty-four Palestinians were killed and dozens wounded, an outcome of new clashes between the parties. The total number of fatalities from October 2006 to May 2007 was 191. Hard liners from both sides did not like the idea of unity government, attempting to undermine unity by escalating clashes in the field. Thus, in March 2007, Fatah militants fired on a Hamas vehicle in the West Bank. There was a heavy exchange of fire between the parties in Beit Hanun in the Gaza Strip. On March 13, Fatah members assassinated a senior Izz al-Din al-Qassam Brigades member in Gaza City. In response, Hamas detonated a large explosive charge outside the house of an important Fatah member. Incidences of mutual violence continued in March, April, and May, increasing the number of casualties among the rival parties.

Hamas Takes the Gaza Strip

The Mecca accord's de facto crash came in mid-June 2007. Despite countless statements from both sides confirming their commitment to the signed agreement, the developments on the ground shaped the future. During the first half of 2007, a violent armed struggle continued between the PA and Hamas adherents. Neither side believed the rival party nor estimated that the Mecca accord could be implemented—that is, that it could be a platform for a functioning unity government in which the president (Abu Mazen) and prime minister (Haniyeh) would cooperate for the benefit of the Palestinian people. The growing interest of both parties was to control at all costs, which is in fact a "zero-sum game."[21]

In a historical analysis, it turns out that Dahlan's request, with Abu Mazen's approval, to allow Israel to supply weapons to Fatah, had a decisive effect on the deteriorating situation in June 2007, when, eventually,

Hamas took control of the Gaza Strip. Various reports claim that the arms shipment included antitank missiles, armored vehicles, and RPGs (rocket-propelled grenades). Hamas, primarily the military force of the movement, did not remain indifferent to these reports. At this point, they understood that their campaign was in fact twofold: one opponent was Israel, which harmed them and helped the Palestinian Authority; the other opponent was the secular camp in the Palestinian arena that was trying to dismantle the movement by force. This all happened when they were enjoying legitimacy following the election victory for the legislative council. On June 7, an armed Fatah activist opened fire toward an ESF patrol in Rafah. This tactical incident, of which there were thousands during a whole year of violent confrontations, sparked a new wave of bloodshed. The situation for many within the Gaza Strip escalated rapidly during the second week of June: An exchange of heavy fire became routine; people (including innocent civilians) were injured or killed. Abu Mazen and Haniyeh called for an immediate ceasefire, but the fighting continued with different methods of killing, as well as kidnapping and bombing (including RPGs and mortars).[22]

These were historic days, days of decision-making. Negotiations passed from the discussion table at the Mecca palace to the Gaza Strip streets. The leadership changed its face. It was no longer the buttoned-down leadership of a president and prime minister but a leadership of street gangs, making physical decisions through fighting—which might bring about changes in government. The Izz al-Din al-Qassam Brigades, the military wing of Hamas, felt during those days that they were fighting for the future of all of Palestine and raided Fatah's Gaza City offices to establish facts on the ground. Ismail Haniyeh's private residence and the presidential compound of Abu Mazen were attacked too.[23] On June 14, the picture became clear. Hamas had taken over key positions across Gaza, including the presidential complex and the headquarters of security forces. The rivals' fates were revealed. The religious stream had taken over the Gaza Strip, and since then reality there has been that of two geopolitical entities that share a common ethos but lack the ability to put internal disagreements aside and focus on national challenges.

Abu Mazen's reply was "too little, too late." By the time he ordered his security forces to defend their posts and positions, Hamas had gained nearly complete control of all the territory of the Gaza Strip. The last outpost, the presidential compound, was seized toward midnight of June 14. The Palestinian president dismantled the unity government (he de facto canceled the Mecca accord) and declared a "state of emergency." This step was decided and announced after hundreds of Fatah representatives, among them senior members, had fled by boat to Egypt.[24]

Perhaps the most amazing step at this point of armed negotiation was taken by Haniyeh. Haniyeh insisted on remaining in his position as prime minister based on Palestinian law.[25] However, he also announced that he was interested in resuming the day-to-day functioning of the government until Fatah and Hamas could enter a reconciliation dialogue. This can be perceived not just as a gesture from the winning side to the losers, but as a move that reflected responsibility and commitment (to the civilians), as well as a political understanding by Haniyeh that Hamas would have to work with Abu Mazen. Haniyeh's stance leads to the conclusion that he clung to the integrative approach and at the same time posited himself personally—and eventually Hamas as a political power—in an equal position to Abu Mazen. The new reality created in Palestinian society and politics—of two separate entities—was henceforth the opening situation in which the next rounds of negotiations between the Palestinian Authority and Hamas would begin.

Chapter 5

Sana'a Declaration, March 2008

New Order on the Ground

The new geopolitical situation required both sides to reassess their policy. Hamas, the winning side of the battle, faced for the first time a new situation, which was to be the opening of phase four in its evolution. From a political player that encountered opposition for many years, it changed into a de facto sovereign state in the Gaza Strip. Hamas leaders, perhaps adopting an attitude reserved for victors, took a conciliatory approach. Khaled Masha'al offered to resume talks between the parties, and Haniyeh made it clear that the movement was fully committed to the Mecca accord. He also instructed the military forces to calm the situation as much as possible.[1]

On the other side, during the first few months after the Hamas takeover of the Gaza Strip, the Palestinian president did not seek dialogue with the national-religious movement Hamas to examine the possibility that the movement would restore power and authority to the PA. "What Hamas did is a crime against the nation and a military putsch and those responsible for these actions are the sacked prime minister and others in the movement. As soon as they admit their responsibility for this coup and change the situation on the ground, we will reconsider, but for the moment there will not be any dialogue with them."[2]

Instead, Abu Mazen focused on an effort to fortify and strengthen West Bank authorities. He issued several presidential decrees aimed at suspending the activity of the legislative council, dominated by Hamas, and removed legislative and judicial oversight by the executive, paving the way for him to decide according to his personal interests. It was a clear signal that he did not believe that Hamas would consent to relinquishing control of the Gaza Strip. It also mirrored his fear of the possibility that Hamas activists in the West Bank would seek to exploit their success in order to undermine his rule. He dismissed Haniyeh from the post of prime minister and appointed Salam Fayyad, a pro-Western moderate, as prime minister of the emergency government. The move received backing from the United States and Israel. The Palestinian president accused Hamas of a coup, breaking the law, and added that there was a group among the people that wanted to destroy them, sow fear, and attack innocents, but that this was a temporary situation.[3]

Under the new circumstances, renewal of negotiations was not a real option. In fact, Abu Mazen shook the foundation of the democratic process that led to Hamas's victory in the legislative council and created two governments, in effect: an elected government in Gaza, headed by Haniyeh, and an appointed government in the West Bank. This situation in effect gave a new status to the government in Gaza, which would operate independently and not under the appointed government. Hamas's power, which seemed equally powerful to that of the PA, would be reflected in the future dialogue between the parties. Abu Mazen also made a change in the security leadership and appointed veteran Fatah members, his contemporaries, to head these apparatuses, among them 'Abd el-Razak Al-Yahya, who became minister of the interior.[4]

Situation in the Gaza Strip

Meanwhile, on the ground, summer and fall 2007 had witnessed significant changes in the Palestinian reality. The Palestinian establishment in Gaza, under Haniyeh's government, tried to get life back to normal. In August 2007, local authorities reopened. In those days, a new phenomenon emerged that placed the PA and Hamas as equals, at least in public. This can be seen, for example, in the case of abducted British journalist Alan Johnston. He was kidnapped in March 2007 and released on July 4. The leaders of both opposing parties were quick to issue a press release on the matter. The PA president said: "Without a shred of a doubt, we are very happy for the release of our friend, the journalist Alan Johnston. This man's detention, and the detention of any other man anywhere, pains and harms us and the entire Palestinian people."

Hamas's prime minister Ismail Haniyeh said: "This case was a priority for the Hamas government. We made a big effort in the past months to free him." Hamas political bureau chief Khaled Masha'al said: "Our message at this moment is that nobody in Palestine—especially in Gaza—is above the law."[5]

The Johnston affair was another tier that made Hamas a state actor no longer subject to Abu Mazen, at least not in the Gaza Strip. Musa Abu Marzook, Hamas Political Bureau Deputy Chief, perfectly portrayed Hamas's leading position at the time, to make them an influential political player: "The attempt to squeeze out Hamas would fail and isolating the Gaza Strip would breed a dangerous, long-term bitterness between Gazans and PA president Mahmoud Abbas's leadership. If they expect peace to come through conferences that exclude Hamas, they are wrong . . . conferences cannot disregard the fact that Hamas is the strongest side on the Palestinian street level."[6]

In Gaza, Fatah members tried to challenge the new regime of Hamas, firing in the air and throwing stones at the Executive Security Force's members. In retaliation, ESF activists amplified their actions against Fatah and the public in general. They dispersed crowds, beat protesters, arrested civilians for no reason, detaining Fatah members, and did not hesitate to open fire on the innocent. When Fatah asked to arrange a rally in Gaza City with the title "freedom of expression," Haniyeh issued a decree banning all kinds of demonstrations without an official license. Despite the decree, three hundred Fatah members held a protest, which was interrupted violently by ESF squads. The annual report of Human Rights Watch of 2008 defined the situation in Gaza:

> Since June 2007, when Hamas forcefully seized control in Gaza, it has conducted arbitrary arrests of political opponents, tortured detainees, clamped down on freedom of expression and assembly, and violated due process rights enshrined in Palestinian law. The victims have frequently been leaders, activists and supporters of Fatah, especially those with suspected ties to a security force or those who sought to undermine Hamas rule.[7]

Hamas as a de facto sovereign-state actor had to face a double challenge: first, to make sure that Fatah did not try to undermine its efforts to control; second, to establish its control through enforcement.

Various incidents that occurred during July 2007 provided Hamas with an opportunity to act. In the first case Hamas activists tracked Fatah members in the Gaza Strip and arrested them from time to time on various grounds. Hamas demanded that Fatah members pay bail for release of one of the detainees, but Ibrahim Abu Naja, a Fatah official in the Gaza Strip, said that his group would not pay. "This is a serious precedent."[8] The incident happened after Hamas activists violently dispersed a crowd of Fatah protesters, firing in the air and beating demonstrators. The second incident occurred on July 31, when a Hamas man shot dead a Hamas activist who took part in a demonstration near the Rafah crossing. The shooting took place when Hamas feared that protesters against the closure of the Rafah crossing were distressed and would attempt to break into Egypt.[9]

The third incident was late in August 2007, when Fatah activists in the main cities of Gaza called for a boycott of Friday prayers in mosques and for starting weekly protests to put pressure on Hamas to cease its persecution policy. Five thousand Fatah members gathered in Gaza City park (August 31), and after the prayers they started a rally, calling out against Hamas and attacking Hamas-controlled buildings with stones and pipe bombs. A similar demonstration with seven thousand Fatah members and supporters took place in Rafah. In response, the ESF of Hamas violently dispersed both protests, firing into the air, beating demonstrators, tossing percussion grenades, arresting scores of protesters, and injuring between ten and twenty people. On September 1, Abu Mazen condemned Hamas's behavior against civilians, stating that the movement had violated all the accepted civil and religious norms of the Palestinian people. He called for an urgent meeting of the executive committee of the PLO to discuss ways to end Hamas operatives' persecution of Fatah members in Gaza.[10]

In addition to the aforementioned incidents, Hamas through its enforcement apparatuses—Izz al-Din al-Qassam Brigades and ESF—acted to remove any political, security, or civil threats. The Palestinian Centre for Human Rights archive documented the many events that took place after the Yemeni initiative was published, from which it can be learned that Hamas strived to be the only sovereign on the ground. The movement adopted the popular slogan of Islam "one man, one vote, one time," and exploited its rise to power democratically to implement authoritarian rule.[11]

The Gaza Strip was witness to countless incidents such as those previously described. Fatah members were beaten, torched, arrested, injured, or killed. Distributors of newspapers printed in East Jerusalem (*Al-Quds*) or in the Palestinian Territories (*Al-Ayyam*, *Al-Hayat Al-Jadeeda*) were detained and banned throughout the Gaza Strip from distributing the newspapers. Public servants such as physicians, lawyers (including the attorney general and his deputy), and independent attorneys were dismissed, questioned, or arrested. All were indicted for misconduct, but the real reason was Hamas's suspicion that they were Fatah supporters.[12]

These events, in essence tactical incidents, were in fact proof of the Gaza situation: there was a new sovereign that did not intend to relinquish control. The political meaning of this situation from then on became clear: any future negotiations between the parties would put Hamas and the PA under Abu Mazen in equal positions. Both could claim the legitimacy of their rule, both had population responsibilities, and both were in leadership positions. Both were also looking to achieve different interests, a situation that reduced the chance of unity.

On November 7, 2007, Hamas decided to convene the legislative council. The meeting was held in Gaza and was attended by six members from the West Bank through a telephone call. Fatah representatives boycotted the meeting, claiming it was illegal.[13] The event sharpened the political rift: Hamas, a majority in the council, sought to express legislative activity—a clear expression of political sovereignty. On the other hand, Fatah people refused to acknowledge this. Such a reality reduced the chances of resuming negotiations, in which both sides would show a mutually positive attitude. By that time, Haniyeh managed to arrange his security mechanism, ESF (four units): police; internal security, providing protection for Hamas officials; national security, mainly in charge of the border with Egypt; and naval police. The total forces numbered around thirteen thousand men.

The West Bank

Both sides continued to disagree on the division of political powers between them. That was the case in mid-July, when Abu Mazen ordered his new prime minister, Salam Fayyad, not to pay a salary to Palestinian officials of the Gaza Strip until they publicly expressed support for him and not Hamas. In response, Sami Abu Zuhri, Hamas representative, said that "the Fayyad government's decision not to give thousands of employees their salaries enforces the political and geographical separation of the Palestinian people."[14]

A symmetrical appearance of governance developed on the ground in both areas: Hamas sought to establish control of the Gaza Strip; the PA sought the same in the West Bank. There were many demonstrations in both areas in which the message was reversed: Hamas people raised banners condemning Abu Mazen and Fatah; Fatah members accused Hamas of betraying the national idea and urged Abu Mazen to regain control of the Gaza Strip. Violence returned to the streets quickly. In the West Bank, PA security continued to hunt Hamas activists, arresting four hundred of them by mid-July. Their primary goal was to dismantle the Hamas infrastructure in the West Bank in order to achieve the main interest—political survival—for Abu Mazen's reign.

Abu Mazen, in turn, chose the behavioral approach, not only during negotiations with Hamas but also regarding changing the characteristics of his rule in the West Bank. A series of warrants that violated the human rights of Palestinians significantly eroded the separation of powers—meaning the legislature and the judiciary—to criticize the PA's policies. The Human Rights Watch report included the following on the West Bank:

> In the West Bank, the Fatah-dominated authorities have committed many of the same abuses, with victims being the activists, leaders and supporters of Hamas and affiliated institutions. Fearful of a Hamas takeover of the West Bank, security forces have detained hundreds of people arbitrarily, tortured detainees, and closed media and organizations that are run by or sympathetic to Hamas. The West Bank security forces have operated with significant support, financial or otherwise, from the United States, the European Union and Israel.[15]

After the publication of the Yemeni initiative (August 5, 2007, discussed later), the PA and Hamas negotiated indirectly, which can be called deaf dialogue. On the declarative level, they exchanged mutual accusations as they claimed responsibility for the political crisis on the other side. On an operational level, the parties adopted a similar policy aimed at establishing and strengthening their control over the territory.

In the West Bank Abu Mazen's policy toward Hamas was exactly as Hamas treated his people in Gaza. Security personnel closed more than one hundred charitable associations, most of them affiliated with Hamas. The official explanation was that these associations committed financial and administrative offenses, but the Palestinian Center for Civil Rights issued a statement expressing concern that it was a course intended to strengthen the Palestinian Authority's emergency measures and violate basic civil rights.[16]

Security apparatuses brutally dispersed demonstrations all over the West Bank. This was the case when women protested in Ramallah demanding that their families be released from Palestinian detention centers (September 2007), and when residents protested in Hebron against the closure of a Hamas TV station.[17] During the latter demonstration, two journalists from the same station were arrested, and the participants protested the PA violating freedom of expression (November 2007). That month, people in Hebron, Bethlehem, Ramallah, and Nablus who protested the Annapolis peace conference, demanding that the Palestinian president refuse to give up national aspirations—which were part of the ethos—were badly beaten. The same PA policy continued in 2008 when the US president visited Ramallah. PA security personnel brutally beat PFLP and PDLP protesters in Manara Square, the central square of the city.[18]

The Unnecessary Way to Sana'a

It was Abu Mazen who made the first move toward renewal of the dialogue. In his speech for the forty-third anniversary of Fatah, he said:

> I bear the supreme national responsibility to erase all the blurring and darkness of our clear image as a people, as an institution, as a cause, and despite criminal practices that conflict with the heritage of our people and our values, by Hamas and its militia that continue to arrest, kill, torture and try to prevent terrorism. Despite all this bitterness, I urge those who started the coup or what they called the military settlement to open the page of a new relationship within our single Palestinian home. A new page that we outline with a credible agreement based on a partnership in life on the homeland and the struggle for its liberation. There is no room for any party to be a substitute for the other party, and there is no

> room for the term coup or military resolution, but dialogue, dialogue and dialogue, until understanding deepens and lasts. Partnership, and I consider this approach an initiative in the name of all the Palestinian people and in the name of all of its brothers and friends who are keen on their interests.[19]

Abu Mazen based his call for a resumption of the dialogue on several components: his position as president; a common ethos for all Palestinians living in the homeland, which he believed was the West Bank and the Gaza Strip as a single unit; and the campaign the Palestinians were facing with Israel and the international system. However, it is highly questionable whether he believed in the ability to reach agreements following the June 2007 split.

Hamas, through Mahmood al-Zahar, accepted Abu Mazen's invitation to resume talks with Arab mediation. In fact, both sides met in Yemen (March 18, 2008) for the first time since Hamas took control of the Gaza Strip. This time the opening conditions were in Hamas's favor. The movement managed to stabilize its reign in Gaza. It also enjoyed popularity in public polls. Palestine Centre for Policy and Survey Research (PCPSR) data from mid-March 2008 showed an increase in Hamas support rates from 31 percent (in the December 2007 poll) to 35 percent, and a 7 percent drop in support for Abu Mazen (from 49 percent to 42 percent). Most of the Palestinian public also expressed opposition to the Palestinian president's political moves and supported the armed resistance Hamas led against Israel.[20] From Hamas's perspective, there was no reason to refuse the Yemeni initiative, especially when it did not require Hamas to give up assets and interests before beginning the dialogue. Abu Mazen, for his part, hoped that his responsiveness to the initiative and expressing a stance on national reconciliation could improve his standing in the public.

Senior Fatah and Hamas officials Azzam al-Ahmad and Musa Abu Marzuq opened face-to-face talks in Yemen, and after five days they signed a reconciliation agreement. Both sides valued Yemen's role as mediator, hoping that Arab states would support their mutual understanding.[21]

Analysis of the Yemeni Initiative

The Yemeni initiative for Palestinian internal reconciliation took effect on the PA and Hamas in early August 2007, less than two months after

Hamas took control of the Gaza Strip. Judging by a historical analysis, the reconciliation was premature. Both sides were preoccupied with political and physical survival, assessing the damages and losses they sustained in the eighteen months of fighting. The political atmosphere was one of total distrust and mutual suspicion. These were not ideal conditions, to say the least, for successful negotiations. Obviously, the two parties were not ready for the Yemeni initiative; however, out of mutual respect, they agreed to consider it. This readiness was granted after only seven months, which elicits a great deal of skepticism.

The Yemeni bargain had seven sections, as follows:[22]

a. Section 1 called for returning the situation in Gaza to what it was before June 6, 2007, adhering to what the Palestine Liberation Organization committed itself to, and holding early presidential and legislative elections. Apparently, the Yemeni proposal could have been terminated here, as this section contained propositions that Hamas refused to agree to: First, Hamas would not renounce its control over the Gaza Strip. The various statements made by the movement's leaders, Masha'al, Abu Marzouk, and Haniyeh (see previous discussion) expressed a clear interest in keeping the Gaza Strip in their hands. Other options, certainly before resuming negotiations with Abu Mazen, were not considered at all. Second, Hamas enjoyed control of the legislative council and there was no apparent reason to jeopardize it through new elections. Even the proposal to hold PA presidential elections—and perhaps to end Abu Mazen's reign—was a proposal that Hamas was not yet ready to accept, due to the need to establish its rule in the Gaza Strip.

b. Sections 2–5 dealt with reorganization of the political and security systems of the PA. Section 2 determined resumption of dialogue on the basis of the Mecca agreement of 2007, with the understanding that the Palestinian people were an indivisible whole, and that the Palestinian Authority consisted of the elected presidential authority, the elected parliament, and the executive authority represented by a government of national unity and commitment to Palestinian legitimacy with all its components. This was not the real picture of the political and geographic situation, as it stood in August 2007. In fact, the Yemeni suggestion did not offer a viable alternative for breaking the deadlock. It reflected the traditional Arab perspective of seeing the Palestinians as one inseparable community, which was an unrealistic interpretation of the social-political conditions in the Palestinian arena. In August 2007, two separate governments functioned in the Palestinian system. Section 3 called for respecting the Palestinian constitution and law and abiding by it all; and section 4 suggests rebuilding the security services on national bases, so that they belong to the supreme authority and the government of national unity, without any faction having a relationship with them. An analysis of section 2 is also relevant to this section. At the time, in August 2007, the Yemeni offer for reconciliation was cut off from reality, certainly after Abu Mazen accused Hamas of instigating a coup, trampling on the law, and committing crimes against innocents. Moreover, the proposed wording was general and murky, enabling Hamas to argue that Abu Mazen violated the constitutional provisions by dismissing a democratically elected government and appointing his own government to manage the situation in the West Bank.

c. Section 5 proposed forming a coalition government of national unity in which all factions would be represented according to their weight in the legislative council and would be able to fulfill all their responsibilities.

d. Section 6 discussed the option of forming a committee through the Arab League consisting of appropriate countries such as Egypt, Saudi Arabia, Syria, and Jordan. Yemen expressed willingness to participate if requested to do so, and its task would be to implement the foregoing. Apparently, this was the easiest section for both sides to agree to. The PA and Hamas regularly sought Arab support—political, economic, and in terms of security—and fulfilling this section would give them credit in Arab capitals. However, a closer look reveals that the fact that the Palestinians'

> opponents accepted this agreement meant that it had an external (Arab) influence on the design of the Palestinian political system.

Disagreement between the parties surfaced on the day the agreement was signed. Despite the solemn declarations, both parties presented materially different interpretations regarding the application of the clauses of the agreement. The PA presidency announced that "Hamas must accept ending its control of the Gaza Strip before any dialogue can take place." The PA interpretation was based on the joint statement in the Sana'a declaration: "We, the representatives of Fatah and Hamas, agree to the Yemeni initiative as a framework to resume dialogue between the two movements to return the Palestinian situation to what it was before the Gaza incidents."[23] For Abu Mazen the declaration was the end of the dialogue, as indicated by the statement he issued: "Resumption of dialogue . . . must take place to implement the Yemeni proposal and not to deal with it as a framework for dialogue because this will not lead to any result. We want the implementation of the proposal. We do not want talks over its articles."[24]

For Hamas, the signed agreement in Sana'a was just the first step in round two of the dialogue after the failure to implement the Mecca accord. The fact that Abu Mazen's position was rigid, demanding that the movement to return sovereignty over Gaza to the PA was unacceptable, in fact, a nonstarter when it came to discussion. Sami Abu Zuhri, Hamas representative, said that "Fatah's comment reflects the presidency's lack of regard for dialogue and it gives the impression that its signature is no more than an act of gratitude toward the Yemenis."[25]

Yemeni president 'Ali 'Abdallah Saleh was aware of the hostile relationship between the Palestinian rivals. Therefore, he decided to start the dialogue after the Arab summit in Damascus (March 29) was over with a supportive declaration for his mediation effort. The fact that he invited the Palestinian parties to talk was, in fact, reflected in Hamas's stance that further discussions were needed on how to summarize the details of the agreement, which were drafted along general lines. In practice, however, a completely different dynamic had developed in the Palestinian territories. Abu Mazen, who realized that the Sana'a declaration was not the end of the negotiations, chose to move in two directions. He did not refuse the invitation of the president of Yemen, and at the same time he acted to effectively cancel the contents of the statement. As a result, even before the Arab League convened in Damascus, demonstrations by thousands (March 26, 28) renewed the call for the parties to resume the dialogue. Khaled Masha'al even invited Abu Mazen to meet with Ismail Haniyeh in Gaza.[26] Instead, Abu Mazen headed to Damascus to participate in the Arab summit. His speech focused on the political deadlock with Israel, and he called for international protection for the Palestinians, warning, "if we don't reach peace by 2008, tensions and instability will spread to all countries in the region."[27]

Hamas rejected Abu Mazen's speech, while at the same time senior executives stepped up their statements on the political conflict with Israel. For the movement, this was another move toward becoming a sovereign-state player. Nearly a year after taking over the Gaza Strip, the movement did not hesitate to challenge the PLOs hegemony, further increasing Abu Mazen's suspicions of its intentions. The following two statements emphasized this change within Hamas: Ghazi Hamad, Hamas spokesperson, said that "the movement is now prepared for a partial truce that would only include the Gaza Strip. In return, Hamas wants Israel and Egypt to open their trade and passenger crossings with Gaza, which have been sealed since Hamas seized control of the territory last June. The proposal has been relayed to Egyptian mediators."[28] In parallel, Masha'al announced that Hamas agreed to the establishment of a Palestinian state in the Palestinian territories that Israel occupied in 1967 if the Palestinian people would accept this in a referendum. But Hamas would not recognize Israel.[29]

To conclude, the Sana'a declaration remained, finally, a dead letter.[30] The Yemeni initiative was offered in August 2007, but the parties managed to meet only seven months later. Despite mutual smiling and a joint declaration based on both an interest in not harming the Yemeni mediator and on a common national ethos, the parties' broad political interests at this time were already different. Hamas saw itself as a legitimate sovereign player after winning the 2006 elections as well as popular support in the Gaza Strip, having achieved the movement's goals since it took over in June 2007. By March 2008, it had already formulated a different political and social vision than those of the PA. Abu Mazen tried to minimize damage through talks in Yemen, but significant differences in interpretation with Hamas of the Sana'a statement tainted the prospect of implementing it. Both sides adhered to a structural (dialogue through mediator) and behavioral (mutual suspicion) negotiation approach, and strategically, out of respect, each came to the same conclusion individually that any concession in favor of the other would result in a win-lose situation.

Chapter 6

Cairo Agreement, 2009

This chapter discusses the Egyptian effort on behalf of PA and Hamas. It was the third round of talks aiming to end the internal Palestinian rift. This time the dialogue continued for three months and took place after a military campaign between Hamas and Israel (Operation Cast Lead, December 27, 2008–January 18, 2009). The Egyptians also changed the structure of the negotiations, bringing together representatives of other Palestinian factions and dividing the participants into five subgroups.[1] Following the failure of the Yemen mediation, the situation within the Palestinian territories remained divided.

Gaza Strip: Hamas's Rule Is Established

Hamas felt free to act to establish its sovereignty in the Gaza Strip. It also expanded its operations against terrorists who did not obey the government's instructions. For example, on May 17, 2008, the Hamas force raided a mosque of Salafi group (global jihad) in the Jabaliya refugee camp, after the imam attacked Hamas policy in the Gaza Strip. The following day a Hamas man fired at a Salafi (global Jihad) activist who tried to launch a Qassam rocket at Israel, at a time when it was in Hamas's interest to fire. In another incident, Hamas forcefully intervened to end a clash between Palestinian Islamic Jihad members in Deir al-Balah and the Nuseirat refugee camp.[2]

In general, the extent of the clashes between Hamas and Fatah supporters had diminished and the latter were coming to terms with the new reality in which the Islamic stream was in fact the sovereign one in the Gaza Strip. Occasionally there were serious incidents, one of which occurred at the end of July 2008, when a bomb was detonated near the home of the Hamas senior Marwan Abu Ras. Three members of Hamas were killed and more than twenty injured. The incident led to further tensions in the Gaza Strip. Hamas arrested two hundred Fatah activists while trying to locate those involved in placing the explosive charge.[3]

Hamas was working on a number of issues in the area to strengthen law and order: it stopped smugglers of goods through tunnels excavated from Egypt to the Gaza Strip; it cleared booths and huts set up by unlicensed residents along the coast; and it followed journalists suspected of supporting Fatah. Security services of Hamas arrested supporters of the Fatah movement, among whom were 15 who occupied leadership positions, including secretaries of districts and the spokesperson of the Fatah movement in Gaza, Dr. Hazem Abu Shanab. Political detainees also included Dr. Ussama al-Farra, governor of Khan Yunis, and Mr. Ahmed al-Qidwa, governor of Gaza. In all these situations, violent, brutal clashes occurred from time to time, such as the two follow examples:

1. A serious shooting incident (August 2) stood out when its armed force engaged in a shootout with members of the Helles clan in central Gaza, which Hamas saw as opposition. In the exchange of fire, 11 people were killed and 103 injured.[4]

2. Bloody clashes took place between the Palestinian police and gunmen from the Dughmosh clan in the Al-Sabra neighborhood in the east of Gaza City. Ten members of the Dughmosh clan, including two children and a police officer, were killed; another forty-two persons, including ten police officers, were wounded.[5]

At that time, Hamas was positioning itself not only as a sovereign, but also as an influential political party against Israel. It announced its willingness to implement a ceasefire with Israel, in order to promote concern for the lives of residents of Gaza. By doing so, it would increase its legitimacy to the population. To this end, Hamas police forces thwarted terrorist groups that aimed to launch rockets at Israel; at the same time preachers at the mosques were instructed to explain to the public during Friday prayers the importance of the ceasefire. Another important move in this regard came at the end of June 2008, when one of Hamas's security leaders discussed with other factions' representatives the possibility of firing at Israel in response to IDF activity in the West Bank. It was, actually, an attempt to signal to residents of the West Bank that Hamas considered itself responsible for them and was not settling for just controlling Gaza.

Escalation in the West Bank

After the failure of the Sana'a negotiations, Abu Mazen continued to adhere to the rigorous policy adopted in June 2007. Fearing for the survival of his regime and his security, Palestinian Authority security forces acted throughout the West Bank to counter threats, real or imagined, to the stability of the PA. They raided homes of wanted activists, detained Hamas activists with no real reason, made large-scale arrests against opposition activists, and continued to monitor journalists. International organizations and human rights institutions continued monitoring violations of the law by PA security apparatuses. The following incidents illustrate the situation within the West Bank during the second half of 2008:

1. A General Intelligence Service (GIS) squad used force to arrest Assed 'Amara, a photographer, in Bethlehem, while he was filming a rally to mark the sixty-year anniversary of the Nakba (May 8, 2008). The official reason for his arrest was working for Al-Aqsa television station, which was affiliated with Hamas. This tactical event embodied Abu Mazen's policy: Despite the demonstration being held within the framework of the national ethos, there was no room for commemorative activity by parties affiliated with the opposition to his rule. The ethos belonged to both sides, but the right to commemoration activity was the PA's alone. On the other hand, the political vision was to regain control of the Gaza Strip and become a dominant political power in the Palestinian arena, contrary to Hamas's vision.[6]

2. On the same day, the GIS arrested two journalists and a columnist in Qalqilya. One of them, Mustafa Sabri, said that he was accused of distributing flyers criticizing Palestinian security apparatuses for their activity. In two other

incidents, GIS squads arrested Issam Shawar, a dentist and a columnist for the *Palestine Daily*, which is published in Gaza and whose distribution in the West Bank had been banned for several months; they also detained Mohammed Darwish, a cameraman for the Associated Press.

3. On September 23, 2008, GIS officers searched Samira Halaiqa's office in Hebron. Halaiqa was a Palestinian Legislative Council (PLC) member of the "Change and Reform" party, affiliated with Hamas. The intelligence squad confiscated documents and video cassettes, arguing that they contained incitement materials against the PA.[7]

The PA's mechanisms continued to monitor and arrest Hamas activists. There was a wide wave of arrests in July 2008, and among those detained were public figures, imams of mosques, schoolteachers, university students, journalists, and elected members of local councils. Several released detainees stated that they were subjected to cruel treatment, including torture. PCHR reported in May 2008 that Palestinians from all over the West Bank were afraid to complain after receiving threats from security officials that if they did so, they would be arrested. It also called for security forces of PA and Hamas in Gaza to stop violating human rights.[8] The security forces of both sides ignored the call and continued rigid security policies to protect the incumbent regime. In one case, Shadi Shahin was arrested on charges of violating public safety, when he tried to set fire to the home of Nabil Amru, former PA information and legislative council member. Shahin, 27, died during detention in Jericho.[9]

The PA's policy against Hamas was not only applied to security-related events. At the end of October 2008, Palestinian education minister Lamees al-'Alami sent a severance letter to over eighty West Bank teachers identified as Hamas. The letter said: "Upon the directives of the relevant authorities, it has been decided that you are to be relieved of your post." One of the teachers said the letter came after the security forces claimed she was linked to Hamas, which she herself denied. A more thorough investigation revealed that one of her relatives committed a suicide bombing during the second intifada (2000–2005) though at the time she did not even live in the Palestinian territories. Her attempts to change the decision failed. Similarly, the PA fired 1,500 teachers for security reasons, namely, because of ties with Hamas or other opposition organizations.[10] The Authority's leadership understood the threat of employing Hamas-affiliated teachers. Educators can make a direct impact on the next generation, and Abu Mazen sought to reduce that impact by dismissing teachers and hiring educators to teach content that served his rule. This was one of the most prominent examples of using the shared national ethos to achieve different goals for realizing different visions; in this case, the goal was to shape the education of the next generation.

The Road to Cairo

Despite the deep rift, as early as July 2008, perhaps in a victorious move, Hamas offered to resume internal Palestinian dialogue. Khaled Masha'al called for resumption of talks in Yemen or in Qatar. He said that Hamas "supports talks to resume the Palestinian dialogue on the basis of the Yemeni initiative with the aim of restoring the Palestinian situation in Gaza and the West Bank to what it was before and remedying all the causes that led to the Palestinian dispute."[11] This statement was certainly too general at the time, when both sides were continuing to tighten their control over a population living in Gaza or the West Bank. Masha'al also failed to soften his position by joining in Hamas's good will toward Abu Mazen, or to show that there was a benefit in renewing the dialogue at that point.

Earlier in October, Ismail Radwan, senior member of Hamas in Gaza, rejected the idea of a technocrat government or new elections. Radwan said that Hamas did not trust that other actors would not fabricate election results for the West Bank. This lack of trust is consonant with the behavioral approach. However, he welcomed the formation of a national unity government as part of a comprehensive dialogue that would also reform the security services in Palestine.[12] In December, Haniyeh, Gaza's prime minister, addressed thousands of people, marking Hamas's twenty-first anniversary: "Brothers and sisters, we confirm with this huge crowd on this great and special day that our people have only grown stronger since the siege of Gaza!"[13]

They both clearly stated Hamas's interest in the possibility of negotiating with the Palestinian Authority: no new elections are necessary, as less than three years have passed since the elections; there is no need for a new government because there is an incumbent government that enjoys the support of most of the legislative council; we are ready to resume the talks. Hamas assumed the uncompromising position of a self-confident, strong political power that considered itself an equal partner, if not superior.

In November, following pressure from Egypt on both sides to resume talks, Hamas refused to send its delegation to Cairo. The official reason was Hamas's allegations against Abu Mazen's security policy. Specifically, Fawzi Baroum, Hamas spokesperson, stated that "Hamas has decided not to attend the dialogue talks in Egypt. We have informed the Egyptian authorities of our decision. Our decision was made because president Mahmud Abbas is continuing to weaken the Hamas movement and he has not released any Hamas detainees in the West Bank."[14]

The PA response was cynical and did not convey a desire for dialogue. PA spokesperson Nabil Abu Rudeina criticized Hamas's decision and blamed the group for being responsible for the failure of the talks, stating: "Hamas carries the responsibility for the failure of the Cairo dialogue and the responsibility for losing the opportunity to regain Palestinian unity and stop the division between Palestinians."[15]

Looking back, it seems that Israel pushed PA and Hamas to negotiate. The military campaign of December 27, 2008, to January 18, 2009, in Gaza (Operation Cast Lead) clarified, again, for the Palestinians, especially those who lived under Hamas's reign, that they needed to recalculate their political moves within the internal arena. The chronology of the escalation went back to June 2008. Israel and Hamas agreed to a ceasefire for six months according to the official announcement of the UN: "Palestinian militants agreed to immediately halt their attacks on Israel and Israel agreed to cease its military operations in Gaza. Israel also agreed to ease its blockade of Gaza and to gradually lift its ban on the import of a large number of commodities."[16] The agreement was reached through Egyptian mediation and was effectively maintained until November 5, when IDF forces detonated a terror tunnel excavated from the Gaza Strip into Israeli territory. Six Hamas activists were killed in this incident, which led to the resumption of fire from Gaza to Israel.[17]

Hamas did not officially announce the end of the ceasefire until December 18, six months after it was signed, although it was clear that the negotiations collapsed as early as November following a massive resumption of intense firing from Gaza to Israel.[18] According to Israel's official position, the goal of Operation Cast Lead was to improve the security reality for the Israeli residents of the south of the country, after more than seven years of missile attacks.[19] The Israeli military operation lasted twenty-one days and cost the lives of at least 1,166 Palestinian in the Gaza Strip.[20] Between six hundred and seven hundred factories, small industries, workshops, and other business enterprises throughout the Gaza Strip were destroyed—plus twenty-four mosques, thirty-one security compounds, and ten water or sewage lines.[21]

Israel announced, unilaterally, a ceasefire (January 18), while Hamas and other Palestinian groups in Gaza accepted it hours later. However, public statements by Hamas senior officials explained Hamas's vision to liberate all Palestine via control of the Palestinian political system. During the campaign Masha'al called for the West Bank population to start the third uprising (intifada) against the Israeli occupation, mentioning Fatah, "which was the first to use rifles, to open the first uprising and to lead the (national) struggle."[22] Masha'al wisely used the armed struggle component of the shared national ethos to call on Abu Mazen–controlled West Bank residents to join Hamas's national struggle against Israel. In doing so, he hoped to agitate the population against two opponents—Israel and the PA. He repeated this call time and again in the following decade after the Operation Cast Lead.[23]

According to the official website of the Palestinian news agency, the first public speech by Abu Mazen in 2009 was on February 4, 2009.[24] In a mirror image of Masha'al's directive, Abu Mazen made sure to tie together both parts of the Palestinian people and present himself as the president of everyone. He described the suffering afflicting the Gaza Strip as the result of the military campaign. He also blamed Israel in the ongoing violation of Palestinian rights of those living in the West Bank and in East Jerusalem. He described the tragic scenes in different cities of Palestine and the continuing damage caused by Israel's policy. Like Masha'al, the Palestinian president used the national ethos to explain the national vision of an independent state in the land in 1967's border and its capital being East Jerusalem. As was the case with the Yemeni initiative, this time Abu Mazen was also the first to call for renewed Palestinian dialogue. He said that "national reconciliation and the formation of a national reconciliation government constitute one of our priorities. We have opened the door to that reconciliation that ends the division and coup and the repercussions of the separation between Gaza and the West Bank."[25]

This conciliatory speech by the Palestinian president came just days after he decided in Cairo to make sure that the Hamas-Israel ceasefire agreement, reached through Egyptian mediation, did not harm the Palestinian Authority and the PLO, as the only representative of the Palestinian people. Hence, following statements by Hamas officials, who set preconditions for renewed Palestinian dialogue and challenged the PLO's dominance. Osama Hamdan, Hamas's representative in Lebanon, said that the "Palestinian Authority must end security coordination and peace talks with Israel before any reconciliation talks between the two rival Palestinian groups can take place."[26] Khaled Masha'al called for creating a new Palestinian "reference" or representative body, to replace the PLO.[27] By that time, the aspiration of Hamas to be the dominant political power within the Palestinian system was clear, and Abu Mazen worked to minimize damages. As in 2008, his public popularity was low compared to Haniyeh: while Abu Mazen's public support dropped from 58 percent in December 2008 to 45 percent in March 2009, Haniyeh's popularity climbed from 32 percent to 58 percent.[28]

In fact, Hamas used Egyptian mediating with Israel to check the odds for resumption of dialogue with the PA. Salah Bardawil, one of Hamas's political leaders in Gaza, announced after visiting Cairo (February 4, 2009) that "Egypt intends to invite Palestinian factions to a meeting on February 22 to clarify how national reconciliation will proceed. Five committees will be formed to deal with specific aspects of the internal Palestinian conflict, including security and the structure of the Palestine Liberation Organization (PLO)."[29] The last point was the significant change that characterized the opening momentum of the negotiations this time compared to the Mecca and Sana'a dialogues. Hamas had challenged the PLO's hegemony. Bringing the issue to the negotiating agenda gave the movement more flexibility and a broader scope during the talks, so that if it were to be waived, it would be a topic to discuss in the future.

The dialogue between the parties started on February 25 under the auspices of Egypt. After two days of discussions both sides (and representatives of another eleven Palestinian factions) agreed to form five committees tasked with the following in order to reach an agreement by the end of March: (1) forming a unity government, (2) holding parliamentary and presidential elections, (3) fostering reconciliation, (4) reforming the security services, and (5) reforming the PLO. All committees were monitored by Egypt, and they held four rounds of discussions between March and May 2009; they agreed on new legislative and new presidential elections (four and five years after the previous elections, respectively). It was also agreed to discuss ways to rehabilitate the Gaza Strip after Operation Cast Lead.

As a step demonstrating seriousness and good will, Salam Fayyad, prime minister of the West Bank, submitted his resignation to Abu Mazen (March 7). This was to enable the unity government to be formed.[30] More than a decade later, it seems that Fayyad's move was too little and apparently too late. Two weeks later, while negotiations continued, one participant leaked that the talks were stuck on the unity government's composition and powers.[31] The parties pledged, as confidence-building gestures, to release detainees of each other's factions (no releases were reported). Despite the basic understandings, the parties disagreed on fundamental issues, such as the parliamentary elections system, the makeup of a new government and division of portfolios, and the unification of the security services. Hamas steadfastly refused to agree that the unity government would accept the terms of the Quartet: recognizing Israel's right to exist and accepting previous agreements.

The conclusion of this chapter is simple: the Egyptian mediation of 2009 failed, as did the mediation efforts of Saudi Arabia and Yemen. Although the Palestinian Authority and Hamas responded to Egyptian pressure to talk and reach agreements, following the damage done to the Gaza Strip after Hamas's confrontation with Israel, the basic positions remained as they were.

Addressing the key features required for successful negotiation, neither party showed flexibility. Both sides clung to the behavioral approach, the one that favors personal interest or that of the movement over national interest. They continued to show suspicion and mistrust of each other, which increased at times during this period, due to mutual counterterrorism and media accusations against each other. None of the negotiation stages examined the integrative approach, seeking to create a win-win situation. The common national ethos expressed during Operation Cast Lead in the face of many victims was not enough to bring about reconciliation within the Palestinian arena. Hamas, which had considered itself the victorious and right side since 2006, ended the third round of talks in Cairo after not giving up a single interest. The movement adhered to its ideology and remained true to the 1988 convention. Abu Mazen and the PA, despite conciliatory statements, were unwilling to relinquish their power, particularly his as president—perhaps also because of the backing he received from regional and international bodies—and thus the internal political crisis continued to affect the

Palestinian system. A resident of the Gaza Strip summed it up this way: "They (Fatah and Hamas) prioritize their movement interest and not the national interest, and the one who suffers is the people. I have a store and people owe me 100,000 new Israeli shekels [more than $25,000]. I have no heart to ask them to pay: no salary, no work."[32]

Chapter 7

Cairo Dialogue, April 2011

This chapter analyzes the Cairo agreement of April 2011, which, according to media reports, was achieved between the PA and Hamas after four years of political rift. The parties agreed on forming an interim government and fixing a date for a general election.[1] Between 2009 and 2011, several low-profile attempts were made to revive the Egyptian mediation initiative, without success. Khaled Masha'al announced (January 3, 2010) that reconciliation was close following a meeting with Saudi officials to discuss the Egyptian proposal. A month later, in February, representatives of all Palestinian factions met in Gaza City after Nabil Sha'ath, a senior Fatah member, visited Gaza in a bid to encourage bilateral dialogue. In March, delegations from both sides met in Damascus. Azam al-Ahamad, heading Fatah, put pressure on Hamas to sign the Egyptian offer but was unsuccessful. Six months later, in September, another attempt failed, again in Damascus.[2] Meanwhile, on the ground the Palestinian arena remained divided.

Situation in the Gaza Strip

In the first months following the failure of the Cairo negotiations, the situation in the Gaza Strip continued to be characterized by tension between Hamas, the sovereign, and the opposition organizations, headed by Fatah. As a rule, the extent of the clashes between Hamas's forces and the opposition parties, headed by Fatah, diminished during the months following the talks in Cairo, which ended in May 2009. Fatah members came to terms with the fact that the Gaza Strip was controlled by a national religious movement. One salient incident occurred on August 14, 2009, near the Ibn Taymiyyah Mosque in Rafah, when Hamas's ESF clashed with Salafi-jihad adherents after Friday prayers. Sheikh 'Abd al-Latif Musa then declared the establishment of an Islamic emirate in the Palestinian territories and denounced Hamas for failing to enforce Islamic law in Gaza. According to the PCHR, twenty-eight people died and more than one hundred were wounded.[3]

Salafi-jihadi elements in the Gaza Strip continued to challenge the rule of Hamas there even after the severe confrontation in Rafah. They claimed that Hamas's rule was not religious enough, and from time to time they terrorized civilians in the Gaza Strip and at cafés (where men and women sat together) and conflicted with Hamas officials. The result was that the traditional confrontation between Hamas and the Palestinian Authority took place in the second half of 2009 and in the first half of 2010 without fanfare within the Gaza Strip.

However, when Hamas felt that there was some danger from opposition factions, it quickly acted. This was the case, for example, in a raid on Beit Lahiya's wedding, after participants posted a photo of a Fatah activist killed by Hamas members, and a week later at another wedding of the nephew of a senior Fatah member, Mohammad Dahlan, in Khan Yunis (sixty-one people were injured). In another case in response to the escalation in Qalqilya (discussed later), Hamas forces raided the homes of Fatah members and arrested them.[4] In early August 2009, Abu Mazen asked the Fatah Central Committee to convene its first meeting after thirty years. Hamas banned Fatah members living in the Gaza Strip from leaving, announcing that any member who left would be arrested immediately upon his return to the Strip territory. This step was taken in response to Abu Mazen's refusal to release all Hamas detainees in the West Bank and reflected the distrust between the parties, which only a few days earlier had returned from Cairo without an agreement to end the rift.[5] In November 2009, Hamas closed the office of Ramattan TV in Gaza and banned the broadcast of a commemoration ceremony marking five years since Yasser Arafat's death. The official reason was that the event was unlicensed, but the threat was in allowing thousands of Fatah supporters to have a political opportunity to protest.[6]

This allowed Hamas to try to act, as an actual sovereign, on a range of civilian issues:

1. Cultivating a culture of resistance. Asking to improve its international image, Hamas focused on cultural initiatives and public relations. Senior officials told a *New York Times* reporter that they were interested in opening a two-day conference on a culture of resistance. Ayman Taha, a former fighter, explained that armed resistance was still important and legitimate, "but we have a new emphasis on cultural resistance. After the war, the fighters needed a break and the people needed a break."[7] Obviously, this served another interest of Hamas, which was continuation of the armed struggle until fulfillment of the vision of liberating all of Palestine.
2. Dialogue with the population. Taha admitted that the decision to halt firing on Israel had been partly the result of popular pressure. People within the Gaza Strip started to wonder about the effectiveness of launching rockets.
3. Ensuring ongoing provision of services to the population. Hamas faced difficulty in providing for Gazans' needs, primarily because of Israel's security policy that imposed restrictions on the entry of goods into the Gaza Strip. Often, when merchandise came in, Hamas worked first and foremost to support its own families and only then to assist Fatah supporters.
4. Perpetuating the national ethos and shaping social norms in the spirit of Islam. Two different occasions, one in April 2010 and the other a month later, illustrated Hamas's policy on the issue. On the first occasion, Hamas banned a show in Gaza, claiming that the organizers did not ask for a license.[8] In May, Hamas prohibited activists from NGOs from commemorating the Nakba anniversary. The official explanation again was an absence of permission from the authorities, but it appears that Hamas was not interested in public activity that did not fit its ideology.[9]

Situation in the West Bank

Abu Mazen, disappointed by the failure of the third round of dialogue, clung to his previous security strategies, striving to minimize potential threats from Hamas. PA security apparatuses continued to put pressure on opposition activists, focusing on Hamas as well as on journalists. On August 15, 2009, for instance, Hamas member Fadi Hamadna from 'Assira (north Nablus) hanged himself in the PA prison of Juneid, after being in custody for two months.[10]

PA security personnel raided Qalqilya (May 30, 2009), clashing with members of the military wing of Hamas. Heavy fighting lasted until the next morning and caused the deaths of six people. The operation's goal was to arrest Mohammed al-Samman, the leader of the Izz al-Din al-Qassam Brigades in Qalqilya and his aide. A PA security services spokesperson argued that the PA's forces had come under attack. He added that the security unit tried to negotiate with the attackers in order to avoid potential harm to civilians, but the negotiation failed. The information obtained from this unusual, essentially tactical incident leads to an inevitable conclusion: distrust prevailed not only between leaders from both parties, but also on the terrain. In this case, Hamas officials chose to fight to the end and not surrender. They did not consider alternatives and remained true to the values of the movement. Following the clash, the PA put Qalqilya under curfew and arrested more than two hundred Hamas members in the city.[11] Tension between the parties escalated a few days later when three more people, two from Hamas and one in the security forces, were killed in an exchange of fire again in Qalqilya.[12]

The brutality in Qalqilya sparked, again, mutual accusations between the parties. Prime Minister Salam Fayyad made it clear that the Palestinian Authority would not apologize for the death of Hamas members, as "security officials have fulfilled their national duty." On the other hand, Hamas argued against the PA's aggression and conspiracies against its people. It used all the elements of the ethos to explain to the public that all Palestinians used to face the occupier, whereas now the Authority had become a traitor and cooperated with the US and Israel to counter the resistance.[13] In total, twelve people died in the West Bank in the second half of 2009 as a result of the ongoing Fatah-Hamas rift.

A few days later, PA security forces revealed what they defined as "a terror plot of Hamas against the PA." According to the investigation, Hamas activists in Nablus admitted to receiving 1.5 million euros to establish infrastructure aimed at undermining Abu Mazen's regime.[14] Severe escalation in the West Bank impelled Egypt to call on Abu Mazen to release Hamas detainees as a gesture of good will toward resumption of talks late in June 2009. Hamas, however, clarified that there would be "no unity without release of all Hamas prisoners in the West Bank."[15] According to another report, which was never verified or approved, Hamas's intention was to kill Abu Mazen.[16]

When the parties met in Cairo (June 29, 2009), Hamas was determined to discuss only the issue of political detention and refused to discuss the other pending dossiers.[17] This stance supported at least two interests of Hamas at that time: (1) releasing its people from PA prisons, and (2) maintaining good relations with Egyptian mediators by accepting the invitation to resume the dialogue. Despite Egypt having scheduled July 9, 2009, for signing an agreement, Hamas emerged as a tough negotiator. The movement refused to accept the terms of the international Quartet and added, from a position of power, a new condition—terminating the security mission of US officer Keith Dayton in the West Bank.[18] It also rejected the PA's demand to allow fifteen thousand of its security forces to return to the Gaza Strip.[19]

The PA's policy of keeping away any potential threats was also directed against the media. After arresting journalists working for Hamas's Al-Aqsa television several times, in July 2009 Prime Minister Fayyad suspended Al-Jazeera's work in the West Bank "due to its flagrant incitement against the Palestine Liberation Organization (PLO) and the Palestinian National Authority (PNA), which implied an attempt at provoking disorder."[20] Fayyad's decision encapsulated the PA stance in all previous dialogues with Hamas: allowing no room for compromising on PLO dominance and hegemony. If someone tried to challenge this, the PA would not hesitate to punish. In order to prevent Hamas's Da'awa activity, the PA has completed its takeover of all mosques in the West Bank. In February 2010, Mahmoud al-Habash, the minister of religion, announced that every imam in the mosque had received a security classification and that the PA was monitoring mosques. He added that Hamas could not perpetuate division, and that the Palestinians must change this reality.[21]

The Road to Cairo Again (April 2011)

Abu Mazen and Khaled Masha'al signed a reconciliation agreement on April 27, 2011, almost two years after the four months of dialogue failed back in 2009. This was the culmination of negotiations between the parties that had continued on and off since the last failure. In September 2009, after visiting Cairo, Masha'al estimated that resumption of talks with PA would likely occur in 2010.[22] At the same time, Hamas welcomed a senior Fatah member's offer to visit the Gaza Strip for talks. There was no real reason for Hamas to refuse the initiative. It was always ready to talk but that did not mean giving up on principles. Beyond that, dialogue in Gaza, which was its home court, was conducted under opening conditions more favorable to it. Moreover, accepting Fatah's suggestion could serve Hamas's interest vis-à-vis Egypt, with the opening of the Rafah crossing helping to provide Gaza's population with relief.

At the same time, Fatah members continued to complain about Hamas's provocation of Abbas. One of the senior officials, Jibril Rajoub, returned to the elements of the Palestinian national ethos to urge Hamas to unite. "We have international resolutions against the occupation, and against the separation fence that Israel has established, and therefore incitement does not serve the national interest."[23] Meanwhile, rumors about signing an agreement on October 15 were spread, but Abu Mazen addressed the Palestinian people on October 11, accusing Hamas of conducting a revolution in the Gaza Strip.[24] In Damascus Masha'al spoke with a double tongue: on the one hand, Hamas was committed to reconciliation, a general statement that did not give up its position, and on the other hand, he attacked the PA for not adopting the Goldstone report.[25]

Both sides entered 2010 without an agreement. The rift between the parties continued and in the reality of geopolitical fragmentation, new elections to the legislative council, four years after the January 2006 elections, were unviable. Hamas opened the year talking in two different voices. Masha'al, who met with senior officials in Saudi Arabia, stated that reconciliation with Fatah was to be closed since "big strides have been achieved."[26] Looking back, his statement was apparently to appease his Saudi hosts. Simultaneously, Hamas launched a strong personal attack on Abu Mazen, claiming that he no longer represented the Palestinian people and calling him the former president. In doing so, Hamas not only sought to express dissatisfaction with the fact that the Palestinian president extended his presidency in early 2009 for another year, but also challenged, once again, the PLO's status as the sole legal representative of the people. For the purpose of upcoming negotiations, Hamas's position toward Abu Mazen's legitimacy raised the question of whether he would be a partner to any future agreement. The official announcement by Hamas also accused Abu Mazen of abandoning the national goals, which made up the national ethos. In this situation, according to Hamas, there was no point in entering a "cycle of arbitrary negotiations that only serve the American and Zionist interests."[27] Hamas's various representatives repeated time and again that the movement was not afraid of new general elections.

In the murky atmosphere between the parties, Haniyeh and Mahmoud al-Zahar, one of Hamas's senior figures, and Nabil Shaath, a senior member of Fatah, met in the Gaza Strip (February 4, 2009), trying to break the impasse.[28] Four days later, the PA announced that municipal elections would be held in July 2010, but Hamas responded that it would not participate. Hamas's decision on the municipal elections issue indicated its political power compared to the PA: there was no room for political decision-making without at least consulting with the Hamas movement. Eventually, the PA postponed municipal elections to 2012. In fact, no breakthrough was achieved in the coming months. Hamas's de facto sovereignty within the Gaza Strip was steady, while Abu Mazen faced popular unrest in response to his willingness to accede to US demands to upgrade peace talks with Israel, while settlement expansion, the Judaization of Jerusalem, and the siege of Gaza continued. Mahmood al-Zahar from Hamas was interviewed on the Asharq al-Awsat (Middle East) website, mapping the obstacles to reaching a reconciliation agreement:[29]

1. Arab parties stand behind the PA. When Abu Mazen believes there is support for his open position, he becomes intransigent and takes hardline positions with regard to the reconciliation.

2. Arab states are not really concerned about the Palestinian issue (al-Malaf al-Filistini). They look at their own interests and do not care about the internal rift within Palestinian society. He mentioned the dispute between Arab leaders on the eve of the Damascus summit (March 29, 2010) on whether to include the Palestinian issue in the agenda.

3. Hamas had no interest in going back to the Mecca agreement of 2007, nor to the Cairo memorandum of understanding of 2009. He gave two indications of how Hamas saw upcoming negotiations, if they happen: first,

the movement must not fail the people again. According to Imam 'Ali guidelines, Hamas's objective is to preserve public legitimacy and commitment, while having discussions with PA representatives. Second, Hamas had a solid position, and its people were surprised to reveal that the final version of the agreement with the Egyptian mediator contained points that were not agreed upon. Again, as Imam 'Ali wrote, Hamas is looking for justice. If the mediator tried to obstruct the movement, how can it be believed in the future by either party?

4. The internal rift primarily affects people's willingness to engage in the struggle against Israel. Focusing on the resistance motive of the ethos, al-Zahar expressed Hamas's priorities in interests and its vision, meaning that liberating Palestine, by all means, remained its top priority, even if the Palestinian people were still suffering. Ahmad Bahr, a prominent member of Hamas in Gaza, supported al-Zahar's messages, responding to rumors about renewal of talks between PA and Israel saying, "it is a betrayal of the nation."[30]

In contrast to Hamas's stiff stance, Fatah officials tried to introduce a softer approach. Nabil Shaath, who met with Hamas leaders in the Gaza Strip in February, tried in May to revive the talks between the parties. He argued that the gaps between them were insignificant and that the national struggle, which included the liberation of Palestine, the return of refugees to their homes, the introduction of goods into the Gaza Strip, and the holding of democratic elections, was in the interests of both parties, requiring reconciliation. "There are continuous meetings between Fatah and Hamas in the West Bank, and a decrease in the number of Hamas detainees in the prisons of the PA, which has become similar to its counterpart in Gaza, and allowed the leaders of Hamas to visit detainees and to communicate with them. The obstacle to reconciliation is the position of Hamas—due to some items in the Egyptian paper, Hamas refuses to sign it."[31] Hamas's response was uncompromising. The movement announced a boycott of the mid-July municipal elections, claiming that the Salam Fayyad government, which decided on them, was illegal and even dismissed some of the West Bank village councils and appointed people on its behalf.[32]

In June 2010, the Palestinian Authority made another effort to resume reconciliation talks. Abu Mazen recruited Munib Al-Masri, a wealthy businessman from Nablus, to reach an agreement with Hamas. In mid-June, the Palestinian media reported that an agreement was reached between the parties. Although details of the agreement were scarce, the report insisted that "only security issues remained at issue, and all that is needed is an OK from Abu Mazen and Masha'al."[33] Hamas welcomed Al-Masri but did not show any willingness to be flexible in its stance; therefore, a close aide of Abu Mazen announced that the Palestinian president was not considering going to Gaza. Hamas's intransigence continued even after Egypt took punitive measures against it, such as refusing repeated calls to open the Rafah crossing. The Egyptians also did not allow Arab aid delegations to enter the Gaza Strip and assist the population.[34] A day after the Egyptian decision, Hamas strongly condemned Salam Fayyad, calling him a traitor after his meeting with Israeli defense minister Ehud Barak. Hamas's announcement stressed that the meeting was weakening the resistance.[35] It was a direct message that the national-religious faction had no fear of challenging the PA, and that it clung to its traditional ideology and activities on behalf of achieving the liberation of Palestine.

Winds of change toward possible renewal of the dialogue between the parties picked up in September 2010. Masha'al met Omar Suliman, head of the General Intelligence Service of Egypt, in Saudi Arabia. At the same time Jamal Khoudari, an independent member of the Palestinian Legislative Council, met Abu Mazen in Amman to discuss the possibility of dialogue with Hamas. He updated Masha'al on the results of his talks with the Palestinian president, and on September 25, a Fatah delegation headed to Damascus to meet Hamas seniors.[36] The joint declaration after the meeting in the Syrian capital said that "Hamas and Fatah are closer than ever to a unity deal." Musa abu Marzook said that agreement was reached on many points.[37]

Two separate incidents, both quite marginal, illustrate the mutual deep distrust between the parties. On October 5, a PA security court in Ramallah sentenced 'Alaa Hisham Diab, an Izz al-Din al-Qassam activist, to twenty years in prison for his participation in a deadly 2009 shootout with Palestinian police, according to a court official. Hamas reacted strongly to the ruling, saying, "On the one hand there is the lack of legality of the courts that issue these verdicts, and on the other these verdicts come while there is talk of coming closer to reaching internal reconciliation."[38] Days later, during the Arab League session, Abu Mazen and Syrian president Bashar al-Assad traded sharp words over Syria's criticism of the PA's decision to return to direct talks with Israel. In protest, Abu Mazen requested that the national unity talks be moved to another capital, but Hamas refused, and talks were delayed indefinitely.

Both events reflect Hamas's choice of the behavioral approach to negotiating. The movement, from a position of strength, sought Hamas's entrée to dialogue (the fourth since 2007) under optimal opening conditions. Hamas was interested in conducting talks in Damascus, where it enjoyed support of the host, rather than Cairo, and was also interested in portraying the Palestinian Authority as an illegitimate entity that could not prosecute civilians (as was the case with Diab). Hamas saw two reasons for the illegitimacy: the PA's power being based on the PLO's decision, and the fact that no elections had been held for more than four years. This automatic response by Hamas casts doubt on its intentions to reach an agreement that would end the rift and satisfy both sides, which, as the integrative approach suggests, would be a win-win situation. Mahmood al-Zahar's interview in mid-December supports this analysis: "We are not in a hurry to buy or to sell our national interest because this is not the proper market. Hamas is focusing its efforts on state-building and providing an example of honest Palestinian governance. We finished five years and we survived, and we stayed, and we faced two wars. So, we can stay, and we can withstand, and we can win. We are the owners of this land."[39]

Abu Mazen's public appearances in the last quarter of 2010 included a number of messages he sought to convey to the Palestinian people in order to strengthen his political power. He made it clear that he would not relinquish the Palestinian people's historical rights (without elaborating on them), and in effect said that he was committed to the elements of the national ethos. However, he did not hesitate to attack Hamas and continue to accuse it of mounting a coup in the Gaza Strip in 2007. He also emphasized that he chose not to respond by force to the coup but to negotiate to settle the talks, yet Hamas refused to sign the Egyptian draft document in April 2009.[40]

Interestingly, independent members of the PLC were skeptical about the chance of reaching an agreement between the parties. Hasan Khreisheh said that "the continued detention confirms that the round of reconciliation talks sells the illusion to the Palestinians of the possibility of Palestinian internal reconciliation."[41]

If the Hamas-Israel military campaign in December 2008–January 2009 accelerated contacts for Palestinian internal negotiations in April 2009, then in early 2011, the intervening external variable that led to talks was the popular protest that broke out in some Arab countries and received the Arab Spring nickname. Egypt, the chief mediator, was entangled in domestic unrest, which eventually led to President Hosni Mubarak's topple in February. The internal situation in Egypt had implications for two opposite trends relevant to the negotiations within the Palestinian arena: First, the attention of the Egyptian mediator was subject to internal issues; therefore, the pressure exerted on the Palestinians lessened during that period. Second, precisely because of the public awakening in Egypt (and earlier in Tunisia), there was an awakening on the Palestinian streets that led to loudly demanding that its leaders reconcile.

Data from a public opinion poll published by a central research institute in Nablus in December 2010 indicated that 39 percent of Palestinians believed that the geopolitical split between the West Bank and the Gaza Strip was irreversible. Fifty percent believed that such a reconciliation was possible, but it would take time. An absolute majority (76 percent) opposed the possibility of having separate general elections in both regions. The clear conclusion from this data was that the Palestinian public clung to the national ethos that saw the parts of Palestine united.[42] Three months later, the data showed that only 21 percent believed the split was permanent. Apparently, the sharp decrease was an outcome of increased public and youth demonstrations in the West Bank and the Gaza Strip demanding an end to the split.[43]

For the first time since the split in June 2007, the pressure came from the streets. On January 1, 2011, a group of students in the Gaza Strip, probably influenced by the popular protest in Tunisia, produced a document to express their grievances with Hamas and Fatah.[44] It was a basic, unsophisticated document in which the writers, all young people, residents of the Gaza Strip, severely criticized Palestinian behavior in both regions (as well as Israel, the United States, and the United Nations). They described the reality of their poor daily lives:

> Here in Gaza we fear being incarcerated, interrogated, hit, tortured, bombed, killed. We are afraid of living, because every single step we take has to be considered and well-thought, there are limitations everywhere, we cannot move

> as we want, say what we want, do what we want, sometimes we even can't think what we want because the occupation has occupied our brains and hearts. Politics is bollocks, it is screwing our lives up. We want three things. We want to be free. We want to be able to live a normal life. We want peace. Is that too much to ask?[45]

By mid-February more than twenty thousand Palestinians supported, through social networks, the students' call for reconciliation. In Ramallah, about one thousand young Palestinians converged, demanding unity between Fatah and Hamas. They held up banners reading: "The people want an end to division."[46]

Fatah spokesman Azzam al-Ahmad said in Ramallah: "We are ready to meet the Hamas leadership so that the Egyptian document can be signed." According to the general atmosphere in Palestinian society, it was only natural to express in public a willingness for reconciliation. The Palestinians continued to call for unity, when thousands of women in Gaza used the Women's Day rally (March 8) to wave slogans for reconciliation between the rival Palestinian parties. But Hamas stuck to the tough line that does not allow concessions in negotiations. In early March 2011, the movement was steadfast in the face of public pressure to reconcile and did not hesitate to attack the Palestinian Authority. It reported on calls through social networks to end Abu Mazen's rule, and Masha'al stated that it was time to create a new reality in Palestine. According to him, "Hamas wants reconciliation that upholds resistance and has a leadership on the path of Jihad."[47]

On March 15, 2011, thousands of people gathered in the central squares of Gaza calling to end the internal rift. It was the largest gathering to date (one hundred thousand people) and was attended by all political parties, ordinary citizens, and members of the NGOs. Hamas's automatic response was to brutally attack the protesters, beat them, arrest some, and hunt down journalists who documented the incidents. In the West Bank, the PA security forces used tear gas on some eight thousand protesters in Ramallah, briefly dispersing them and injuring twenty. The next day, Ismail Haniyeh called Abu Mazen and invited him to visit Gaza, an indication that the Hamas leader in the Gaza Strip understood that the call from the public for reconciliation was authentic.[48] Abu Mazen accepted the invitation, making it clear, however, that he would go to Gaza to make a deal, not for discussion.[49] In fact, he did not rush to travel to Gaza and explored alternatives for maximizing his interest if negotiations with Hamas resumed. The Palestinian president sent a delegation to Cairo to discuss the details of the agreement, and at the same time met with a delegation of Hamas officials in the West Bank and discussed the possibility of going to Gaza. In doing so, he adopted a positive attitude toward both the Egyptians and Hamas.

Direct dialogue without the presence of a mediator in the room started, for the first time since 2007, on April 6 in Gaza. As the parties reported progress in talks, the Palestinian Authority made concessions to Hamas—one of the most prominent being the release of eleven Hamas detainees from detention facilities on April 17, which was Palestinian Prisoners Day. Ten days later, an Egyptian official confirmed that Fatah and Hamas had reached an agreement on all of their differences, including elections and the formation of the new government. Azzam Al-Ahmad, member of the Fatah central committee who had been leading the Fatah delegation in the Cairo talks with Hamas, confirmed reaching an agreement. Hamas leader Izzat Ar-Rishq confirmed the initial agreement.[50]

Analysis of the Agreement

The signing ceremony was on May 3 in Cairo. The 2011 agreement contained the following details:[51]

1. Elections

    a. Establishment of an elections commission. Both Fatah and Hamas agreed to identify the names of the members of the Central Election Commission in agreement with the Palestinian factions. This list would then be submitted to the Palestinian president, who would issue a decree on the reformation of the commission.

    b. Electoral Court. Fatah and Hamas agreed on the nomination of no more than twelve judges to be members of the Electoral Court. This list would then be submitted to the Palestinian president so that the necessary legal actions would be taken to form the Electoral Court in agreement with the Palestinian factions.

    c. Timing of Elections. The legislative, presidential, and Palestinian National Council elections would

> be conducted at the same time exactly one year after the signing of the Palestinian National Reconciliation Agreement.

Neither side had a real reason to refuse the election paragraphs. General elections symbolized democracy; it gave Fatah an opportunity to regain legitimacy and political power, perhaps even to undermine and challenge Hamas in Gaza. On the other hand, it provided Hamas with an occasion to confirm its dominance in Gaza and to enhance its public legitimacy in the West Bank.

2. Palestine Liberation Organization. Fatah and Hamas agreed that the tasks and decisions of the provisional interim leadership could not be hindered or obstructed—nor could they conflict with the authorities of the Executive Committee of the Palestine Liberation Organization. In other words, in April 2011 Hamas agreed to postpone its vision of creating a new reality in Palestine, as Masha'al declared. On this specific point, Hamas chose the integrative approach (a win-win situation), not because the movement gave up on its interest in challenging the superior PLO position, but because Hamas was not ready and politically strong enough to insist on this issue.
3. Security. It was emphasized that the Higher Security Committee would be formed in response to a decree by the Palestinian president and would consist of professional officers acting in consensus. No matter how this sentence is read, it is a general formulation that one could find no reason to oppose. Who is not interested in a committee where senior officer members discuss ways to improve public safety? According to this wording, there was no agreement on the distribution of security powers between the opposing parties, no details on the number of security personnel in each region (the West Bank and the Gaza Strip), no determination by which a government ministry would control them, nor was there an account of what powers the government and the president would have in relation to the issue of security. Therefore, there was no problem or solution on which to agree or disagree. The implementation stage

would, however, involve a reasonable division of powers—and once again, disagreements would begin.

4. Government

   a. Formation of the government. Fatah and Hamas agreed to form a Palestinian government and to appoint the prime minister and ministers in a consensus between them.

   b. Functions of the government

      i. Preparing necessary conditions for conducting presidential, legislative, and Palestinian National Council elections.

      ii. Supervising and addressing the prevalent issues regarding the internal Palestinian reconciliation resulting from the state of division.

      iii. Following up on the reconstruction operations in the Gaza Strip and the efforts to end the siege and blockade that was imposed on it.

      iv. Continuing the implementation of the provisions of the Palestinian National accord.

      v. Resolving the civil and administrative problems that resulted from the division.

      vi. Unifying the Palestinian National Authority institutions in the West Bank, Gaza Strip, and Jerusalem.

      vii. Fixing the status of the associations, nongovernmental organizations, and charities.

5. Legislative council. Fatah and Hamas agreed to reactivate the Palestinian Legislative Council in accordance with the Basic Law.

All sections dealing with the Palestinian government and the legislative council, except for section 4b (iii), were also drafted with general outlines. There was no waiver of any opening positions, principles, or interests that any Palestinian—whether PA supporter, Hamas supporter, or unaffiliated—would disapprove of. Hence, the unavoidable question is: If this was the language of the agreement, why did it take two years to reach these understandings? Article 4b (iii) reflected the interest of Hamas as a sovereign in the Gaza Strip, committed to caring for the population, and of Abu Mazen, who considered himself president of all Palestinians. In any case, it depended to a considerable extent on the good will and policy of Israel, which controlled the crossing points to the Gaza Strip. It should be noted that Abu Mazen's permanent and traditional condition was not included in the agreement: to have Hamas's obligation to recognize the conditions of the international Quartet: recognizing Israel's right to exist and accepted previous agreements.

Eventually, neither side gave up any substantial and important interests. This agreement came as a result of pressure exerted by the Palestinian streets and both parties' fear that popular protests that erupted in Arab countries could also reach the West Bank and Gaza Strip. Due to widespread protests in March 2011, Gaza and Ramallah accelerated the negotiations, but the signed agreement did not end the mutual suspicion and mistrust between the parties. It is a fact that the Cairo 2011 agreement did not come into effect, and within a year the two parties found themselves negotiating a fifth round of negotiations, this time in Doha, the capital of Qatar.

Chapter 8

Doha Agreement, 2012

This chapter discusses the fifth round of negotiations between the parties, this time in Doha, Qatar, in February 2012. In fact, this dialogue continued in Cairo, three months later. The Doha agreement was signed by both leaders, Abu Mazen and Khaled Masha'al, and the May 2012 supplemental agreement in Cairo set timetables for the implementation of the agreements. Despite the personal involvement of the leaders, this agreement failed when both sides were not ready to make any substantial concessions for ending the ongoing crisis.

Aftermath to Cairo 2011

Obstacles to implementation of the agreement emerged just days after the signing in Cairo. Al-Zahar, on behalf of Hamas, said that the reconciliation offered not integration but mere "coexistence between Hamas's and Fatah's contradictory and conflicting programs." A Fatah negotiator admitted that "after fighting each other and being divided for years, a piece of paper signed after a few hours of negotiation doesn't mean much. It was just headlines, full of holes."[1]

Politically, Abu Mazen enjoyed the immediate fruits of the reconciliation. A public poll that was conducted in mid-June indicated that most of the Palestinians were pleased with the agreement with Hamas and believed it would be implemented. At the same time, the Palestinian president decided to go to the UN for recognition of the Palestinian state in September. Also, most of the Palestinian people (69 percent), troubled by international sanctions against the PA, favored a new Palestinian government of specialists to implement the president's and the PLO's peace program and policy rather than that of Hamas.[2] Abu Mazen published a special article in the *New York Times* for the sixty-third anniversary of the Palestinian Nakba, explaining, "We are now compelled to turn to the international community to assist us in preserving the opportunity for a peaceful and just end to the conflict. Palestinian national unity is a key step in this regard."[3] On May 28, addressing a conference of the Arab follow-up committee, he clarified that the new government would be composed of technocrats, and there would be no room for figures who are affiliated with political organizations.[4]

Disagreements between the parties over the implementation of the agreement started in June 2011. The Palestinian president said that he had the right to choose the head of the new interim government and specifically named the current prime minister of the West Bank, Salaam Fayyad. He added that he had the right to form a government that represented his policies. In response, Ismail Haniyeh stated that the proposed unity government should not threaten the resistance, and Hamas spokesperson Sami Abu Zuhri accused Abu Mazen of making a false statement. He claimed that PA security apparatuses had resumed political arrests and political prosecution of Hamas members and supporters. Hamas also insisted that the new government must receive PLC approval, dominated by the Hamas since its victory in January 2006's elections.[5]

Interestingly, both sides, aware of the disagreement between them, headed to Turkey looking for support for their positions and hoping that Ankara would pressure the other side to compromise. Abu Mazen arrived in Turkey on June 20, 2011, and Masha'al a day later. Originally, they were supposed to meet in Cairo, but the meeting was postponed due to controversy. It is doubtful whether Turkey, as an intermediary, had put pressure on both parties to implement the agreement signed in Cairo just a month earlier; it is clear, however, that the parties were negotiating indirectly, which was not necessarily fruitful as far as reaching an agreement was concerned but was aimed, rather, at getting the mediator to support their positions. Proof of this was the fact that the two Palestinian leaders were in the Turkish capital at that time and did not meet to settle their disputes.[6]

The maximum Abu Mazen was able to extract from the Turks was his offer to Hamas to postpone the implementation of the reconciliation agreement until September. He probably speculated that there was no real chance of implementing the Cairo 2011 understandings at the time, but that it was perhaps possible that after Palestine became recognized internationally as a state (during the UN General Assembly), through international and regional backing, pressure could be put on Hamas to accept the agreement's terms. He wasn't looking for a win-win solution but was at most hoping to preserve the status quo and prevent a new crisis in party relations.[7] Interestingly, in mid-September the Palestinian president enjoyed a peak in popularity with the public. Fifty-nine percent said they would vote for the PA president if elections were held, compared to only thirty-four percent who had supported Ismail Haniyeh.[8]

Eventually, the major obstacle was the reappointment of Fayyad as prime minister. Hamas refused to accept that because the movement considered him to be pro-Fatah and a close ally of the US. Abu Mazen insisted on Fayyad's continuation as prime minister, arguing that he had no political affiliation and that he met the criteria for a technocrat. When representatives of the parties met in Cairo (August 7), it was after the PA announced that there would be municipal elections in October, which Hamas rejected. The Central Election Commission (CEC) officially informed the government in Ramallah that there was no real need to prepare for elections within the Gaza Strip.[9] The discussions in Cairo focused on several issues: (1) release of prisoners, (2) general elections, (3) compensation for killings, and (4) passports for Gazan residents prevented from travel and who were forced out of Gaza after the events of 2007. In an unconventional move, Abu Mazen rang Haniyeh (August 11) to discuss the need to implement the reconciliation agreement, affirming his intention to make progress on the issues of political prisoners and passports. Haniyeh in turn said it was important to maintain a positive atmosphere. Simultaneously, Masha'al visited Doha to update the emir of Qatar on developments in Palestine, including the reconciliation efforts. It was the second time that Qatar mediation was considered by at least one of the parties (after Sana'a 2008).[10] As had happened in the past, this time the general consensus was that they were just paying lip service. Two weeks after the phone call between Abu Mazen and Haniyeh, Diab Al-Luh, one of the Fatah officials in the Gaza Strip, announced the suspension of talks until September. The official reason was the security escalation between Hamas and Israel.[11]

The PA leadership devoted its attention in September 2011 to the international community. Therefore, little, if anything, was done to carry out the May 2011 agreement. Abu Mazen and his closest aides were under international community pressure to stick with the implementation, which was supposed to give Hamas an internal political legitimacy within the Palestinian arena, without accepting the Quartet's terms. Hamas in turn had shown no hesitation, stating on the eve of Abu Mazen's speech in the UN General Assembly (September 23) that the Palestinian statehood bid was not acceptable. The announcement by the leadership in Damascus said that it had no objection to Abu Mazen's vision of a Palestinian state (on 1967 lines, with East Jerusalem as its capital), but the fact that the PA appealed to the UN without consulting with Hamas and other political forces was not acceptable. This stance by Hamas illustrated again its political interest within Palestinian society. The movement sought to be part of the decision-making cycle. At the same time, supporting the PA's bid for a Palestinian state was not considered a concession regarding its vision to liberate all of Palestine.[12]

On September 16, Abu Mazen addressed the Palestinian people, explaining his decision to ask that the UN recognize Palestine as an independent state, emphasizing that the PLO would remain the only legal and legitimate representative of the people until this goal was achieved. It was a clear message to Hamas that he had no intention to compromise on this point or to allow Hamas to become an equal partner.[13] Abu Mazen's speech at the UN General Assembly (September 23) dealt largely with the history of the Israeli-Palestinian conflict. He mentioned international resolutions of the conflict and blamed Israel for failing to negotiate between the parties; he also asked UN secretary-general Ban Ki Moon to discuss the Security Council's request to accept the PA as a member of the organization. As for the reconciliation agreement with Hamas, a brief mention was made in which he said he hoped to achieve it soon.[14]

One tactical incident, which occurred in Gaza, demonstrated how deep the rift was between the parties. On September 20, Hamas announced that both parties agreed not to take to the streets to avoid a split while Abu Mazen headed to New York.[15] On that very day Fatah issued its own statement claiming that there was no agreement between the parties.[16] On the ground, Hamas security forces in the Gaza Strip banned restaurants showing Abu Mazen's speech in New York. In one case, they arrested Jamal Salim Abu al-Qumsan, who owned a restaurant, accusing him of airing Abu Mazen's speech.[17]

Hamas reacted coldly to Abu Mazen's speech to the UN. The movement made it clear that its request to recognize Palestine should include "all of Palestine, including the lands in the territories of Israel." Haniyeh, for example, made it clear that there was no need to beg for Palestine, and that its release should come first.[18] As time went on, both sides clung to ideological messages and showed no willingness to bend in their positions or to discuss the implementation of the Cairo agreement of May 2011. At the beginning of October, Masha'al, visiting Tehran, made it clear that there was no alternative to armed resistance, while Fatah members focused their comments on possible political scripts following Abu Mazen's speech. Both sides realized that the implementation of the agreement was not going to happen soon. As Khalil al-Hayya, a senior member of Hamas, described it: "A date has been set for new rounds of talks between the Hamas and Fatah parties, emphasizing the need for talks that include all Palestinian factions. We are in urgent need of such talks to clarify to ourselves, first, to discuss our affairs, and then decide the next steps."[19] Bardawil followed al-Hayya, calling the PA to carry out necessary reforms within the PLO's institutions and to allow partnership in decision-making, pointing exactly to one of the major obstacles.[20]

Toward Doha via Cairo

No real progress was made between the parties until mid-November, when Musa Abu Marzook, Masha'al's deputy, announced that the Hamas leader and Abu Mazen would meet in Cairo soon. He did not forget to lower expectations, saying, "Abbas was the one impeding progress of the reconciliation by insisting on Salam Fayyad as the premier of the transitional, unity government." In response, Mohammad Nahal, a Fatah member, said that a new government would be formed after the two leaders met.[21]

Abu Mazen arrived early in Cairo and met with Muhammad Tantawi, head of the Egyptian Supreme Council of the Armed Forces (November 23), in order to coordinate positions with the Egyptian realtor before meeting with Masha'al. Following the meeting between the two leaders, the first meeting in six months, the Egyptian media could not provide details. However, it was reported that the identity of the next prime minister (Hamas objected to Fayyad's reappointment) was not discussed. Instead, they discussed general political issues and ways to simultaneously appease the Gaza Strip and the West Bank.[22] Apparently, both of them chose to publicly present an image of joint interests and vision, perhaps even an integrative approach to negotiation, while they focused on the positive atmosphere between them. The Palestinian president said that they "discussed everything, particularly political developments facing the Palestinian cause in great detail. We want very much to work as partners, and we have a joint responsibility toward our people and cause . . . there are no differences between us at all on any of the issues. You will see all of this in the coming days and weeks." Masha'al added, "I want to reassure our people inside and outside that with this meeting we have opened a new page of a high level of understanding, concern for partnership, and seriousness in implementing not only the terms of the reconciliation agreement, but all that has to do with organizing the Palestinian home and dealing with the present and future stages."[23]

Analyzing the details leaked from the meeting between Abu Mazen and Masha'al reveals, again, general formulations, which were not enough to force the parties to give up their principles and positions of power that had strengthened over the years:[24]

1. Truce in the West Bank and Gaza Strip, including halting political arrests. Neither side had a real reason to oppose this formulation, simply because that would leave their security forces with broad discretion as to when to make arrests and whom to arrest. They can always explain that detention was for security reasons only, even if it served political purposes. In fact, Fawzi Barhoum, a Hamas representative, accused the PA of arresting more Hamas members after the meeting between Abbas and Masha'al in Cairo.[25]

2. Vowing to increase "popular resistance" to oppose Israel's settlement expansion and construction of the separation wall. Traditionally, popular resistance was the cornerstone of Abu Mazen's ideology, as he was opposed to terror. As for Hamas, there was no reason to refuse popular resistance, as long as the movement did not have to relinquish armed struggle.

3. Pledging further talks among the factions in order to agree on the next patterns of activity by popular resistance. Obviously, both sides realized that all Palestinian factions shared the same ethos and vision, so the more the factions understand each other, the stronger the consensus around the agreement.

The smiling pictures that came out of the meeting in Cairo did not hold up for long. Senior members of Hamas made it clear that popular resistance did not replace armed struggle against Israel, and in order to carry out such struggle, the PA must stop security coordination with Israel.[26] Ismail Haniyeh used Friday prayers at the mosque to embrace Abu Mazen, calling on him to lean on Arab-Muslim support rather than on the US and Israel, which have no plans that would benefit the Palestinian people.[27] Delegations of the rival parties met at the beginning of December to discuss various aspects of Cairo's mutual understanding between Abu Mazen and Masha'al. Diab al-Luh, a senior member of Fatah, described the meeting as important, declaring that both parties were committed to reaching reconciliation.[28] At the same time, 'Azzam al-Ahmad, chief negotiator of the PA, stated that the unity government must come before new elections, because it was not legal to have elections when the Palestinians had two separate governments. Visiting Nablus for updating Fatah cadres of the city, he stressed the national goal of bringing back unity in order to fight the unjust occupation.[29]

As in the past, these negotiations were characterized by ups and downs. On December 12, the two sides announced that the discussions were proceeding slowly, and that the likelihood of reaching agreements satisfactory to both parties was questionable. It seems that the PA's and Hamas's representatives sought the integrative approach to end the rift—according to the decree following the Cairo leaders' meeting. But, in fact, the parties remained in conflict over the hard-core issues, and Abu Mazen and Masha'al had to return to Cairo for the second round of talks in a month. The meeting was set for December 21, but even before that an event took place that made it clear that the atmosphere between the parties was strained. Al-Ahmad ordered representatives of eight Palestinian organizations, who were invited by the Egyptian mediator, to leave the discussion table on the grounds that they were not members of the PLO. Beyond the personal insult, Abu Mazen conveyed the message that the Palestinian factions, which might challenge the PLO's positions in the negotiations, should not be part of the discussions.[30]

On December 21, Hamas representative Fawzi Barhoum said that the parties had reached an agreement on six steps toward the reconciliation:[31]

1. Forming a new Central Elections Commission. Hanna Nasser will be the head of the commission and the other members will be divided between the West Bank and the Gaza Strip (each region having four members). The new

composition of the commission requires Abu Mazen's approval.

2. A unity government should be sworn in by the end of January 2012.
3. All political prisoners will be released by January 31, 2012.
4. An interfactional committee will be formed to deal with freedom of movement and passport issues. This committee will be active and initiate practical steps.
5. PLO membership will be discussed between Abu Mazen and Masha'al.
6. The parties agree to endorse a social reconciliation committee to carry out their work. The committee was formed in 2009 to address cases of people who have suffered as a result of the political split.

Apparently, no real progress had been achieved. A close look at these agreements indicate that no party had to make any painful concessions. The spirit of the agreement was quite general. It left quite a bit of leeway for the leaders to make decisions about concrete measures, such as the release of prisoners or the establishment of a government. The controversial main issues, such as the identity of the next prime minister or the granting of a foothold for Hamas in the PLO's institutions, were left unresolved by the parties.

Abu Mazen and Masha'al met on December 22. It was a meeting in which there was a real breakthrough, since the parties agreed to: (1) form the interim unity government by the end of January 2012 (a ratification of the agreement between the delegations that would meet the day before); (2) bring elected Hamas-affiliated legislators back into the PA's parliament, the Palestinian Legislative Council; and (3) sit together on the commission that would prepare for the next elections of the PLO's parliament-in-exile, the Palestinian National Council (PNC). This move was agreed on in order to facilitate Hamas's and the Islamic Jihad's membership.[32]

Hamas, almost immediately, announced that the movement would consider joining the PLO. This announcement had two immediate implications: First, Abu Mazen, for the first time, agreed to open the door for Hamas to the PLO and to allow it to be part of the organization he considered the sole legitimate representative of the Palestinian people. Hamas, for its part, saw this as a political opportunity to upgrade its status and gain power that would enable it to become the leading political force in Palestinian society in the future. As it turned out, however, this required Hamas to compromise, especially on the issue of armed struggle, which it found difficult. Masha'al himself said, publicly, that this time he was optimistic regarding reconciliation. He used features of the national ethos, mainly the centrality of Palestine as a connecting thread between all Palestinian factions. He also called Fatah and Hamas brothers, and said that the great sacrifices of their people would not be in vain. Masha'al invited all Palestinian factions to join the reconciliation process. However, he stressed that Hamas had the right to armed resistance.[33]

In contrast to Masha'al's optimism, Abu Mazen had doubts regarding the formation of unity governments. In fact, at least according to one report, during the talks in Cairo he linked internal Palestinian agreements with the PA's interest vis-à-vis the international community. The Palestinian president said that "the formation of the national accord government depends on the responses received from the Quartet about the future of the negotiations with Israel." He justified his stance by explaining that he did not want to give Israel any justification for accusing him of using the formation of the national accord government.[34] Abu Mazen's position actually revealed some of his interests in both arenas. He was interested in a message from the Quartet that saw Israel as responsible for the failure of the negotiations, thus gaining international backing for the Palestinians' moves. In doing so, he expressed his lack of belief in the possibility of resuming diplomatic negotiations with Israel as long as the right-wing government was in Jerusalem. At the same time, he may have asked to hold off on the implementation of the understandings vis-à-vis Hamas, because he realized that it had the potential to harm the PLO's hegemony. In fact, it seems that the Palestinian president could not decide which one of his interests to prefer when he declared that "all options are open."[35]

On the ground, apparently as a gesture, PA senior member Nabil Sha'ath visited Gaza (January 2, 2012) and met al-Zahar. Sha'ath said that an independent government of technocrats was needed by the end of January to prepare the coming general elections, planned for May. After the elections, a national unity government would be formed. He added that Fatah and Hamas were close to resolving the issues of political detainees and passports for Gaza residents, which meant that

Gazans would have the right to hold Palestinian passports, issued by the PA.[36] At the same time, as happened in previous rounds of talks, tactical incidents threatened to collapse the fragile understanding. Such an event occurred on January 6, when a delegation of four Fatah members asked to enter the Gaza Strip but had to wait for an escort since they had not coordinated their visit in advance. The quarrel at the Beit Hanoun crossing point ended when they turned back to the West Bank. Hamas was aware of the potential damage the incident could cause, so it published an official statement explaining, "The Ministry of Interior and National Security asserts the freedom of movement into and out [of] the Gaza Strip for all Palestinians, and we do not and will not prevent any eligible individuals from traveling. We do not object to the visit of the Fatah delegation to the Gaza Strip."[37]

Abu Mazen referred to the reconciliation with Hamas during his speech to the Advisory Council of the Fatah movement (January 12). He chose to share with the audience details from his dialogue with Masha'al, opening with Hamas's demand that the truce be applied to the West Bank just as it applied to Gaza. This simply meant that both sides ceased political arrests. However, Abu Mazen made it clear that smuggling weapons, money, or explosives to the West Bank would be prohibited, and that anyone who did so would be arrested and would go to the judiciary. This was the issue of arms for anyone, regardless of political affiliation.[38] That was a direct message to Hamas that the PA under his reign objected to armed resistance, and that any violation of that rule, when it came to the security of the territory he oversaw, would not be allowed. The Palestinian president stressed that reconciliation was in both sides' interest, and he hinted to Hamas to make sure that no incident like the one in Beit Hanoun would occur.

One way or another, the talks in Cairo paved the way for a third meeting between Abu Mazen and Masha'al on February 5, 2012, in Doha, the Qatar capital. They signed a deal to form a unity government of independent technocrats for the West Bank and Gaza, headed by Palestinian president Mahmoud Abbas. This understanding enabled the parties to get past the obstacle of Fayyad as the next prime minister. However, the timetable for implementation was not set.[39] Truly, Masha'al's agreement that Abu Mazen would also be president and prime minister ignited a fierce dispute within Hamas. Members of the Gaza Strip were outraged for not having been consulted. Beyond that, they realized that the move endowed Abu Mazen with even greater political power and reduced the government's ability to monitor the decisions of the Palestinian president. Al-Zahar, for instance, said that the agreement was a mistake.[40] Masha'al, who seemed to have the courage needed for moves that could end the internal rift and lead the Palestinian system toward unity, was influenced by the pressure exerted by his friends in the Gaza Strip, and asked Abbas to delay the implementation of the agreement for several months. The result was that the Doha agreement was fully published after only three months, this time in Cairo.

Soon security activity in both areas escalated again. Hamas arrested Fatah activists in Gaza and the West Bank renewed waves of Hamas arrests. An extremely serious incident was reported on May 1, when an anonymous man tried to assassinate Kadura Musa, the governor of Jenin. He was not injured but later died of a heart attack.[41] The escalation after a long period of relative relaxation led to an acceleration of contacts aimed at reconciliation. Delegations of the rival parties headed to Cairo in mid-May to publish a signed agreement on May 20, which included the following text:[42]

A) Central Election Commission will start working on May 27.

B) Representatives of the parties will meet on May 27 to discuss the structure and the composition of the new government.

C) The final stage of a government assembly will be a meeting between Abu Mazen and Khaled Masha'al in Cairo, no later than ten days after the announcement of the new government composition.

D) The election commission in charge of preparing the National Assembly Elections Law will resume its work as of May 27, 2012, in order to be able to complete its work and to prepare for conducting the presidential, legislative, and National Assembly elections simultaneously.

E) The date for holding the elections is determined by consensus between all the Palestinian factions and forces, taking into consideration the completion of the work of the Central Election Commission.

F) The work of the government to be formed is limited to a period of no more than 6 months to implement the agreed-upon tasks, including elections and starting the reconstruction of Gaza; the duration of this government will be linked to the agreed-upon date for conducting elections.

G) In case the elections are not held on the planned date for any reason beyond the will of the parties, the two parties will meet to discuss the possibility of forming a new national unity government headed by an independent person to be agreed upon.

H) The importance of implementing what is stated in the agreement regarding preparing the atmosphere for conducting elections is emphasized, through speedy work to implement the recommendations of the Public Liberties Committees in the West Bank and Gaza Strip and of the National Consensus Government. The issue of public freedoms will be completed in full as quickly as possible before the elections are held according to the law.

I) What is stated in this agreement is one package, and the signatures contained therein are binding on the two parties, and Egypt, for its part, will monitor and supervise the implementation of each party's obligations, including issues of public freedoms.

Azzam al-Ahmad signed the agreement on behalf of Fatah. Musa Abu Marzook did the same on behalf of Hamas. A close look at the content leads to the conclusion that it was a tactical and technical agreement. Some sections include clear schedules, some schedules are formulated more vaguely. The language of the accord does not reflect a willingness of either party to give up power, authority, or ideological principles. The issue of the identity of the next prime minister remains unanswered, and the general agreement on an independent person, that is, a person without political affiliation, does not guarantee that in due course any candidate will be acceptable to both sides. Both sides found a win-win integrative approach with the Egyptian mediator and agreed to give him a mandate to monitor the progress of the implementation of the agreement—but in their direct interface, the underlying suspicion did not allow for a more detailed agreement. Fear of new security escalations in both areas seems to have pushed the parties to sign an agreement after a year of debilitating discussions, which eventually also failed to implement the accord on the ground.

Chapter 9

Cairo Accord, 2013

This chapter deals with the Cairo agreement of 2013. Both sides found themselves negotiating under Egyptian auspices for the third time in four years. This time, as in 2009, the resumption of the dialogue was, inter alia, a result of another military campaign between Israel and Hamas in the Gaza Strip (Operation Pillar of Clouds, November 14–21, 2012).

Aftermath of the Signature in Cairo

The first month following the ceremony in the Egyptian capital was quite promising. On May 28, 2011, as agreed, the Central Election Commission started to work in Gaza. The commission found out that approximately 250,000 people in Gaza had neither Palestinian identity cards nor passports, since the PA had stopped issuing documents as a response to Hamas's control of the Gaza strip. A week later (June 5), representatives of Fatah and Hamas met, with Egyptian mediation, to discuss details of the new government. In mid-June things started to deteriorate again: on June 13, Fathi Hamad stirred up the surroundings when he addressed new police officers and told them, "There will be no peace with secularism. The only peace is first with God, then with Jihad, then with resistance, then with the people and with martyrs." Hamas's prime minister, Haniyeh, tried to decrease tensions by stating, "We will not allow a return of chaos, whether in Gaza or the West Bank."[1] At that point, Fatah, like Haniyeh, stressed its commitment to the signed accord, calling the period of rift "the black era."[2] No real effort was made by Abu Mazen and Masha'al to reduce tensions between the parties.

Earlier in July, Hamas withdrew the CEC's activity in Gaza, accusing Fatah of intimidating Hamas supporters in the West Bank to discourage them from participating in the election process. In response, the PA announced municipal elections in October 2012, and Hamas replied that the PA was disrupting reconciliation.[3] Rival parties that had honest intentions and real interest in reconciliation ought to be able to find a way to contain such tactical events, but, as in the past, basic distrust led to mutual accusations. Fatah released an announcement (July 2) blaming Hamas for failing to reconcile. Fatah spokesperson Faiz Abu 'Ita told reporters that Hamas's decision came as a surprise, and that it was a disappointment, especially when the Palestinian people have expectations of a new government as agreed to in Doha and Cairo. He denied Hamas's allegations and verified that registration of eligible voters in the West Bank had not stopped.[4]

Hamas made things between the parties even worse after demanding to change the composition of CEC members on the ground, so that the commission was imbalanced. Al-Zahar, on behalf of Hamas, claimed that the CEC was dominated by Fatah members, effectively allowing the PA to supervise the electoral process. In response, the youth movement (al-Shabiba) of Fatah in the West Bank characterized al-Zahar's claim as political bankruptcy, maintaining that it showed that Hamas had no real intention to reconcile.[5] This demand by Hamas had carried a covert message for future negotiations: it essentially expressed Hamas's reluctance to reach an agreement because it alleged that Hamas insisted on technical and substantive issues that could easily be resolved in a negotiated situation where two parties seek an agreement that serves both. On July 10, the PA decided on municipal elections within three months, and Hamas almost automatically condemned the decision, claiming that such a unilateral move put more obstacles in the way of reconciliation.

While this blame game continued, no real advance was achieved in the summer of 2012. In fact, the schedules of the parties indicated that the behavioral approach dictated their activity. Abu Mazen was troubled by the potential financial crisis of the PA and therefore went to Saudi Arabia (July 11). The Saudi king granted the PA one hundred million dollars to overcome the crisis.[6] Abu Mazen visited Hebron on August 2 and gave a long speech, part of which dealt with reconciliation with Hamas. He described the negotiations in Doha (February) and Cairo

(May) between him and Khaled Masha'al. He also reported that the Central Election Commission had almost completed preparations for elections, which were the basis for reconciliation in his view, and registered three hundred thousand new voters in the Gaza Strip. The Palestinian president said: "I am the president of everyone. I don't care who they choose, the main thing is to exercise their right to vote." A day before the CEC's job was completed, one of Hamas's representatives announced the cessation of work. He added: "The truth was that for a moment, I have no idea why." In an attempt at the soft approach, Abbas urged Hamas to change its mind and allow preparations for elections to end.[7]

Despite this attempt, bilateral accusations continued. Various speakers on behalf of Hamas argued that Abu Mazen was back to a "language of preconditions," and that this was the reason that reconciliation had been halted. Taher Nunu, a Hamas government spokesperson in Gaza, attacked Azzam al-Ahmad, the chief negotiator of Fatah, after the latter claimed that there was no real siege on the Gaza Strip. Nunu replied, saying, "We will not be drawn into this factional discourse, and we will remain most adamant on the supreme national interest."[8]

Hamas was inspired by the victory of the Muslim Brotherhood in the elections in Egypt in June 2012. Ismail Haniyeh declared that Mohammad Morsi, the new Egyptian president, would no longer allow a siege on the Gaza Strip.[9] When Egypt faced a terror attack in Sinai (August 5, sixteen Egyptians killed), Hamas offered assistance. A Hamas delegation (Abu Marzook and Bassam Na'im, minister of health) headed to the Muslim Brotherhood's Guidance Bureau (August 28) to meet with leaders of the group, including Supreme Guide Mohamed Badi'e. Hamas asked for assurance that the Muslim Brotherhood had nothing to do with the attack on the border checkpoint in Rafah.[10]

At the same time, as it moved closer to Iran, Hamas's self-confidence increased. Haniyeh and Abu Mazen received an invitation to attend the annual Non-Aligned summit in Tehran (August 26–31). While Haniyeh confirmed his participation, the PA rejected the invitation, blaming Iran for deepening the internal Palestinian rift. Salam Fayyad published an unusual statement mentioning that the PLO was the sole legitimate representative of all the Palestinian people. In response, Haniyeh's spokesperson Mohammed 'Awad published a statement saying that Haniyeh had no intention of responding to Fayyad.[11] Eventually, Haniyeh did not fly to Iran, explaining that he was "more concerned about the Palestinian cause and did not want to contribute to Palestinian division."[12]

Two important statements by Ghazi Hamas, the deputy foreign minister and a senior Hamas official, at the beginning of September 2012, indicated that Hamas had already delineated different courses to achieve its different interests, perhaps even another vision in comparison with the PA. First, he said that Hamas preferred Egyptian mediation for reaching a unity government "because of geographic proximity and the new regime," implying that it was much more convenient for the movement to lean and rely on a regime with the same ideology. In another statement, he confirmed that Hamas was seeking diplomatic ties, including appointing its diplomats around the world.[13] By mid-September, the different visions became clearer when Faysal Abu Shahala, a senior Fatah member from Gaza, said that his organization still supported the "two states for two peoples" solution with Israel and al-Zahar declared that the goal of Hamas was the destruction of Israel.[14] At that point in the fall of 2012, Hamas also received great encouragement from the historic visit made by the Qatar ruler, Sheikh Hamad bin Khalifa al-Thani in the Gaza Strip (October 23), in which the sheikh promised generous financial assistance for the rehabilitation of physical infrastructure. The Qatari visitor called on Hamas and the PA to quickly resume their reconciliation dialogue: "Why are you staying divided? There are no peace negotiations, and there is no clear strategy of resistance and liberation. Why shouldn't brothers sit together and reconcile?"[15]

This visit served Hamas's interests in two ways: first, it contributed to its image as a sovereign actor that took care of the Gazans; second, it promoted Hamas's effort to enlarge its regional support from Sunni regimes.

On the other side of the conflict, PA seniors kept the reconciliation process alive, while Salam Fayyad said he was ready to resign if that was the will of the people. His statement came after a series of protests in the West Bank in response to the rising cost of living, but Fayyad knew that Hamas perceived him as pro-Fatah and refused to accept him as prime minister.[16] It was too little for Hamas, which felt itself more powerful after the Muslim Brotherhood won the Egyptian elections. A public opinion poll on September 15 showed that only 51 percent of Palestinians believed that reconciliation of the Palestinian Authority with Hamas would be achieved in the near or distant future.[17]

Meanwhile, on the ground, the strained relationship between Hamas and the PA minimized the chance of a reconciliation agreement being implemented. Both sides, like tango dancers, took a step forward and retreated two. The behavioral approach once again directed them to act for survival and to thwart any activity by the opponent in which they identified a threat to government stability. PA security forces continued to monitor Hamas personnel. They gathered intelligence on them, conducted arrests, and ignored court orders to release Hamas detainees:

1. On June 28, 2012, PCHR expressed its concern about the lives of six detainees, who started a hunger strike within the PA's prison. Four of them were Hamas activists from Hebron, who were arrested in September 2010, accused of harming national unity. They decided on a hunger strike after the PA refused to release them, although a Palestinian court ruled to free them.[18]
2. On June 30, security squads used force to disperse a peaceful demonstration in the center of Ramallah, protesting against the Palestinian president for his meeting with Shaul Mofaz, Israeli deputy prime minister at that time. Members of civil society organizations and journalists were also attacked. GIS arrested seven people, among them Mohammad Jaradat, a journalist who was severely beaten. The day after, a second rally was organized, this time to protest the violence by security forces. PA police used force again and three of the protesters were arrested.[19]
3. On September 19, PA security forces carried out extensive arrests of Hamas operatives across the West Bank. Seventy-one Hamas members, including leaders of Hamas, reconciliation figures, ex-prisoners, journalists, youth activists, and university students, were arrested: nineteen in Salfit (south of Nablus), eighteen in Tulkarm, fifteen in Qalqilya, eleven in Nablus, six in Hebron, one in Jenin, and one in Ramallah.[20]

Hamas in the Gaza Strip did the same to Fatah. Two prominent incidents are worth mentioning in this context: the movement banned a mass marriage ceremony in Gaza (August 31), organized by Fatah. The official reason was that "arrangements for the ceremony were coordinated with the Palestinian police, but the decision to prevent its organization was made in the end when the police noticed that the number of attendants was higher than expected." It was a cover for the real reason, which was to prevent Fatah from social achievement—and the proof of that was supplied in November when Hamas banned Fatah activists from holding a ceremony marking eight years since Arafat's death.[21]

Operation Pillar of Clouds

Operation Pillar of Clouds was an Israeli military operation in the Gaza Strip, which began on November 14 and ended on November 21, 2012. The operation began with the elimination or targeted assassination of Ahmad Ja'abari, at the actual headquarters of the Hamas military wing. Israel attacked targets in the Gaza Strip, and at the same time, about 1,500 rockets were fired and launched from Gaza at Israel; also, for the first time, missiles were fired at the center cities of Tel Aviv and Jerusalem. For the second time in less than four years, Israel had an impact on the internal rift within Palestinian politics.

The security escalation that led to the military clash between Israel and Hamas started early in November. On November 6, an IDF soldier was wounded after a sabotage charge was fired at the vehicle in which he rode, during an operation near the perimeter fence. On November 8, in an IDF operation in the Gaza Strip, a thirteen-year-old Palestinian boy was killed in an exchange of gunfire, and then an explosive tunnel was blown up. On November 10, a Milan antimissile missile was fired at a military patrol jeep, wounding four soldiers. In response, the IDF bombed the Gaza Strip, killing seven Palestinians, five of them civilians.

According to the Israeli army, 177 Palestinians were killed, of whom approximately 120 were combatants, and over 900 were injured. In addition, Israel carried out over 1,500 airstrikes against targets in the Gaza Strip, including "19 senior command centers, operational control centers, Hamas's senior-rank headquarters, 30 senior operatives." The Israeli military campaign hit Hamas's military infrastructure: "command and control centers, hundreds of underground rocket launchers, 140 smuggling tunnels, 66 terror tunnels, dozens of Hamas operation rooms and bases, 26 weapons manufacturing and storage facilities, and dozens of long-range rocket launchers and launch sites."[22] The Human Rights Council official report mentioned 174 killed and heavy damage for civil infrastructure, such as hospitals and schools.[23]

On the third day of the campaign, Abu Mazen gave a speech in which he returned to the common national ethos. Seeing himself as the president of all Palestinians, he talked about the massacre Israel was carrying out in the Gaza Strip, and he updated the Palestinians in respect to the PA's efforts vis-à-vis various world leaders to stop Israel's military operations. He described the Palestinian resistance in the Gaza Strip as steadfastness (*sumud*), another feature of the national ethos, and blamed Israel for thwarting the Palestinian national goal. He took the opportunity to call on Hamas (and other political or military groups) to remind them that the Israeli aggression was against all Palestinians, and he urged them to stand together and make an extra effort to reconcile. He added: "I tried to call Khaled Masha'al and Ismail Haniyeh but failed to reach them."[24] This time, as a result of the Israeli offensive, the Palestinian president chose, at least for a short term, an integrative approach in order to resume dialogue.

Shortly after Israel and Hamas agreed to a ceasefire, a new round of intra-Palestinian dialogue began. Both sides decided on mutual gestures of good will: Hamas decided to release those accused in cases related to the division that occurred in 2006. It also allowed the return of Fatah activists who fled Gaza in 2007 clashes. In response, the PA would release Hamas members who did not commit any criminal offense. This was also an indirect admission that the PA was making political arrests. Sha'ath also said that Abu Mazen met (November 24) with Hamas seniors in the West Bank and would soon visit Gaza.[25] Sha'ath himself joined Haniyeh to attend a ceremony to honor bereaved families (November 27). The PA let Hamas supporters in the West Bank mark Hamas's anniversary (December 14).

A week later, Khaled Masha'al visited the Gaza Strip for the first time in forty-five years, escorted by Abu Marzook and Rishq. Representatives of all political factions, including Fatah, welcomed him at the Rafah crossing point.[26] In his speech on December 9, the anniversary of the 1987 intifada outbreak, he seemed to continue the reconciliation line that Abu Mazen sought to advance after the Israeli military operation in the Gaza Strip. Masha'al said that "free and democratic elections are a necessary step for the Palestinians. We all shared responsibility and one of the key factors is mutual understanding. However, we should not neglect the national constants. Dialogue with the PA, under Egyptian auspices, will resume soon, this time with Arabic and Islamic support. Again, previous disputes between us and Fatah partners will not recur. We will continue to fight for the liberation of Palestine, and we will stick to jihad and resistance."[27]

Fatah described Masha'al's speech as "very positive." Azzam al-Ahmad, the chief negotiator, said that the Hamas leader concentrated on topics that the parties already agreed on in Doha and Cairo (February and May 2012). "We want to put an end to the rift and to have one authority, one president, one government, one PLC, and one legitimate source, which is the PLO."[28] Despite the friendly atmosphere, the parties remained suspicious of each other. While Fatah suggested (December 19) canceling the next round of discussions in Cairo, as a result of the internal turmoil in Egypt, Salah Bardawil from Hamas rejected that. He explained that Egypt was the natural mediator (it was comfortable for Hamas to hold this stance since at that time Egypt was under the reign of the Muslim Brotherhood) and raised speculation that "Abu Mazen is waiting for a new peace initiative before heading toward reconciliation."[29]

Eventually, Hamas security forces in the Gaza Strip decided to approve the Fatah ceremony to mark its forty-eight-year anniversary. On January 2, 2013, Ismail Haniyeh met the Fatah delegation to discuss security arrangements for the Fatah ceremony, scheduled two days later. He said that "this time Gaza is witnessing the launch ceremonies where the Hamas movement has revived its launch. It will coincide with the days of the Fatah movement festival, and when Fatah submitted a request to commemorate the movement's anniversary, we agreed, based on the enhancement of the positive climate in which we live in Palestine, and on an investment for victory, and I hope this will be a day of national celebration and enhance the national spirit."[30] It was the biggest, most impressive, and powerful Fatah rally since the violent split of 2007, when hundreds of thousands gathered at the central square of Gaza near the Governor Building (Saraya) to express their support of Fatah. They waved flags of the Fatah movement, pictures of Yasser Arafat, and listened to Abu Mazen's televised speech.[31]

Egyptian president Mohammad Morsi invited Abu Mazen and Masha'al to Cairo to discuss next steps for implementing the previous understandings between the PA and Hamas. The Egyptian president met them both, separately, on January 9, 2013. Subsequently, the two Palestinian leaders met without the Egyptian mediator but failed to formulate measures to implement the agreement signed in May 2012. Abu Mazen stated after his meeting with Morsi, "We discussed the Palestinian conditions and the means to achieve reconciliation through implementing the agreed-upon steps according to the Doha and Cairo agreements."[32]

Azzam al-Ahmad revealed (January 17) the agreements reached by Abu Mazen and Khaled Masha'al during their meeting in Cairo:[33]

1. The Central Election Commission will resume its work no later than January 30, 2013 and continue its normal work in the West Bank.
2. The meetings of the Committee on Public Liberties and the Committee for Social Reconciliation will begin no later than January 30.
3. Consultations to form a government will begin at the same time, that is, no later than January 30.
4. Negative media statements issued by some people will stop, as this hinders the reconciliation process.
5. A Fatah-Hamas committee, under Egyptian supervision, will be formed to implement the reconciliation agreement.

Analysis of these paragraphs indicates that there is no essential change from the previous agreement (Doha to Cairo, 2012). Basically, these mutual understandings were tactical. However, sections 4 and 5 told the true story in which both sides consciously, once again, chose the behavioral approach to negotiating: both respected the Egyptian mediator; both agreed on general formulations. They also understood, however, that the atmosphere between them was tense, more so because of the war of mutual accusations carried out in public. Both also felt that the chances of implementing the understandings were low, and therefore agreed on a committee headed by the Egyptian mediator to oversee the progress of the process.

On January 18, Hamas and Fatah agreed to implement by the end of January the previous reconciliation agreement signed by both parties. They also decided that the Central Election Commission would resume the registration of voters within the Gaza Strip.[34] But senior analysts were skeptical about the odds that this time both sides would succeed where they had already failed five times in the past. Aaron Miller, a former senior official in the US State Department, said that "unity is again being driven by tactical considerations, not by a sincere desire to unify ranks. Unity talks will start, stop, start again, and perhaps even result in a formal accord. But beneath this faux process, the players will continue to dig in their heels." His analysis met the criteria of the behavioral approach, as the parties did not believe each other. Diana Buttu, a lawyer in Ramallah who used to work with Abu Mazen, explained that the Palestinian president had an interest in accepting financial support from the Gulf states; therefore, the reconciliation was not real. It was no more than an instrumental move to serve a much more important interest. Her explanation fit the rational choice approach as well as prioritizing of interests.[35]

On the ground, during the last ten days of January 2013, things seemed to be moving toward the implementation of the agreement clauses. Hamas allowed greater numbers of Fatah members to return to the Gaza Strip. Ismail Haniyeh announced that he was preparing for the general elections and that he would allow the Central Election Commission to resume voter registration across the Strip. Izzat al-Rishq, a senior member of Hamas, verified that the parties agreed on a cabinet of "independents" before Palestinians will have a new election.[36] However, new obstacles emerged early in February after 'Aziz Dwaik, PLC representative and Hamas member, decided to call an assembly of the PLC. Faysal Abu Shahala, a senior Fatah member from Gaza, replied, saying that this move was an excuse to obstruct reconciliation. He stressed that the Cairo agreement provided for the formation of the government first, and then the legislative council would convene in a month.[37]

Interestingly, although not surprisingly, as the steps to realize the reconciliation progressed, Hamas leadership stressed in public its strict policy stance that showed how different its vision was from that of Abu Mazen. Khaled Masha'al said in a speech broadcast on Jordanian television that Hamas would neither give up Palestine nor recognize temporary borders such as, for instance, the 1967 borders. Haniyeh said Hamas would never give up the right of return. These statements were meant, first and foremost, for the Palestinian president to clarify the political power the movement had garnered since 2007.[38]

Delegations of the rival parties met again in Cairo (February 9), this time under two umbrellas: Egypt as a host and mediator and the PLO as a provisional governing body. Wassel Abu Yussef, one of the members of this forum, described the gaps between the parties: "Fatah wants the [transitional nonpartisan] government [tasked with organizing the elections] formed at the same time as a decree setting the date for elections. Hamas wants the government to be formed first to end the division before the date of elections is decided."[39] As happened before, the parties failed to agree on this tactical issue, which in fact illustrated the strategic rift between them. Khalil Assaf, independent coalition chief, said that Palestinian factions had not done enough to fulfill the ambitions of the Palestinian people. "None of the agreed-upon points have been implemented. Unity talks should take place publicly."[40] This was an interesting proposal, allowing the people to decide which party was not interested in reconciliation. Lack of trust between the parties increased in those days, after the PA security forces arrested twenty-five Hamas activists throughout the West Bank.[41]

The CEC renewed its work on the Gaza Strip (February 11), and Haniyeh declared, "We were able to register voters, and this step would not have taken place had it not been for the positive atmosphere surrounding the dialogues in Cairo."[42] By the end of March, Qatar accelerated the reconciliation process, offering to form a "mini" Arab summit in Egypt to negotiate reconciliation between rival Palestinian factions.[43] The Qatari offer was accepted by the parties, but Abu Mazen, again, took the behavioral-rational approach, refusing to attend the proposed meeting in Cairo if Hamas participated.[44] The Palestinian president asked to maximize two different interests: One was tactical—for him to receive the honor he deserved as president, not to share it in a meeting with other Arab leaders. The second interest was strategic—to make sure that only the PLO represented the Palestinian people.

Despite his threat, by mid-April a series of events within the Palestinian political system paved the path to meet in Cairo: first, Salam Fayyad resigned from his office as prime minister; second, all Palestinian factions in the Gaza Strip urged Abu Mazen to form a new unity government and to authorize this government to set a date for presidential and parliamentary elections; third, Masha'al and Haniyeh headed to Doha to consult with the Qatari on the latest development.[45] On April 27, 2013, Abu Mazen announced the start of consultations to form a consensus government. Hamas's automatic reply was that the movement had no intention of being run by remote control: "We heard about Abu Mazen's decision over the media. No one has consulted with us. We warned Fatah against unilateral moves."[46] Eventually, on May 14, both sides signed a new agreement. In fact, it was a confirmation of the 2012 agreement, which was achieved with Qatari-Egyptian mediation. This time the parties agreed to set a timetable for the formation of a unity government within three months. There was no clear indication of how this timetable would fare better than previous unrealized plans. Hamas representative Sami Abu Zuhri told that Hamas had decided to "finalize all reconciliation issues in three months, including that of the national unity government . . . and legislative and presidential elections."[47]

From a historical perspective, the May 2013 agreement was in fact a continuation of understandings from their previous agreements. Since both parties failed to implement the previous mutual understandings, except for the completion of voter registration in Gaza, the only innovation in the agreement was setting the timetable to establish a unity government within three months. Even after the agreement was signed, it became clear that mutual suspicion and mistrust continued to dictate the moves of both parties, and a unity government only emerged after more than a year.

Chapter 10

Al-Shati Agreement, 2014

This chapter analyzes the negotiation process between the PA and Hamas from mid-2013 to mid-2014, when the parties reached the Al-Shati agreement.[1] This agreement came after more than a year of stagnation due to internal political developments in the West Bank and the Gaza Strip and both regional and international changes, mainly the toppling of the Muslim Brotherhood's regime in Egypt and efforts by US secretary of state John Kerry to resume the peace process between Israelis and Palestinians.

Aftermath of the Signing in Cairo: Continuation of the Blame Game

The optimism that followed the signing of the Cairo agreement (May 2013) lasted about a week. On June 2, Abu Mazen announced his intention to appoint Rami Hamdallah as prime minister instead of Salam Fayyad.[2] Hamas and all other major Palestinian factions in Gaza rejected Abu Mazen's decision and called it illegal, claiming that "formation of a new government proves that the Fatah leadership is willing to maintain and prolong the state of disagreement."[3] Yusuf Rizka, a close advisor to Haniyeh, declared that the new government was an extension of the Fayyad government mistake—imposing a political rather than legal government.[4] Hamas's suspicion of Abu Mazen increased even more after Palestinian security apparatuses arrested seven Hamas activists in the West Bank (June 5).[5] But Abu Mazen ignored the criticism, and on

June 7 a new PA Cabinet was sworn in. The Palestinian president said: "This is my government and you have all my trust and protection."[6]

The Palestinian political system received another surprise on June 20, when Hamdallah announced his resignation. The official reason was that he was not satisfied with the powers he received. Abu Mazen accepted the resignation but asked Hamdallah to continue his duties until a new government could be formed.[7] On the other side of the barricade, Hamas had not publicly addressed the issue of reconciliation. At the end of June, Ismail Haniyeh made it clear that the movement would never recognize Israel. "We went through two wars, hundreds were killed, and we didn't recognize Israel." During his speech in Gaza, he did not even mention the internal Palestinian rift. Political developments in Egypt, during which the Muslim Brotherhood's regime ended, may have had a negative effect on Hamas, which lost an important arm, but the movement said it was not afraid of the new situation in Egypt.[8] The fact that Egypt, the main Arab mediator, had experienced internal upheaval led to stagnation in the Palestinian arena. Neither party had a real interest in promoting reconciliation, and the mediator had other interests to promote, so his attention to intra-Palestinian reconciliation had waned in the summer of 2013.

Meanwhile, on the ground, tension between the rivals escalated as the result of a series of mutual statements reflecting the current of mistrust beneath the political rift that did not allow reconciliation based on the common national ethos:

1. Hamas renewed its call for the PA to stop security coordination with Israel (July 13). It was a polite move by Hamas, and it treated Fatah and the Palestinian Authority as siblings: "We call on our brothers in Fatah and the PA in the West Bank to shoulder their responsibilities before our people and our prisoners and take bold steps against the occupation."[9] Four days later (July 17), Rizka admitted that there was no contact between the parties, since Abu Mazen was busy with US secretary of state John Kerry and was not available for negotiation with Hamas. He also rejected the statement by Mohammad Al-Shtayyeh, a senior member of Fatah, that August 14 was the deadline for reconciliation. Rizka and Sami Abu Zuhri accused the PA of selective implementation of the Cairo accord, calling on Abu Mazen

not to bet on negotiations with Israel.[10] These statements reflected Hamas's attitude toward reconciliation: a lack of confidence in Abu Mazen, who found it difficult to choose between full reconciliation and negotiations with Israel. This indecisiveness also pointed to Abu Mazen's lack of leadership and commitment to the people, a necessary trait according to Imam 'Ali.

2. When Abu Mazen accepted John Kerry's initiative to resume talks with Israel, Hamas spokesperson Fawzi Barhoum warned that this decision endangered Palestinian unity. He also argued that the PA's decision was not legitimate because the Palestinian people refused to have a dialogue with Israel. "Israel and the US are the main reason for the stagnation of the reconciliation process between the PA and Hamas, because they put pressure on Abu Mazen not to converge with Hamas."[11] Different speakers from the religious movement continued to pressure Abu Mazen to say no to Kerry, drawing a link between "political suicide" and the PA's potential acceptance of the American plan for internal reconciliation. Hamas's interest was in enhancing its political influence, while at the same time offering all Palestinians a different vision, which would not be a political settlement and compromise with Israel.

3. On July 28, Hamas closed the offices of Al Arabiya television and Ma'an News Agency (affiliated with the PA), on the grounds of broadcasting fake news based on Israeli sources and on Lines Media Company. Ismail Jaber, the group's attorney general, released a statement explaining that the decision came "because these two media offices had published fabricated news, rumors and inaccurate information that posed a threat to civil peace and negatively affected the Palestinian people and resistance." For instance, Ma'an News Agency published a news item claiming that leaders from the Muslim Brotherhood in Egypt had infiltrated Gaza.[12]

4. Following Abu Mazen's indication that he would allow a meeting between Palestinian and Israel delegations in

Washington (July 20), Osama Abu Hamdan, Hamas's representative in Beirut, accused him of leading "a serious scheme to drive a wedge between Gaza and Egypt, as part of a systematic policy to take revenge on the Hamas movement." He added that Hamas had managed to get official documents to prove the PA's involvement in a conspiracy in coordination with the US and Israel to liquidate the Palestinian cause.[13] Al-Zahar repeated these allegations in Gaza later in August. Such serious accusations against the Palestinian president were sure to prolong the stalemate with regard to reconciliation because they expressed Hamas's basic distrust of Abu Mazen's policy.

5. Majed Abu Shamalah, PLC member of Fatah, revealed (August 9) that Hamas security forces had raided houses of Fatah members in Gaza, warning of a large-scale operation against his colleagues and calling the arrests political.[14] The Palestinian Centre for Human Rights confirmed that Hamas arrested sixteen Fatah activists and questioned them about giving money to Fatah families.[15]

6. Azzam al-Ahmad, the chief negotiator of the PA, in all previous rounds of dialogue between the parties, declared that Hamas was not ready for reconciliation. He said that the parties had signed an agreement on May 14 to implement reconciliation talks with the formation of a unity government of independent technocrats headed by President Mahmoud Abbas no later than August 14.[16] He accused Hamas of not abiding by this agreement.

7. Interaction between the parties continued to be edgy when Husam Badran, a senior Hamas member from Nablus, called for escalating resistance in the West Bank, aware of the possibility that the PA would attempt to block it.[17] On the surface, it was an ordinary statement, one of dozens, but Badran's call suggested that Hamas sought to bring together a combination of qualities in the population—such as the courage to protest, the character to accept struggle and self-sacrifice, the will to be uncompromising and to have no intention of giving up. Such qualities shaped patterns of national struggle, a Palestinian identity and vision other

than the one that Abbas sought to lead. Moreover, Badran's call expressed courage even at the cost of a confrontation with PA security forces.

8. Abu Mazen was interviewed on Egyptian television, exposing the fact that the PA had received information that Hamas's activists were involved in terror attacks in Sinai against the Egyptian army. However, it was up to the Egyptian judiciary system to rule on this issue: "If Egypt asks, we will provide the information."[18] This statement not only confirmed Hamas's earlier claims that it was trying to drive Hamas into Egypt but further jeopardized the prospect of reconciliation. The behavioral approach, which Hamas is regularly suspected of using, also dictated Abu Mazen's moves in this case.

New Signs of Reengagement

By the end of 2013, the internal atmosphere had changed, mainly because of a financial crisis within the Gaza Strip. On December 17, informed sources revealed to Ma'an News Agency that Hamas informed President Abu Mazen of the movement's formal approval to form a national unity government in preparation for holding presidential and legislative elections. According to this report, Masha'al and Haniyeh called the Palestinian president, separately, to update him on the decision. It was two weeks after Masha'al said that Israel and the US were obstructing the path to reconciliation.[19] This time, the parties agreed to extend the period of Rami Hamdallah's government to six months before the upcoming elections. Hamas did not deny the report, and Abu Mazen headed to Cairo to discuss the latest development with Adly Mansour, interim Egyptian president. Four days later contact over resumption of a reconciliation dialogue came out into the open when Mohammad Al-Shtayyeh, a senior Fatah member, confirmed a phone call between Abu Mazen and Haniyeh, and stated that "Fatah is ready for reconciliation at any price."[20]

Both parties entered 2014 without agreements regarding the next moves to implement reconciliation. Despite this situation, Hamas decided to make more gestures of good will. Islam Shahwan, Interior Ministry spokesperson in Gaza, announced (January 8) that seven Fatah detainees would be released soon and that all Fatah members who fled the Gaza Strip in 2007 could return, without going to trial, except those who killed Hamas activists.[21] The justification for Hamas's decision was the difficult economic situation in the Gaza Strip, which in early 2014 forced Hamas to compromise, tactically, in order to try to increase its external sources of funding.

Hamas continued these gestures, allowing PLC members of Fatah to enter Gaza for the first time since 2007. Rawhi Ftooh and Majed Abu Shamalah arrived in the Gaza Strip (January) to discuss reconciliation with Hamas.[22] Early in February, Haniyeh approved another visit, this time of a Fatah delegation of four members who met with their cadre. Haniyeh instructed his security forces to make the necessary arrangements to ensure that their visit was carried out as planned. Following the visit, Nabil Sha'ath, a senior member of Fatah, said he was optimistic regarding the reconciliation.[23] However, it appears that for Fatah the visit was not enough. The movement published (February 12) an official statement accusing Hamas of evading the reconciliation under feeble pretexts and excuses. The statement stressed that Fatah was ready for immediate implementation of the previous agreements and announced, "We have the feeling that Hamas aims to gain more time."[24] A week later, Amin Maqbul, head of Fatah in Nablus, said the reconciliation was not close and that Azzam al-Ahmad would not travel to Gaza before Hamas accepted the concept of general elections and a unity government. He also argued that "it has become clear that Haniyeh and the political politburo of Hamas are in disagreement."[25]

When the parties seemed to find the way to realize the reconciliation, Hamas took a step back. Hamas hardened its stance about possible reconciliation at the beginning of March. Marwan Abu Ras, PLC member of the Change and Reform Bloc, said that Egypt was no longer a neutral party, which would overshadow all reconciliation rounds if they were held. "We cannot rely on Egypt if it prefers one side over another."[26] Following this declaration, Hamas prohibited Fatah members in Gaza from having a festival in support of Abu Mazen (March 16). Amal Hamad, a Fatah activist, said the ban weakened negotiations and that it was time for Hamas to side with the Palestinians.[27]

In mid-March 2014, Abu Mazen gave a speech addressing the issue of reconciliation. He made it clear that internal reconciliation was in the interest of all Palestinians and blamed Hamas for not wanting it. "I suggested that we form a temporary government and hold elections in three months. They asked for elections in six months. I agreed. I sent them a letter asking for immediate reconciliation and they replied that they could not accommodate that. They had leadership inside [in Gaza] and outside [Masha'al], and they disagreed on the issue. Hamas disagrees and the people pay the price."[28] A month later, Hamas denied reports on an upcoming visit by a Fatah delegation to Gaza in order to restart a reconciliation dialogue. Hamas also again urged the PA to stop security coordination with Israel as a response to Israeli prime minister Benjamin Netanyahu, who ordered Israeli officials to halt cooperation with Palestinian officials.[29]

Eventually, the breakthrough came from Abu Mazen. In March he appointed a new delegation for the resumption of negotiations. Representatives of other Palestinian organizations joined al-Ahmad in order to put pressure on Hamas and to pass on its reservations from the 2013 Egyptian offer for Palestinian reconciliation.[30] Real progress toward a new direct dialogue between the parties was made on April 21 when Musa Abu Marzook arrived at the Gaza Strip. On the same day, Azzam al-Ahmad confirmed in Cairo that a high-ranking delegation from Fatah and representatives of other Palestinian groups would travel to Gaza within forty-eight hours. Al-Ahmad said that this time there was a place for optimism: "We are going to Gaza not to propose new suggestions, but rather to carry out a clear mission which is to end the state of disagreement and address three decisive issues: formation of a national consensus government, elections, and restructuring the PLO so we can dedicate our efforts to confronting Israeli occupation."[31] Both sides announced that they agreed on a historic unity government in a historic deal, and Al-Ahmad said that he hoped the deal would be a true beginning and a true partnership.[32] A senior Hamas official speaking anonymously with a news site also expressed optimism, explaining that "the living conditions in Gaza have reached an unprecedented level of suffering and there is no light at the end of the tunnel with regard to the deteriorating relationship with Egypt. This has sped up the reconciliation. Hamas wants to liberate itself from the regional and international isolation it has been experiencing since the fall of Morsi in Egypt."[33] That senior official, in fact, hinted that Hamas was being forced into reconciliation with the Palestinian Authority, and that reconciliation actually constituted an instrument for promoting three important interests at the same time, in April 2014, that were equivalent to enacting an armed struggle to liberate Palestine: the first concern was to improve the state of the Gaza Strip, where Hamas was the de facto sovereign; the second was to improve the deteriorating relationship with Egypt; and the third was to break out of regional and international isolation.

The April 2014 agreement became known as the Al-Shati agreement because the discussions were held at the home of Ismail Haniyeh, a resident of the Al-Shati refugee camp. It had a preamble, in which several features of the national Palestinian common ethos were mentioned: Israel's attacks on the Al-Aqsa mosque, Israel's intention to Judaize Jerusalem and to diminish Jerusalem's Arab identity, the expansion of the Jewish settlements on Palestinian lands in the West Bank, and the ongoing aggression of the Israeli army against Palestinians—who were the victims. On this basis, "National reconciliation, the end of Palestinian division, the restoration and strengthening of national unity, and the establishment of controls that ensure stability, continuity, and growth have become a national duty."[34]

The clauses of the agreement establish the following agenda:

1. To emphasize a commitment to all that was agreed upon in the Cairo agreement—and the Doha declaration, and [these agreements] shall be considered a reference for implementation [of reconciliation]. There are several reasons why the opening clause mentions previous understandings: (1) The understandings of 2012 were still relevant because they were never fully implemented. (2) The wording agreed on in the first paragraph did not require both parties to waive any of their opening positions in the negotiations. (3) The rejection of the previous agreements was basically a criticism, also indirectly, of Egypt and Qatar. Both sides—the PA and Hamas—had previously assisted in both countries and were not interested and wanted to maintain a good and close relationship with them.

2. The government: President Mahmoud Abbas will begin consultations to form a government of national consensus, in line with his history, and it shall be declared within the legally specified period of five weeks, based on the Cairo agreement and the Doha declaration, and it will carry out all of its obligations. This section was also not supposed to run into opposition, because it was drafted in general terms, and it set a date for establishing a unity government. It did

not specify shared powers between the Palestinian president and the government, and the parties were not required to relinquish powers and political power according to the terms agreed upon.

3. Elections: To emphasize that legislative, presidential, and National Council elections will be held simultaneously and the president is authorized to set a date for elections, in consultation with the national forces and actors, and the elections shall be held at least six months after the formation of the government. This shall be discussed in the PLO Activation Committee, during its next meeting, and the requirements for holding said elections shall be completed.

4. Palestine Liberation Organization: It was agreed that the Palestinian Liberation Organization Activation and Development Committee will meet, to exercise its functions stipulated in the agreements, within five weeks as of this date, and it was confirmed that its meetings would continue periodically thereafter. These two subjects, which deal with the PLO's powers, do not clearly refer to the involvement of Hamas members in the discussions. Paragraph 3 emphasized that Abbas could set a general election date in consultation with all political parties, that is, with Hamas as well. Paragraph 4 of the agreement does not mention whether Hamas members would participate in the PLO's discussions and thus have the potential for disagreements between the parties in the future.

5. Social Reconciliation Committee: The immediate resumption of work on social reconciliation, including the work of subcommittees, based on what was agreed upon in Cairo.

6. Freedoms Committee: An emphasis on the application of what was agreed upon in Cairo, concerning the issue of public freedoms. The Public Freedoms Committee in the West Bank and the Gaza has been called upon to resume work immediately and implement its decisions.

7. The legislative council: An emphasis on the application of what has been agreed upon, to activate the Palestinian Legislative Council, in order to carry out its duties. The

> last three paragraphs are a kind of complement to the main agreements and should reflect the good will of both parties to improve their relationship and serve the Palestinian people. This is done through popular committees that represent all Palestinian factions and the legislative council elected by the public in January 2006.

This time, in contrast to previous agreements, the reconciliation agreement was implemented. The unity government did materialize within five weeks of the agreement and even began functioning within a few months; then the suspicion and distrust of both parties again started to dictate political behavior—until the agreement collapsed and Hamas formed a shadow government. The two sides did not meet for another round of negotiations until more than three years later, in September 2017. Despite the fact that this round of negotiations ultimately achieved significant progress, the inevitable conclusion is that once again lack of trust and a preference for personal interests (Abu Mazen) and organizations (Hamas and Fatah) led to the continuation of the political crisis between the two sides.

Chapter 11

Cairo Agreement, October 2017

The final chapter of this study discusses the period between April 2014 to September 2017, when the PA and Hamas announced, for the eighth time in ten years, a reconciliation agreement. This time, they needed, again, Egyptian mediation and Cairo as the arena for dialogue. This agreement, like all the previous ones, did not reach the point of implementation. As this study was sealed, the geopolitical and ideological rifts within the Palestinian sociopolitical system had not come to an end.

Forming a Unity Government

As expected, the signing ceremony of the Al-Shati agreement had immediate consequences. On the very same day as the signing, April 23, Israel attacked Abu Mazen's decision, blaming him for choosing Hamas instead of peace. US State Department spokesperson Jen Psaki said that the "US was disappointed by the move," and a senior administration official added that this move was anticipated. But Abu Mazen rejected the US position, saying that the unity agreement did not contradict talks with Israel.[1] He continued to approach Hamas and gave public expression to their positive relations when, during his visit to Qatar (May 5), he met with Masha'al, and the two praised each other. The Palestinian president took advantage of the visit to update the Qatari host on the reconciliation process and to pay tribute to the effort he made to promote intra-Palestinian reconciliation. In this case, Abu Mazen chose the win-win approach, in which he respected both his mediator and his political opponent.[2] Abu Mazen is likely to be encouraged and incentivized to reconcile with Hamas, based on a public opinion poll published in early June, in which half of the Palestinian public expressed increasing confidence in the Palestinian Authority in a scenario of reconciliation with Hamas.[3]

On the ground, rapid progress was recorded. Faiz Abu 'Ita, the Fatah spokesperson in Gaza, announced (May 10) that al-Ahmad would return soon to the Strip to discuss further implementation steps, stressing that "the reconciliation train is on its way and there is no way back."[4] Following his meetings with Hamas officials in Gaza, al-Ahmad stated that the Rafah crossing would be reopened immediately after the unity government was sworn in.[5] This statement was to serve two different interests of the PA: to convince the Gazan population that Abu Mazen was aware of their needs and was working for them, and to put pressure on Hamas to accelerate the pace for implementing the agreements. Haniyeh confirmed that both sides were approaching a unity government and highlighted that Hamas signed the reconciliation agreement on its own, without pressure.[6]

The new unity government of Rami Hamdallah was sworn in at a ceremony in Ramallah on June 2, 2014. Abu Mazen declared that a "black page in history has been turned. Today we restore our national unity. We are all loyal to Palestine. We want to keep its banner hoisted high."[7] At the same time, the former prime minister, Haniyeh, made a speech in Gaza, stating that Hamas had shown great flexibility in making this government successful. We are leaving the chairs, but not leaving the role, he stated. He added that the new government had a long way to go and many important missions, such as lifting the siege on the Gaza Strip and preparing for the next general elections.[8] Three days later Haniyeh unintentionally provided the real reason for the reconciliation: Hamas's economic hardship. He announced that the Qatari ruler had undertaken to support the national reconciliation government and paid its employees' salaries, especially those of the previous government in the Gaza Strip.[9] Qatar's financial support was at this point of primary interest to Hamas, therefore the movement was content with a brief laconic response in which it accused the PA of arresting sixteen Palestinians across the West Bank.[10]

Hamdallah's unity government had twenty portfolios but only eighteen ministers, including Hamdallah, all allegedly technocrats or independents. In fact, most of the ministers were loyal to Abu Mazen and at least two ministers—Hussein al-Sheikh and Ziad Abu Ein, were Fatah members. The prime minister was also interior minister, which meant that all security apparatuses were under his direct supervision. Four ministers were from the Gaza Strip and the others from the West Bank.[11]

Operation Protective Edge

The euphoria that prevailed in the Palestinian system following the signing of the unity government was very short-lived. The new government had two significant and pressing challenges to address: one involved payroll for government employees in the Gaza Strip, and the other face was dealing with threats from Israel to impose various sanctions in response to the agreement between the Palestinian Authority and Hamas. The functioning of the government became more complicated on June 12, 2014, when three Israeli teenagers were kidnapped in Gush Etzion, near Bethlehem. This terror attack led to a massive security escalation on the ground. Since mid-June, Hamas and Israel had been attacking each other. In the West Bank, Israel embarked on a large-scale military operation to locate the kidnappers. In the Gaza Strip, the characteristics of the confrontation, at this stage, were Israeli airstrikes on Hamas targets there and, on the other hand, high-trajectory firing by Hamas into Israeli territory. During the operation, 11 Palestinians were killed and 51 were wounded in 369 Israeli incursions into the West Bank through July 2, and between 350 and 600 Palestinians, including nearly all of Hamas's West Bank leaders, were arrested.[12]

Moreover, the kidnapping of the three provided an opportunity for the Palestinian rivals to cling to their basic principles, interests, and ideology. Abu Mazen called the Israeli prime minister, condemning the terror attack. He lauded the Palestinian security forces for their efforts to "stop the PA from being dragged into disorder and prevent the factions from taking advantage of the situation for non-nationalistic purposes." Netanyahu told the Palestinian president that he expected him to help bring the abductees back home, which meant that Israel expected the Palestinians to continue the security coordination, despite their reconciliation with Hamas.[13] On the other hand, Izz al-Din al-Qassam Brigades called the Palestinian people to stand and not be afraid of the Israeli threats, promising to demonstrate more determination to resist the Israeli enemy. The announcement made it clear that Hamas was still striving to release all prisoners—a feature in the national ethos—from Israeli jails.[14] Masha'al supported the call to the military wing as he published a declaration that blessed the hands of those who kidnapped the three teenagers. He accused the Israeli prime minister of ignoring the Palestinians and said, "If Netanyahu had listened to the suffering of the hunger-striking prisoners and had not opposed the national reconciliation agreement, the Palestinian situation would have become less tense."[15]

The security threat escalated further on June 30, when the bodies of the three boys were found in the Hebron area. Israel blamed Hamas for the murder, and Netanyahu warned that the militant group would pay a heavy price for the deaths.[16] On July 2, the body of a Palestinian teenager was found burnt. The police investigation led to the arrest of six Jews; later it was found that this terror act was in response to the kidnapping of the three Israelis.[17] A week later, Israel launched the longest military campaign against any Arab enemy. On July 8, Israeli prime minister Netanyahu stated, "Hamas terrorists have fired hundreds of rockets at Israel's civilians. No other country lives under such a threat, and no country would accept such a threat. Israel will not tolerate the firing of rockets on our cities and towns. We have therefore significantly expanded our operations against Hamas and the other terrorist organizations in Gaza. This comes after our repeated efforts to restore calm were met with increased Hamas rocket fire."[18]

Operation Protective Edge lasted for fifty days of combat, which included 4,258 rockets launched toward Israel, 735 Iron Dome interceptions, 5,226 Israeli air strikes, 32 terror tunnels destroyed, 74 dead on the Israeli side, and about 2,200 dead Palestinians.[19] It ended with the August 26 announcement by Egyptian foreign minister Sameh Shukri that both sides accepted Cairo's offer to halt fire and to allow the start of indirect negotiations within a month to discuss issues such as the rehabilitation of the Gaza Strip.[20]

Operation Protective Edge had direct and indirect implications for Palestinian reconciliation: (1) It diverted the attention of Hamas and Palestinian leadership to the needs of the population in the Strip. (2) The high level of casualties and massive destruction of infrastructure led both parties to try to acquire financial, humanitarian, and logistical assistance for the reconstruction of the ruins, which has yet to be completed. For instance, both Abu Mazen and Masha'al met (August 21) in Doha with the Qatari ruler, Tamim bin Hamad al-Thani, and discussed the possibility of a long-term ceasefire and Qatari aid to the Palestinians. A few days later the Qatari decided to give one thousand US dollars to all families who lost their homes as a result of the military campaign.[21] (3) The operation effectively delayed the process of intra-Palestinian reconciliation and led to failure to complete preparations for holding new elections for the legislative council and the Palestinian presidency.

Following the ceasefire, the PA and Hamas went back to the mutual understandings of the Al-Shati agreement. Abu Marzook announced that the PA would pay the salaries of Hamas civil servants in Gaza and that the unity government would be responsible for the rehabilitation process of the Gaza Strip.[22] Despite this confidence-building move, things became unclear again a week later when Abu Mazen, during a visit to Cairo, threatened to cancel the unity deal, claiming that "he cannot trust Hamas." He blamed Hamas for failing to work with the unity government and said: "We won't accept a partnership with them if the situation continues like this in Gaza where there is a shadow government . . . running the territory. The national consensus government cannot do anything on the ground." The reason, according to the Palestinian president, was that Hamas did not allow the unity government to act properly within the Gaza Strip. It was, again, a typical situation of mutual suspicion on both sides: On the one hand, Hamas, for the first time since June 2007, had to share power in the Strip, a new situation that was hard for the movement to adjust to. On the other hand, Abu Mazen stuck to his instincts and showed a lack of patience and trust toward his traditional rivals.[23]

This blame game between the parties accelerated quickly. On the same day (September 7), Hamas called on Prime Minister Hamdallah to come to the Gaza Strip and assume responsibility for paying salaries to public officials. Hamdallah himself said he had received threats to his life if he came to visit and confirmed that the international system that helps the Palestinians threatened to boycott him if he paid civil servants who were also members of Hamas.[24] On September 11, the fact that Hamas started to pay the salaries of forty thousand employees, while the movement expected the unity government to pay, did not help, to say the least, to improve Hamas-PA relations. The Hamas government, although it had technically stood down on June 2, remained the de facto power and was able to make a partial payment after collecting tax monies and receiving financial support from Qatar.[25]

Delegations of the parties met in Cairo (September 23) to discuss unsolved issues such as payment for civil servants in the future and reconstruction of the Gaza Strip after the military campaign of the summer. Only days later, Hamdallah announced that an international third party would pay the salaries of the employees in the Gaza Strip, adding that "the payment process will take place in coordination with the Palestinian Authority."[26] It looked, for a short period, as if the parties managed to put their disagreements behind when the unity government held its first session in the Gaza Strip, discussing the rehabilitation of the region. All Palestinian factions were satisfied with the visit, stressing that it was an important move for enhancing Palestinian unity. They also said that they expected the government to work as quickly as possible to improve the situation in all aspects of the Gazan population. Hamdallah left Gaza ahead of time for Cairo to participate in the Gaza donors' conference. It was an expression of his government's responsibility to take care of all Palestinians.[27]

On the ground, the pace of progress in implementing the agreement did not satisfy Hamas. The movement criticized the PA for not taking all the necessary steps to lift the siege on the Gaza Strip, specifically to reopen the Rafah crossing and to allow the entry of raw materials in order to speed up reconstruction works. At this point's in mid-October, political issues such as new general elections were not discussed. Musa Abu Marzook prioritized Hamas's interests, saying that the most important task for the unity government was to reconstruct Gaza. He added that Hamas's stance was to refuse to allow any obstacle to the entry of construction material. In fact, Hamas asked Hamdallah's government to put pressure on Israel to change its security positions on various issues related to the Gaza Strip. His statement came after Hamas accused the PA security forces of cracking down on members and attacking rallies.[28]

Unity Government: The End

Despite the on-and-off blame game, both sides maintained the effort to hold on to the unity government. By the end of 2014, after more than seven years of geopolitical and ideological rift, it was obvious that they had different interests, different identities (secular/religious), and different allies and different visions (a political solution with Israel versus armed struggle to free all of Palestine)—although they shared the same national ethos. The PA tried to keep the agreement alive to garner more points as the representative of all Palestinians, while Hamas did the same, hoping to have support for its authority in Gaza not only from the population but also from regional players, such as Egypt, Saudi Arabia, and Qatar. Hamas could certainly have been encouraged by the results of a December 2014 poll, which was published in January 2015, saying that if a presidential election were held then, it would have easily won (Haniyeh with 53 percent and Abu Mazen with only 44). In this context, the figure also shows that Haniyeh overpowered Abu Mazen in the West Bank.[29]

The real significant sign of the end of unity was late in November 2014 when it appears that the parties had different interpretations regarding the reconciliation agreement. Sami Abu Zuhri, Hamas representative, stated that the unity government mandate had expired after six months, and that no new elections had been held, nor, therefore, had a new parliament and government been elected. In response, Faysal Abu Shahala of Fatah said, "It was never agreed that the unity government would last only six months. If Hamas had backed away from the reconciliation agreement and ended the division, this is another matter."[30] In mid-December, Masha'al admitted that Hamas was not happy with the reconciliation and in fact there was no rupture with Fatah, but that the situation was painful mainly because external powers—Israel and countries both international and regional—put up obstacles and had an interest in maintaining divided Palestinians. Masha'al returned, almost as usual, to the common ethos of the Palestinians, confirming that "Fatah and Hamas are partners, although we do have some disagreements."[31] Hamas felt under pressure toward the end of December due to two developments: First, Abu Mazen was holding consultations with Arab states on the renewal of the peace dialogue with Israel. Hamas senior member Izzat al-Rishq rejected the move, making it clear that any decision made by the PA without consulting all factions would cause damage to national goals. This was an expression of the different interests and visions of both sides. Second, and at the same time, Qatar announced its decision to cease its financial support for Hamas in order to pressure it to stop incitement against Egypt and to increase its enforcement against armed smuggling from the Sinai Peninsula into the Gaza Strip and in the opposite direction.[32]

The reconciliation process remained in question early in 2015. On January 6, Abu Zuhri accused the PA of allocating the money that was meant for Gaza reconstruction to the PA budget. He also said that the "PA are exploiting the suffering of Gaza's people." This accusation came two days after Hamas blamed the PA and Abu Mazen personally for adopting a policy of discrimination and neglect when it came to the Gaza Strip.[33] A week later Hamas signaled its dissatisfaction as it initiated a restart of the legislative council through a meeting in Gaza for the first time since the unity government in June 2014 was sworn in. This meeting was attended exclusively by Hamas legislators and reflected the high tensions between the parties. Moreover, Ahmad Bahr, the deputy speaker of the PLC, detailed to the participants a delineation of the top three priority interests of Hamas: lifting the siege on the Gaza Strip, rehabilitation and construction of the Strip, and establishing a constant financing source for around fifty thousand Hamas civil servant employees. Abu Shahala, a senior Fatah member, had a response to this meeting that was both critical and cynical: "Partnership according to Hamas means that Hamas can do whatever it wants and whenever it wants and all others should only be supportive."[34]

Simultaneously, Hamas had not forgotten its long-term strategic interest in becoming the dominant force in the Palestinian arena by taking over the PLO. Osama Hamdan indirectly confirmed this when he said: "We want to rebuild the PLO and therefore give the unity government an opportunity."[35] Early in February, the general feeling within the Palestinian political system was that the reconciliation agreement was deeply stagnant. Ahmad Majdalani, a PLO executive committee member, accused Hamas of refusing to allow the PLO delegation to visit Gaza in order to reactivate the agreement. When Hamas approved the visit (February 4), all factions discussed civil affairs (siege, reconstruction, salaries) rather than political matters (elections). Majdalani urged Hamas to hand over security control of the crossings to the Palestinian Authority, a move that he considered a condition for the unity government's ability to help rebuild the Gaza Strip.[36]

Hamas's suspicions of Abu Mazen's moves were, again, publicly expressed in early March. The movement blamed the PA and Egypt for incitement against the Palestinian armed resistance. Various Hamas representatives also claimed that Abu Mazen's security forces were sharing information with Israel in order to arrest Hamas activists in the West Bank. On the ground, PA security apparatuses arrested dozens of Hamas members.[37]

In response to Osama Hamdan's allegation that the PA was delaying the reconstruction work in the Gaza Strip, Prime Minister Hamdallah and two of his ministers arrived at Gaza for a three-day visit. The reception he received was chilly, when Sami Abu Zuhri stated, "So far the Unity Government has failed in its mission to be the government of all Palestinians." The Palestinian prime minister said, "We have come here today to strengthen national reconciliation and to restart dialogue with all Palestinian factions," admitting, in fact, that the reconciliation process was seriously stalled.[38] Another delegation of the unity government arrived at Gaza (April 19) to discuss the same civil affairs, but this effort failed too. Both sides immediately blamed each other: the PA ministers told the press they were confined in a hotel in Gaza and Hamas claimed that Hamdallah did not authorize his ministers to sign an employees' deal. In fact, the PA delegation left the Gaza Strip as quickly as possible before Hamas security forces could take further steps against them.[39] The fragile relationship between the parties suffered another blow a few days later, when Abu Mazen canceled the results of the Bir Zeit University student council elections, in which Hamas won. Hamas issued a statement accusing the Authority of tyranny, claiming that the only alternative to Fatah's rule is national unity.[40] The prolonged delay in the work of rehabilitating the Gaza Strip, also due to political controversy, did not go unnoticed by the Palestinian public in the Gaza Strip. On April 29, four thousand Palestinians protested political unity and Hamas forces dispersed them by force.

Haniyeh attempted the win-win approach to save the unity government when he called for Saudi Arabia's intervention. His call to the Saudis indicated that Hamas's interest was in removing Egypt from its traditional role as mediator and tightening its relations with the Saudis.[41] But Haniyeh's call was too little, too late. The gaps between the parties were unbridgeable, and both sides were unwilling to divide political power between them. On June 17, Abu Mazen announced that the unity government would resign, because Hamas did not allow the government to work in the Gaza Strip according to its interests.[42] Following Mazen's meeting with French foreign minister Laurent Fabius in Ramallah (June 21), Fabius stated: "Abbas told me that this government of national unity could only include women and men who recognize Israel, renounce violence and who are in agreement with the principles of the (Mideast) Quartet." He further noted that "those conditions ruled out Hamas."[43] His statement indicated that Abu Mazen, in fact, admitted indirectly that between him and Hamas there was an ideological abyss, and despite the ethos that rests on a shared historical past, his interests and vision and those of Hamas were radically different.

This time, too, the behavioral approach was dominant in the decision-making of the parties and reflected, as in all previous rounds, the underlying mistrust between them. Admittedly, the al-Shati agreement was the only one that came to fruition, albeit partially, but it also failed the reality test, and both sides found themselves negotiating internal reconciliation toward the end of 2017.

Long Disengagement before the Final Round

The internal Palestinian rift turned into a long period of disengagement until January 2017. During the second half of 2015 and the year 2016 no significant progress was made. Each party focused on different issues; Abu Mazen enhanced his power within Fatah institutions and his reign in the West Bank. Hamas's attention was primarily on getting any possible support for reconstructing the infrastructure—buildings and roads—in the Gaza Strip and ensure salaries for civil servant employees were paid. It is worth mentioning that in July 2015, Azzam al-Ahmad made it clear that a condition for reconciliation was to hand over control of the Gaza Strip to the Palestinian Authority, but Hamas spokesperson Sami Abu Zuhri rejected the demand and called, in response, for Palestinians in the West Bank to launch an insurgency against Abu Mazen's security forces.[44]

Azzam Al-Ahmad tried to reinitiate reconciliation in December 2015 and reached an agreement with Egypt that the Rafah crossing checkpoint would reopen on the condition that Hamas hands over the security responsibility and the administration of the site. Haniyeh replied that Hamas was willing to do so on the basis of political partnership rather than on regime change or replacement, which meant that Hamas was ready to share power but not to give up all of it.[45] Hamas's constant interest in opening the Rafah crossing prompted it to announce in January 2016 the establishment of a committee to look into ways for all parties to cooperate in bringing about a permanent opening of the crossing. However, Hamas did not indicate that it was willing to deliver political power on the Gaza Strip to the PA, as Abu Zuhri had said.[46]

The next dialogue was held in late October 2016 when Abu Mazen, Masha'al, and Haniyeh met in Doha. Hamas's statement after the meeting stressed that the movement "offered a complete vision for achieving reconciliation via certain techniques and steps to uphold previously signed agreements, including comprehensive elections on all levels and an agreement between the political parties on a political and resistance agenda to face the occupation."[47] The positive atmosphere during the meeting did not lead to any sort of rapprochement between the parties, which remained divided both politically and ideologically. As in previous rounds of negotiation, both parties responded positively to the Qatari foreign minister hosting them at his private home but refrained from committing themselves to making any concessions toward the other side. The PA's response to Hamas's announcement confirmed their well-known and traditional interest in forming a unity government, which would accept Abu Mazen's basic principles for a political solution with Israel.

In January 2017, Ismail Haniyeh ended a five-month tour and returned to the Gaza Strip, but not before meeting in Cairo with Egyptian officials. He delivered to the Egyptians Hamas's plan for strategic change in the region. The plan had three different configurations, which in fact, were interwoven: inter-Palestinian reconciliation, understandings with Egypt, and an arrangement with Israel.[48] The October 2017 agreement between the PA and Hamas cannot be understood without analyzing the most important internal change within Hamas leadership in the Gaza Strip. This occurred in February 2013, when Yahya Sinwar was elected as the new leader of Hamas in Gaza, while Haniyeh replaced Masha'al as the head of the politburo of the movement. The first public statement by Sinwar was delivered on the thirteenth anniversary of Sheikh Ahmad Yassin's death, in which Sinwar promised to follow Yassin's path and to deter the enemy (Israel).[49]

In fact, Sinwar changed Hamas policy in some key areas: he sought reconciliation with Egypt, understanding that this was necessary to Hamas for its possible rapprochement with Abu Mazen and for serving Hamas's interest in reopening the Rafah crossing as soon as possible to allow the Gazan population free and open access to the world, and to facilitate the entry of raw materials for reconstruction works.[50] On May 1, 2017, Hamas published a political document entitled A Document of General Principles and Policies. It aimed to adapt Hamas's basic ideology and concepts to the current strategic reality. An analysis of the political document shows that there was no real change in the ideology, which saw all Palestine as one territory without any room for concessions to the enemy. In order to achieve this goal, the movement supported armed struggle. However, in the current situation, this is not the most important interest, because Hamas is required to promote other issues. The document presented a softer approach by Hamas to interaction with the PA:

1. Accepting the PLO as the legitimate representative of the Palestinian people, to be protected.
2. Readiness for a Palestinian independent state within the 1967 borders. This, however, is just the first stage toward an independent state throughout Palestine instead of the Zionist project.
3. Giving the green light to appeal to the UN to promote a political solution for Palestinians, although Hamas does not believe in such an appeal.[51]

This paper, as Hamas defined it, was "a document" rather than "a charter"—which is a more binding term. The document did not offer any change of ideology, but it raised the potential for internal reconciliation. Sinwar asked to use this document to support other interests of Hamas, which still have not been fully achieved: rapid and full rehabilitation of the Gaza Strip, removing the blockade, opening the Rafah crossing, increasing the number of hours of electricity supplied to the Strip, and establishing a regular source of funding for paying salaries of public officials. The new approach toward Egypt, the willingness to help Cairo stop the smuggling of weapons and ammunition into the Sinai Peninsula, and the declaration of PLO recognition were a reasonable price Hamas was willing to pay to advance its interests. All this, without giving up ideological principles and without sharing its power in the Gaza Strip with Abu Mazen.

During the months following the publication of the Hamas document, interactions between the rival parties remained tense. Hamas refused to participate in municipal elections (such participation did not promote any of its interests within the Gaza Strip), and Abu Mazen intensified the pressure on Hamas to relinquish its control by suspending monthly pay to nearly three hundred Hamas prisoners.[52] Abu Mazen's decision in this case hurt the prisoners, who were integral to the national ethos. It was made for political reasons and illustrated once again that the Palestinian president did not really abandon the behavioral approach while dealing with Hamas. Later in June, Ahmad Barrak, attorney general of the PA, ordered the closure of at least eleven news websites in the West Bank, most of them affiliated with Hamas.[53] A month later, Abu Mazen continued to pressure Hamas in his decision to cut the salaries of thirty-seven Hamas PLC members from the Gaza Strip. He also threatened to impose what he called "immediate financial sanctions on Hamas leaders in Gaza," accusing them, as he did in 2007, of staging a coup against the PA. In response, Hamas's Ahmad Bahr described the decision as a "declaration of war."[54]

The catalyst for the October agreement was the eventual rapprochement between Hamas and Mohammad Dahlan, the senior Fatah figure in the Gaza Strip and a bitter political opponent of Abu Mazen. The engagement between Dahlan and Hamas was mainly because of their longstanding acquaintance with Sinwar. In August 2017, the Palestinian president resumed the reconciliation dialogue, which lasted until October with help from Egypt as mediator. During September, delegations of the parties met in Cairo and Hamas agreed to hold general elections for the first time since 2006.[55] From that point progress toward a new agreement was fast. Sinwar warned publicly that "Hamas will never be a party to the division, and I will break the neck of everyone who does not want reconciliation, whether from Hamas or others. We will make very large concessions, and every concession will be staggering and surprising, greater than the one before, in order to achieve reconciliation. Division must end as soon as possible."[56] Sinwar did not forget to mention all the components of the national ethos, explaining that Hamas has built its power in order to make the liberation dream come true.

The PA government of Hamdallah held its meeting in Gaza (October 4) for the first time since November 2004. Hamdallah announced that delegations from the parties would meet again in Egypt. "We are ready to remove all pending issues to the Cairo meeting. The only way to statehood is through unity. We are coming to Gaza again to deepen the reconciliation and end the split."[57] The PA insisted on having complete control of the Gaza Strip, including its security, borders, and crossing points. Hamas was willing to acquiesce to the PA demand but made it clear that removing weapons from its twenty-seven thousand people was not negotiable.[58] This was a red line for the movement because if Hamas had agreed to give up its weapons, it would have meant giving up on armed struggle for Palestine—which would mean conceding part of its ideological principles.

The joint announcement on the new agreement was made on October 12 in Cairo. Unlike with previous agreements, the parties did not reveal the details, but Abu Mazen said that he had received them from the Fatah delegation to Cairo and he considered the agreement to be the end of the division.[59] The Egyptians said that the parties agreed that Gaza civilian control—including the crossings—would be handed over to the unity government on December 1, 2017. Hamas senior member Salah al-'Aruri admitted, "We decided to follow a step-by-step strategy to implement the reconciliation. These talks were aimed at allowing the unity government to operate fully in the Gaza Strip and the West Bank."[60] Other details, inasmuch as the parties disclosed them, were: (1) The PA will lift sanctions imposed during 2017 on Hamas. Looking back, these sanctions increased the PA's flexibility while negotiating with Hamas. (2) The parties will build a joint police force to patrol Gaza. (3) The Egyptians will summon the parties in November to discuss a new unity government. Neither side mentioned such central political issues as new elections, reactivation of PLO institutions, and the future of the PLC.

Aftermath of the Agreement

Naturally, the news from Cairo on a new reconciliation led to celebration both in the Palestinian media and on the street. When Hamas kept its part of the deal and handed over control of the Gaza Strip border crossing to PA security forces (November 1), it seemed for a short time that this time things might go forward and not backward as had happened in the past. Apparently, this was no more than a symbolic gesture by Hamas. PA and Hamas leaders did not look for real integration and a win-win situation, which would have allowed them to promote political and civil affairs for the benefit of the population. Abu Mazen evaded his commitment to remove the sanctions imposed on the Gaza Strip when Hamas transferred its weapons to the PA—which it did not do. However, Hamas had made it clear before signing the Cairo agreement that this issue was not to be part of the understanding between the parties.[61] The Palestinian president, who had already asked Israel in June 2017 to reduce the supply of electricity to the Gaza Strip as part of the sanctions on Hamas (to which Israel responded positively), did not rush to request an increase in electricity—and did not do so until January 2018.

Hamas too, was in no hurry to promote the implementation of the agreement, especially after it took the first step in letting the PA enter the crossings. In response to Abu Mazen's procrastination, Hamas banned the Palestinian Authority from collecting taxes in the Gaza Strip and did not allow the return to their workplaces of its twenty thousand public service workers until 2007. Moreover, other issues like responsibility for reconstruction work in Gaza and preparations for new general elections for the Palestinian presidency and the legislative council were not discussed. When the parties met in Cairo again (November 21), they could not agree this time on a joint statement. Azzam al-Ahmad admitted that the issue of the military wing of Hamas was an obstacle to moving forward, and a month later Sinwar declared, "The reconciliation project is falling apart. Only a sightless person wouldn't see that."[62]

Conclusion

The Palestinian Authority and Hamas were in continual negotiations for ten years, from 2007 to 2017. It was direct negotiation, which included eight rounds of negotiations analyzed throughout the book (the 2012 Doha and Cairo negotiations were, in fact, one case study). Negotiations included indirect ones, in which the parties communicated with each other through public messages, trying to break deadlocks and cause the other party to make concessions that would lead to national reconciliation, based on the same ethos of shared history.

As presented in chapter 1, there are five different theories for analyzing negotiation between at least two parties: structural, strategic, behavioral, processual, and integrative. Analyzing the PA and Hamas dialogue over a decade, my conclusions are:

1. Both sides always clung to the behavioral approach. Declaratively, both parties demonstrated commitment to national interests through statements that frequently used the elements of the national ethos (seeking an independent state, liberation of Jerusalem, return of refugees, and an end to Palestinian victimhood). When things got to the stage of negotiation and the need to show flexibility to promote those interests through the fusion of the internal rift, the suspicion and distrust between the parties overcame rational thinking. Every time, when the parties reached an agreement, they were unable to implement it fully. Like two tango dancers, they moved one step forward and two back. After the final round of October 2017, they walked the greatest distance ahead but failed to break through the barrier of distrust.

2. Processual and integrative approaches were never a real option for either side. They tried to show interest in the progress of the agreement through tactical gestures such as releasing political detainees, approving public events, security easements, and communicative mutual meetings, but these were only tactical measures. My conclusion here is that at no point was there any real progress and interest in real strategic reconciliation.

3. Except for mutual distrust, they had (still have, in fact) different visions. Since the late 1980s, two different ideologies have emerged within the Palestinian social and political systems. After June 2007, the secular and religious camps divided into two separate geopolitical entities. Despite a common ethos, both sides have different visions: one is interested in a political solution with the enemy; the other, based on religious ideology, seeks to destroy it.

4. Neither party ever considered alternatives to enhancing their political dominance, whether in the West Bank or the Gaza Strip. If they showed commitment, it was primarily to personal or political frameworks (Fatah, Hamas) but to neither their population nor to the national cause.

5. The structural theory can explain the use by both parties of the services of a mediating Arab country such as Egypt, Saudi Arabia, Qatar, or Yemen. The PA and Hamas chose to honor the brokerage efforts, with an appreciation of past relations and the understanding that in the future they will again need political, economic, or diplomatic assistance.

6. Abu Mazen saw Palestinian reconciliation as a precondition for a political settlement with Israel, as he wrote in May 2011: "Negotiations remain our first option, but due to their failure we are now compelled to turn to the international community to assist us in preserving the opportunity for a peaceful and just end to the conflict. Palestinian national unity is a key step in this regard."[1] That was just one of the reasons that prompted him to almost always initiate another reconciliation attempt, after Hamas took over the Gaza Strip. He hoped he could regain the prestige and po-

litical power within the Palestinian Authority that he lost in June 2007. In fact, his goal was to co-opt Hamas under his presidency, but he failed to achieve that goal.

7. Hamas shifted from an inferior player to an equal player after forcibly taking over the Gaza Strip. It always displayed a positive approach to reconciliation, never giving up its ideological principles or political power in the Gaza Strip. When it was necessary to decide between loyalty to its values and a reconciliation that required a material concession, the movement regularly clung to a vision based on a rigid religious subset.

8. Although Israel has had a direct and significant influence on the Palestinian arena since June 1967, it has not always directly influenced the reconciliation process. After the three Israeli military operations in the Gaza Strip (Cast Lead, 2008–2009; Pillar of Clouds, 2012; Protective Edge, 2014), a dialogue was held between the Palestinian Authority and Hamas to unite forces. However, between 2007 and 2017, there were another six rounds of negotiations that were not the result of an Israeli move that changed the political or security status quo in the Palestinian arena.

Finally, a successful negotiation requires from the participants demonstrations of patience, tolerance, courage, responsibility, and flexibility. These are more than virtues. These are assets for any negotiator or leader who leads his or her people to fulfill the national vision. In the Palestinian case study, the leaders strayed from the way Imam 'Ali outlined for successful negotiation, and the results were an ongoing failure that consumed a whole decade and entailed the dismantling of Palestinian society into two separate political entities.

Notes

Introduction

1. James K. Sebenius, "BATNAs in Negotiation: Common Errors and Three Kinds of 'No,'" *Negotiation Journal* 33.2 (2017): 89–99.

2. Hisham Sharabi, *Palestine and Israel: The Lethal Dilemma* (New York: Pegasus, 1969), 195–200.

3. Kobi Michael and Omer Dostri, "The Process of Political Establishment of Sub-state Actors: Hamas' Conduct between Sovereignty and the Continuation of Violence," *Journal for Interdisciplinary Middle Eastern Studies* 3 (2018): 9.

4. Philip Leech, "Re-reading the Myth of Fayyadism: A Critical Analysis of the Palestinian Authority's Reform and State Building Agenda, 2008–2011," Research Paper (2012), https://www.dohainstitute.org/en/lists/ACRPS-PDFDocumentLibrary/Rereading_the_Myth.pdf (dohainstitute.org); Natalia Simanovsky, "The Fayyad Plan: Implications for the State of Israel," *Palestine-Israel Journal* 17.12 (2012), http://www.pij.org/details.php?id=1317; Nu'man Kanfani, "As If There Is No Occupation," *Middle East Report Online* (2011), https://merip.org/2011/09/as-if-there-is-no-occupation/; Elie Podeh, *Chances for Peace: Missed Opportunities in the Arab-Israeli Conflict* (Austin: University of Texas Press, 2015); Uzi Arad, "The Process of Arrangements from Oslo to the Present: A Historical View and a Strategic Perspective," in *Negotiations with the Palestinians: Deadlock or a Window of Opportunity?* (Ramat-Gan: Begin-Sadat Center for Research, Bar-Ilan University, 2014); Udi Dekel and Emma Petrack, "The Israeli-Palestinian Political Process: A Return to the Process Approach," *Strategic Assessment* 19.4 (2017): 29–42.

5. Ahmad Safi, *Assessment of the Environmental Impact of the War on Gaza Using a Participatory Method* (Ramallah: Development Work Centre, 2015), http://www.pengon.org/uploads/articles/3.pdf; Joshua L. Gleis and Benedetta Berti, *Hezbollah and Hamas: A Comparative Study* (Baltimore: Johns Hopkins University Press, 2012); Andrea Nüsse, *Muslim Palestine: The Ideology of Hamas* (Abingdon: Routledge, 2012); Eitan Shamir and Edo Hecht, "Gaza 2014: Israel's Attrition

vs. Hamas' Exhaustion," *Parameters* 44.4 (2014): 81–90; Harel Chorev and Yvette Shumacher, "The Road to Operation Protective Edge: Gaps in Strategic Perception," *Israel Journal of Foreign Affairs* 8.3 (2014): 9–24; Ghassan Wishakh and Mohammad Al-Qudra, *Al-Tahwalat al-Mawdayya fi al-Qad'ia ba'ad Oslo* (2016) (Substantive Transformation in the Palestinian Question), Palestinian Information Center, https://www.palinfo.com/Uploads/Models/Media/book/2017/war/war.pdf; Sherifa Zuhur, "Gaza, Israel, Hamas and the Lost Calm of Operation Cast Lead," *Middle East Policy* 16.1 (2009): 40–50; Jim Zanotti, *Israel and Hamas: Conflict in Gaza (2008–2009)* (Darby, PA: Diane, 2010). All translations, unless otherwise noted, are the author's.

Chapter 1. Theoretical Framework for Negotiation

1. *Merriam-Webster Dictionary* (Springfield, MA: Merriam-Webster, 1994); Henry Mintzberg, "Patterns in Strategy Formation," *Management Science* 24.9 (1978): 935.

2. Fred Charles Iklé and Nathan Leites, "Political Negotiation as a Process of Modifying Utilities," *Journal of Conflict Resolution* 6.1 (1962): 19–28.

3. Roger Fisher, William L. Ury, and Bruce Patton, *Getting to Yes: Negotiating Agreement without Giving In* (New York: Penguin, 2011), 15.

4. Fisher, Ury, and Patton, *Getting to Yes*, 42.

5. Adam Galinsky, Michael Schaerer, and Joe C. Magee, "The Four Horsemen of Power at the Bargaining Table," *Journal of Business and Industrial Marketing* (2017): 606.

6. Lauren A. Rivera, "Ivies, Extracurriculars, and Exclusion: Elite Employers' Use of Educational Credentials," *Research in Social Stratification and Mobility* 29.1 (2011): 71–90.

7. Martin Kilduff and Daniel J. Brass, "Organizational Social Network Research: Core Ideas and Key Debates," *Academy of Management Annals* 4.1 (2010): 345.

8. Roger Fisher, Elizabeth Kopelman, and Andrea Kupfer Schneider, *Beyond Machiavelli: Tools for Coping with Conflict* (New York: Penguin, 1996), 74–85.

9. Robert Axelrod, *The Evolution of Cooperation* (New York: Basic Books, 1984), 4.

10. Gadi Hitman, "The West and the Middle East: Liberal Nationalism, Instrumental Nationalism," *Cultural and Religious Studies* 4.3 (2016): 161–174.

11. The Holy Qur'an, Surat Al-'Alaq, verses 1–5.

12. Saeb Erekat, "Imam Ali Bin Abi Taleb and Negotiation," *Journal of Peace Research* (2015): 26–35.

13. Al-Sharif al-Radi, Nahj al-balagha (Peak of Eloquence, 166), www.sufi.ir. English version available from http://dawoodi-bohras.com/pdfs/Nahjul-Balagah-English.pdf.

14. The Holy Qur'an, Surat Al-Mujadila, verse 11.
15. John Burns, *Leadership* (New York: Harper and Row, 1978), 425.
16. Al-Radi, Nahj al-balagha, 22.
17. Erekat, "Imam Ali Bin Abi Taleb and Negotiation," 72–75.
18. Al-Radi, Nahj al-balagha, 170.
19. Al-Radi, Nahj al-balagha, 291.
20. Erekat, "Imam Ali Bin Abi Taleb and Negotiation," 79.
21. Kieron O'Hara, "A General Definition of Trust," working paper, University of Southampton, Southampton, Great Britain, 2012, 1–2.
22. Erekat, "Imam Ali Bin Abi Taleb and Negotiation," 26.
23. Ilai Alon and Jeanne M. Brett, "Perceptions of Time and Their Impact on Negotiations in the Arabic-Speaking Islamic World," *Negotiation Journal* 23.1 (2007): 55.
24. Alon and Brett, "Perceptions of Time," 56.
25. The Holy Qur'an, Surat Al-Bakara, verse 64.
26. Robert H. Lauer, *Temporal Man: The Meaning and Uses of Social Time* (New York: Praeger, 1981), 22.
27. Pierre Bourdieu, "The Attitude of the Algerian Peasant toward Time," in *Mediterranean Countrymen: Essays in the Social Anthropology of the Mediterranean*, ed. Julian Pitt-Rivers (Paris: Mouton, 1963), 59.
28. Fuad I. Khuri, "The Etiquette of Bargaining in the Middle East," *American Anthropologist* 70.4 (1968): 698–706.
29. Tanya Alfredson and Azeta Cungu, "Negotiation Theory and Practice: A Review of the Literature," in *Rome, Italy: Food and Agriculture Organization of the United Nations*, 2008, http://www.fao.org/docs/up/easypol/555/4-5_negotiation_background_paper_179en. pdf.
30. Dictionary.com Unabridged (v. 1.1), https://www.dictionary.com/browse/strategy?s=t.
31. Morton Deutsch, "Trust and Suspicion," *Journal of Conflict Resolution* 2.4 (1958): 271.
32. Alfredson and Cungu, "Negotiation Theory and Practice," 15.

Chapter 2. The National Palestinian Ethos

1. Aristotle, *Nicomachean Ethics*, book II, http://classics.mit.edu/Aristotle/nicomachaen.2.ii.html.
2. Amitai Etzioni, "Minorities and the National Ethos," *Politics* 229 (2009): 100–110; Eyal Lewin, "The Importance of National Ethos in Military Victories," *Social Sciences* 5.3 (2016): 45.
3. Tami A. Jacoby, "A Theory of Victimhood: Politics, Conflict and the Construction of Victim-Based Identity," *Millennium* 43.2 (2015): 511–530.

4. Masi Noor, Johanna Ray Vollhardt, Silvia Mari, and Arie Nadler, "The Social Psychology of Collective Victimhood," *European Journal of Social Psychology* 47.2 (2017): 121–134.

5. Alba Jasini, Ellen Delvaux, and Batja Mesquita, "Collective Victimhood and Ingroup Identity Jointly Shape Intergroup Relations, Even in a Nonviolent Conflict: The Case of the Belgians," *Psychologica Belgica* 57.3 (2017): 98; Daniel Bar-Tal, Lily Chernyak-Hai, Noa Schori, and Ayelet Gundar, "A Sense of Self-Perceived Collective Victimhood in Intractable Conflicts," *International Review of the Red Cross* 91.874 (2009): 229–258.

6. Nur Masalha, "Remembering the Palestinian Nakba: Commemoration, Oral History and Narratives of Memory," *Holy Land Studies* 7.2 (2008): 123–156.

7. For instance: Amit Cohen, "If Arafat Dies, We Will Become Orphans," November 5, 2004, NRG, https://www.makorrishon.co.il/nrg/online/1/ART/815/366.html; https://www.mako.co.il/news-world/arab/Article-68e3ed1bc88ae11006.htm.

8. Ervin Staub and Daniel Bar-Tal, "Genocide, Mass Killing and Intractable Conflict: Roots, Evolution, Prevention and Reconciliation," in *Oxford Handbook of Political Psychology*, ed. D. O. Sears, L. Huddy and R. Jervis (New York: Oxford University Press, 2003), 722.

9. See, for example: Honaida Ghanim, "Poetics of Disaster: Nationalism, Gender, and Social Change among Palestinian Poets in Israel after Nakba," *International Journal of Politics, Culture, and Society* 22.1 (2009): 23–39; Elias Khoury, "Rethinking the Nakba," *Critical Inquiry* 38.2 (2012): 250–266.

10. Maurice Halbwachs, *On Collective Memory* (Chicago: University of Chicago Press, 1992), 5.

11. Daniel Bar-Tal and Dikla Antebi. "Beliefs about Negative Intentions of the World: A Study of the Israeli Siege Mentality," *Political Psychology* (1992): 633–634.

12. Noa Schori-Eyal, Yechiel Klar, and Yarden Ben-Ami, "Perpetual Ingroup Victimhood as a Distorted Lens: Effects on Attribution and Categorization," *European Journal of Social Psychology* 47.2 (2017): 180–194.

13. Noor et al., "Social Psychology."

14. Arnon Grois and Roni Shaked, *PA Textbooks: The Reference to Jews, Israel, and Peace*, 2017, https://www.terrorism-info.org.il/app/uploads/2017/12/H_259_17.pdf, 17, 23, 24, 41, 120, 170, 179, 187.

15. Winston Churchill, "An Address to the House of Commons," May 13, 1940, in *Blood, Toil, Tears and Sweat: The Speeches*, ed. David Cannadine (London: Penguin, 1989), 149.

16. Tommy Franks, "The Meaning of Victory: A Conversation with General Franks," *National Interest* 86 (2006): 8–11.

17. Theodora A. Maniou, Irene Photiou, and Elena Ketteni, "Mediating Patriotism and Triumph through the National Press: Newspaper Content and

Journalistic Perceptions." *International Journal of Social Science Studies* 4 (2016): 65–75.

18. Gabriella Blum, "The Fog of Victory," *European Journal of International Law* 24.1 (2013): 393.

19. Amended Palestine National Charter (1968) in English: http://ecf.org.il/media_items/677.

20. Baljinder Sahdra and Michael Ross, "Group Identification and Historical Memory," *Personality and Social Psychology Bulletin* 33.3 (2007): 385.

21. Chris Shilling and Philip A. Mellor, "Durkheim, Morality and Modernity: Collective Effervescence, Homo Duplex and the Sources of Moral Action," *British Journal of Sociology* (1998): 193–209.

22. Karen E. Fields, "The Elementary Forms of Religious Life," 1995, https://www.academia.edu/14655183/The_Elementary_Forms_of_Religious_Life.

23. Musa Alami, "The Lesson of Palestine," *Middle East Journal* 3.4 (October 1949): 373 405.

24. My discussion does not address the question already discussed in previous studies: When did a unique Palestinian national identity begin to take shape? Some scholars claim that this happened as early as the eighteenth century. Others mark 1917 as the year when it began. The premise is that each group formulates its own identity and defines itself as it sees fit.

25. Fawaz Turki, "To Be a Palestinian," *Journal of Palestine Studies* 3.3 (1974): 3–17; Hamid Rashid, "What Is the PLO?," *Journal of Palestine Studies* 4.4 (1975): 90–109.

26. Rashid, "What Is the PLO?," 92.

27. Helga Baumgarten, "The Three Faces/Phases of Palestinian Nationalism, 1948–2005," *Journal of Palestine Studies* 34.4 (2005): 31.

28. *Filastinuna* 2 (November 1959): 10.

29. *Filastinuna* 9 (July 1960): 2.

30. Yezid Sayigh, "Reconstructing the Paradox: The Arab Nationalist Movement, Armed Struggle, and Palestine, 1951–1966," *Middle East Journal* 45.4 (1991): 609–614; Baumgarten, "The Three Faces/Phases."

31. In June 1967, 150,000 Palestinians left and another 100,000 from July 1967 to February 1968. For more see: Yoav Gelber, "The Project That Lost Its Train: Gaza Exit after the 1967 War," June 2, 2016, https://mida.org.il/2016/06/02/%D7%99%D7%A6%D7%99%D7%90%D7%AA-%D7%A2%D7%96%D7%94-%D7%90%D7%97%D7%A8%D7%99-%D7%A9%D7%A9%D7%AA-%D7%94%D7%99%D7%9E%D7%99%D7%9D/, retrieved: March 11, 2020; Tom Segev, "The June 1967 War and the Palestinian Refugee Problem," *Journal of Palestine Studies* 36.3 (2007): 6–22.

32. Lieutenant Colonel M., "Operation Inferno—Battle of Jordan's East Bank, March 1968," *Ma'arachot* 293 (March 1984): 20–21; 32.

33. See, for instance: Rashid Khalidi, "Observations on the Right of Return," *Journal of Palestine Studies* 21.2 (1992): 29–30.

34. National Palestinian Covenant, July 1968, Al Jazeera, https://www.aljazeera.net/specialfiles/pages/25de66cd-075b-4c8e-9bc3-ddf5ef253676.

35. Aharon Yaffe, "The Arabs in the West Bank and Gaza Strip: Ten Years of Terror," *Nativ* 119 (November 2007): 32–33.

36. Lori Allen, "Getting by the Occupation: How Violence Became Normal during the Second Palestinian Intifada," *Cultural Anthropology* 23.3 (2008): 459–462.

37. Assaf Moghadam, "Palestinian Suicide Terrorism in the Second Intifada: Motivations and Organizational Aspects," *Studies in Conflict and Terrorism* 26.2 (2003): 74.

38. Mariam abdul-Dayyem and Efrat Ben-Ze'ev, "The Shahid as a Palestinian Icon: Negotiating Meanings," *British Journal of Middle Eastern Studies* (2019): 1–19.

39. http://info.wafa.ps/ar_page.aspx?id=8987.

40. *Al-Quds*, October 1, 2000; *Al-Hayat Al-Jadeeda*, October 2, 2000.

41. The text of the speech of Palestinian President Yasser Arafat before the emergency Arab summit conference, %2C+https%3A%2F%2Fwww.albawaba.com%2Far%2F%D8%B3%D8%A7%D8%AE%D8%B1%D9%88%D9%86%2F%D9%86%D8%B5-%D9%83%D9%84%D9%85%D8%A9-%D8%A7%D9%84%D8%B1%D8%A6%D9%8A%D8%B3-%D8%A7%D9%84%D9%81%D9%84%D8%B3%D8%B7%D9%8A%D9%86%D9%8A-%D9%8A%D8%A7%D8%B3%D8%B1-%D8%B9%D8%B1%D9%81%D8%A7%D8%AA, October 21, 2000.

42. A small Palestinian organization affiliated with Ba'ath regime in Iraq.

43. *Al-Hayat Al-Jadeeda*, November 8, 2000; *Al-Quds*, November 10, 2000.

44. "Arafat Cuts Phone Call to CNN Correspondent," Al Jazeera, https%3A%2F%2Fwww.aljazeera.net%2Fnews%2Farabic%2F2002%2F3%2F30%2F%D8%B9%D8%B1%D9%81%D8%A7%D8%AA-%D9%8A%D9%82%D8%B7%D8%B9-%D8%A7%D8%AA%D8%B5%D8%A7%D9%84%D8%A7-%D9%87%D8%A7%D8%AA%D9%81%D9%8A%D8%A7-%D9%85%D8%B9-%D9%85%D8%B1%D8%A7%D8%B3%D9%84%D8%A9-cnn.

45. *Al-Ayyam*, April 22, 2002.

46. *Al-Quds*, April 23, 2002.

47. *Al-Quds*, May 2, 2002.

48. *Al-Ayyam*, October 22, 2000.

49. *Al-Hayat Al-Jadeeda*, October 29, 2000; *Al-Hayat Al-Jadeeda*, November 13, 2000.

50. *Al-Quds*, February 12, 2001.

51. *Al-Hayat Al-Jadeeda*, March 30, 2001.

52. *Al-Quds*, January 7, 2002.

53. *Al-Hayat Al-Jadeeda*, May 3, 2002.

54. *Al-Quds*, May 16, 2003.

55. *Al-Hayat Al-Jadeeda*, September 18, 2003.

56. *Al-Ayyam*, November 2, 2000; *Al-Hayat Al-Jadeeda*, November 8, 2000.

57. *Al-Quds*, November 6, 2000.

58. *Al-Ayyam*, January 1, 2001.

59. President Yasser Arafat's speech to the sixteenth Arab summit in Tunis, May 22, 2004, http://www.palembassy-lb.net/_news.php?news_id=232.

60. Glenn E. Robinson, "Hamas as Social Movement," in *Islamic Activism: A Social Movement Theory Approach*, ed. Quintan Wiktorowicz, Charles Tilly, and Mark A. Tessler (Bloomington: Indiana University Press, 2004), 115.

61. David Hakham, "And the Country Is Full of Hamas," Haifa University (2006).

62. Hakham, "And the Country," 30–31.

63. Hamas covenant, 9, https://www.terrorism-info.org.il/Data/pdf/PDF_06_032_2.pdf.

64. Hamas covenant, 11.

65. Hamas covenant, 12.

66. Mouin Rabbani, "A Hamas Perspective on the Movement's Evolving Role: An Interview with Khalid Mishal: Part II," *Journal of Palestine Studies* 37.4 (Summer 2008): 61.

67. Rabbani, "Hamas Perspective," 62. Ayyash was a prominent leader of the military apparatus of Hamas in the West Bank.

68. Terrorist suicide bombers during the Israeli-Palestinian conflict (September 2000–December 2005). Intelligence and Terrorism Information Center, January 2006, 5, 12.

69. Hakham, "And the Country," 31.

70. Daniel Byman, "The Decision to Begin Talks with Terrorists: Lessons for Policymakers," *Studies in Conflict and Terrorism* 29.5 (2006): 410.

71. Rochelle L. Rosenberg, "Why Camp David II Failed: A Negotiation Theory Perspective," *Harvard Negotiation Law Review* (2012): 2.

Chapter 3. The Political-Security Escalation within the Palestinian Authority

1. Suheib Hasan, "Between 1996 to 2009: A Scene Repeated," July 2005, https://www.paldf.net/forum/showthread.php?t=435398.

2. Hasan, "Between 1996 and 2009."

3. "Preventive Security Apparatus Abuses the Leaders of Hamas and Exposes Them to Ghosts during the Investigation," Palestinian Information Center, https://web.archive.org/web/20150619175541/https://www.palinfo.com/site/pic/newsdetails.aspx?ItemId=8766.

4. Islam Nasr, "Political Detention Is a Crime," September 2005, https://www.paldf.net/forum/showthread.php?t=300624.

5. Camp David 2 Summit (July 11–25, 2000) was a trilateral meeting (the US represented by President Bill Clinton, Israel by Prime Minister Ehud Barak, and the PA by Chairman Yasser Arafat). The US, the mediator, tried to reach a final status agreement between the parties after the five-year interim agreement had ended.

6. Jeremy Pressman, "The Second Intifada: Background and Causes of the Israeli-Palestinian Conflict," *Journal of Conflict Studies* 23.2 (2003): 116.

7. Rema Hammami and Salim Tamari, "The Second Uprising: End or New Beginning?" *Journal of Palestine Studies* 30.2 (Winter 2001): 5.

8. Dennis Ross, "The Middle East Predicament," *Foreign Affairs* (2005): 62–63.

9. "The Sharem Summit Is Closed: Sharon and Abu Mazen Announce the Cessation of Violence," *Globes*, February 8, 2005, https://www.globes.co.il/news/article.aspx?did=881964.

10. https://www.palestinianbasiclaw.org/downloads/2005-elections-law.pdf.

11. Mahjoob Zweiri, "The Hamas Victory: Shifting Sands or Major Earthquake," *Third World Quarterly* 27.4 (May 2006): 676.

12. "An Interview with Mahmood al-Zahar," *Al-Shark Al-Awsat*, August 18, 2005, https://www.memri.org/reports/interview-hamas-leader-dr-mahmoud-al-zahar.

13. "New Hamas Puts Terror on Hold for Shot at Polls," *Daily Telegraph*, January 15, 2006.

14. Riad Malki, "The Palestinian Elections: Beyond Hamas and Fatah," *Journal of Democracy* 17.3 (July 2006): 131–137.

15. *Al-Hayat*, May 21, 2006.

16. Hasan Ibahis and Wael Sa'ad, eds., *Security Developments in the Palestinian Authority, 2006–2007* (Beirut: Zaytoona Centre for Research, 2008), 15.

17. "We Are Approaching the Killers of My Children, and We Will Find Them and Take Their Lives Wherever They Are," Dunya al-Watan, https://www.alwatanvoice.com/arabic/news/2007/03/23/80491.html.

18. Roni Shaked, "Religious War in Gaza," April 2, 2007, Ynetnews, https://www.ynetnews.com/articles/0,7340,L-3360655,00.html.

19. A press release issued by the Islamic Jihad Movement on the Palestinian dialogue, January 4, 2007, in Palestine Documents for the Year 2007, Zaytoona Centre for Research, Beirut, 2009, 32.

20. *Al-Hayat*, May 11, 2006.

Chapter 4. Mecca Agreement, February 2007

1. Michele K. Esposito, "16 November 2006–15 February 2007," *Journal of Palestine Studies* 36.3 (Spring 2007): 144.

2. United Nations, Division for Palestinian Rights, Chronological Review of Events Relating to the Question of Palestine, December 2006, https://www.un.org/unispal/document/auto-insert-195339/.

3. https://www.qassam.ps/update-7-In_the_42nd_anniversary_of_Fatah_Dahalan_attack__H.html, January 7, 2007.

4. "Proposal for Creating Suitable Conditions for Ending the Conflict," *Palestine-Israel Journal*, https://pij.org/articles/988/proposal-for-creating-suitable-conditions-for-ending-the-conflict.

5. "A Close Associate of the Presidency Was Issued: Abu Mazen Is Ready to Meet Meshal on the Basis of Forming a Unity Government That Haniyeh Cannot Assume," Dunya al-Watan, January 15, 2007, https://www.alwatanvoice.com/arabic/news/2007/01/15/70929.html.

6. An interview with Khaled Masha'al on the internal conflict within the Palestinian Society, in Palestine Documents for the Year 2007, Zaytoona Centre for Research, Beirut, 2009, 47–48.

7. Richard Silverstein, "Meshal Accepts Israel as 'Reality' and 'Matter of Fact,' Concedes Right of Palestinian State to Recognize It," *Tikun Olam* (blog), January 11, 2007, https://www.richardsilverstein.com/2007/01/11/meshal-accepts-israel-as-reality-and-matter-of-fact-concedes-right-of-palestinian-state-to-recognize-it/.

8. Hamas: Our People in the West Bank Received Threats, Zaytoona Centre for Research, Beirut, 2009, 87; 103–104.

9. Abu Mazen's Speech at the Opening Meeting in Mecca, February 7, 2007, Zaytoona Centre for Research, Beirut, 2009, 117–118.

10. Ramzi Baroud, "The Mecca Agreement between Hamas and Fatah: What Should We Expect?" *Global Research*, February 17, 2007.

11. Khaled Masha'al's Speech at the Opening Meeting in Mecca, February 7, 2007, Zaytoona Centre for Research, Beirut, 2009, 119–120.

12. Mecca Agreement, February 8, 2007, https://web.archive.org/web/20080212122709/http://www.jmcc.org/documents/meccaagree.htm; see also: arabic.people.com.cn/31662/5387212.html, February 9, 2007; https://ecf.org.il/issue/1195.

13. Mecca Agreement, February 8, 2007.

14. "Abu Mazen's Speech after the Signing of the Mecca Agreement for National Accord to Thank the Saudi Monarch for His Efforts," WAFA News Agency February 8, 2007, http://info.wafa.ps/ar_page.aspx?id=5865.

15. "Abu Mazen's Speech at the Fifty-Ninth Anniversary of the Palestinian Nakba," WAFA News Agency, May 8, 2007, http://info.wafa.ps/ar_page.aspx?id=5865.

16. "Terror Arrives in Eilat: Three Killed in Suicide Attack," Ynetnews, January 29, 2007, https://www.ynet.co.il/articles/0,7340,L-3358163,00.html.

17. "Excavations of the Israel Antiquities Authority," February 6, 2007, http://www.antiquities.org.il/Article_heb.aspx?sec_id=25&subj_id=240&id=1181&hist=1.

18. Hisham Abu Taha and Mohammed Mar'i, "Palestinian OK Unity Govt," *Arab News*, March 18, 2007 from: https://www.arabnews.com/node/296042.

19. Avi Issachroff and Amos Harel, "Fatah to Israel: Let Us Get Arms to Fight Hamas," *Haaretz*, June 7, 2007, https://www.haaretz.com/1.4824399.

20. Taghreed el-Khoday and Isabel Kershner, "Palestinian Interior Minister Resigns Monday, Unable to Control Factions," *The Tech*, May 15, 2007, https://thetech.com/2007/05/15/long5-v127-n26.

21. For this expression, see: John von Neumann, "A Certain Zero-Sum Two-Person Game Equivalent to the Optimal Assignment Problem," *Contributions to the Theory of Games* 2.0 (1953): 5–12.

22. 'Ali Wakd, "Haniyeh Survived an Assassination Attempt," Ynetnews, June 12, 2007, https://www.ynet.co.il/articles/0,7340,L-3411545,00.html.

23. Carol Schachet, "Gaza Drowns in Blood because of the Conflict between Fatah and Hamas Movements," Grassroots International, June 14, 2007, https://grassrootsonline.org/blog/newsbloggaza-drowns-blood-because-conflict-between-fatah-and-hamas-movements/; Chronological Review of Events Relating to the Question of Palestine, monthly media monitoring review, June 2007, https://www.un.org/unispal/document/auto-insert-209128/.

24. Nidal al-Mughrabi, "Abbas Declares State of Emergency," Reuters, June 14, 2007 from: https://uk.reuters.com/article/uk-palestinians/abbas-declares-state-of-emergency-idUKMAC32084020070614?src=061407_1507_TOPSTORY_crisis_in_gaza.

25. May Zuebi, "Three Power Government," Al-Jazeera, https://www.aljazeera.net/specialfiles/pages/89b5fa41-7567-4d64-82b3-84a346b40944.

Chapter 5. Sana'a Declaration, March 2008

1. "Haniyeh: Hamas Is Committed to the Mecca Agreement and a Broad Arab and International Welcome," *Al-Ukaz*, June 16, 2007.

2. United Nations, Division for Palestinian Rights, Chronological Review of Events Relating to the Question of Palestine, monthly media monitoring review, July 2007, https://unispal.un.org/DPA/DPR/unispal.nsf/0/9F83B1413FFAF52E8525737600688B9B.

3. "Abu Mazen: Fayyad's Government Will Handle the Situation," www.arab48.com, June 16, 2007.

4. Mark Mackinnon, "Abbas's Choice for New PM Angers Hamas," *Globe and Mail*, June 16, 2007, https://www.theglobeandmail.com/news/world/abbass-choice-for-new-pm-angers-hamas/article1087105/; Michele K. Esposito, "Quarterly Update on Conflict and Diplomacy: 16 May 2007–15 August 2007," *Journal of Palestine Studies* 37.1 (Autumn 2007): 144.

5. United Nations, Division for Palestinian Rights, Chronological Review of Events Relating to the Question of Palestine, monthly media monitoring review, July 2007, https://unispal.un.org/DPA/DPR/unispal.nsf/0/9F83B1413FFAF52E8525737600688B9B.

6. United Nations, Division for Palestinian Rights, Chronological Review of Events Relating to the Question of Palestine, monthly media monitoring review,

July 2007, https://unispal.un.org/DPA/DPR/unispal.nsf/0/9F83B1413FFAF52E 8525737600688B9B.

7. Human Rights Watch, *Internal Fight: Palestinian Abuses in Gaza and the West Bank*, July 29, 2008, https://www.hrw.org/report/2008/07/29/internal-fight/palestinian-abuses-gaza-and-west-bank.

8. United Nations, Division for Palestinian Rights, Chronological Review of Events Relating to the Question of Palestine, monthly media monitoring review, September 2007, https://www.un.org/unispal/document/auto-insert-198967/.

9. "Teen Killed in Mass-Hamas Rally Near Rafah," *Jerusalem Post*, July 31, 2007, https://www.jpost.com/Middle-East/Teen-killed-in-mass-pro-Hamas-rally-near-Rafah.

10. *Al-Watan* (Saudi), September 1, 2007.

11. See, for instance: Reese Erlich, "One Man, One Vote, One Time," Common Dreams Organization, February 14, 2011, www.commondreams.org/views/2011/02/14/one-man-one-vote-one-time; Lisa Blaydes and James Lo, "One Man, One Vote, One Time? A Model of Democratization in the Middle East," *Journal of Theoretical Politics* 24.1 (2012): 110–146.

12. https://www.pchrgaza.org/en/?p=2832; https://www.pchrgaza.org/en/?p=2825; https://www.pchrgaza.org/en/?p=2821; https://www.pchrgaza.org/en/?p=2811; https://www.pchrgaza.org/en/?p=2802; https://www.pchrgaza.org/en/?p=2792.

13. https://www.pchrgaza.org/en/?p=2749.

14. https://www.pchrgaza.org/en/?p=2749.

15. https://www.pchrgaza.org/en/?p=2749.

16. "PCHR Seriously Concerned by the Closure of 103 NGOs," Palestinian Centre for Human Rights, August 29, 2007 https://www.pchrgaza.org/en/?p=2797.

17. https://www.pchrgaza.org/en/?p=2783; https://www.pchrgaza.org/en/?p=2750.

18. Anne Paq, "Mr. Bush's Trip to Ramallah," *Electronic Intifada*, January 16, 2008, https://electronicintifada.net/content/mr-bushs-trip-ramallah/7304.

19. "Mr. President's Speech on the 43rd Anniversary of Fatah," WAFA News Agency, December 31, 2007, http://info.wafa.ps/ar_page.aspx?id=5865.

20. Palestine Centre for Policy and Survey Research, March 13–15, 2008, https://www.pcpsr.org/en/node/226.

21. "Hamas, Fatah Confirm Importance of Arab Support to Sana'a Declaration," Yemen News Agency (SABA), March 24, 2008, from: https://www.saba.ye/en/news150131.htm.

22. "The Yemen Initiative to Resume Dialogue and End the Palestinian Separation," WAFA News Agency, August 5, 2007, http://www.wafainfo.ps/ar_page.aspx?id=4920.

23. Mohamed Sudam, "Fatah and Hamas Sign Reconciliation Deal," Reuters, March 23, 2008, https://uk.reuters.com/article/uk-palestinians-yemen-deal/fatah-and-hamas-sign-reconciliation-deal-idUKL23831120080323.

24. "Excerpts: Fateh/Hamas Reconciliation? Cheney: 'Palestinian State Long Overdue,'" *IMRA*, March 24, 2008, https://www.imra.org.il/story.php?id=38690.

25. Sudam, "Fatah and Hamas."

26. United Nations, Division for Palestinian Rights, Chronological Review of Events Relating to the Question of Palestine, monthly media monitoring review, March 2008, https://www.un.org/unispal/document/auto-insert-195406/.

27. "The Arab Summit Ends in Syria with the 'Damascus Declaration,'" BBC, March 30, 2008, from: http://news.bbc.co.uk/hi/arabic/middle_east_news/newsid_7321000/7321374.stm.

28. "Hamas Calls for Gaza-Only Ceasefire," *Jerusalem Post*, April 22, 2008, france24.com/en/20080425-hamas-ready-six-month-truce-gaza-israelnytimes.com/2008/04/22/world/middleeast/22mideast.html.

29. "Masha'al: Hamas Agrees to Palestinian State but Will Not Recognize Israel," Ma'an News Agency, April 22, 2008, www.maannews.net/en/index.php?opr=ShowDetails&ID=28875.

30. Jean-Pierre Filiu, *Gaza: A History* (Oxford: Oxford University Press, 2014), 333.

Chapter 6. Cairo Agreement, 2009

1. "Palestinian National Unity Talks Resume in Cairo," February 25, 2009–May 18, 2009, https://www.paljourneys.org/en/timeline/overallchronology?chronos[]=10802&nid=10802#12537.

2. Michele K. Esposito, "16 May–15 August 2008," *Journal of Palestine Studies* 38.1 (Autumn 2008): 191, https://www.palestine-studies.org/sites/default/files/attachments/jps-articles/jps.2008.38.1.190_0.pdf.

3. "A Car Explosion in Gaza Kills Three Hamas Fighters," International Middle East Media Centre, July 26, 2008, https://imemc.org/article/56205/.

4. "11 Palestinians, Including 8 Members of the Helles Clan and 2 Police Officers, Killed and 103, including 17 Children and 6 Women, Wounded in Armed Clashes between the Police and the Clan in Gaza," Palestinian Centre for Human Rights, August 3, 2008, https://www.pchrgaza.org/en/?p=2651.

5. "11 Palestinians, Including 2 Children and a Police Officer Killed and 42 Others Wounded in Clashes between the Police and Wanted Persons in the Gaza Strip," Palestinian Centre for Human Rights, September 16, 2008, https://www.pchrgaza.org/en/?p=2637; https://www.un.org/unispal/document/auto-insert-194856/; https://unispal.un.org/DPA/DPR/unispal.nsf/0/371D0DE4CD823F2E852574F00072116D.

6. "PCHR Condemns Detention of 3 Journalists and a Columnist by the Palestinian General Intelligence in the West Bank," Palestinian Centre for Human Rights, May 8, 2008, https://www.pchrgaza.org/en/?p=2678.

7. "General Intelligence Service Raids Hebron Office of PLC Member Samira al-Halaiqa," Palestinian Centre for Human Rights, September 23, 2008, https://www.pchrgaza.org/en/?p=2634. See also: Sara Roy, *Hamas and Civil Society in Gaza: Engaging the Islamist Social Sector*, vol. 50 (Princeton: Princeton University Press, 2013), 311.

8. "PCHR Calls for Investigating Arbitrary Arrests and Torture by Security Forces in the West Bank," Palestinian Centre for Human Rights, May 7, 2008, https://www.pchrgaza.org/en/?p=2681.

9. "Investigation Demanded after Prisoner Dies in PA Custody," *Electronic Intifada*, October 8, 2008, https://electronicintifada.net/content/investigation-demanded-after-prisoner-dies-pa-custody/3396.

10. Elias Sa'adeh, "How 1,500 Teachers, Palestinian Teachers, Were Dismissed after the Hamas-Fatah Split," Arab Reporters for Investigative Journalism, May 14, 2013, https://en.arij.net/report/how-1500-palestinian-teachers-were-dismissed-after-the-fatah-hamas-split.

11. "Hamas Chief Calls for Palestinian Dialogue," *Arabian Business*, July 13, 2008, https://www.arabianbusiness.com/hamas-chief-calls-for-palestinian-dialogue-185689.html.

12. "Hamas: No Early Elections or Technocrat Government," Ma'an News Agency, October 4, 2008, www.maannews.net/en/index?opr=ShowDetailes?ID=32313.

13. Eric Westervelt, "Hamas-Fatah Rift Deepens, Threatens Peace Efforts," NPR, December 18, 2008, https://www.npr.org/templates/story/story.php?storyId=98449470.

14. "Palestinian Unity Talks Stall after Hamas Boycott," Al Arabiya, November 8, 2008, https://www.alarabiya.net/articles/2008/11/08/59723.html.

15. "Palestinian Unity Talks Stall after Hamas Boycott," Al Arabiya, November 8, 2008, https://www.alarabiya.net/articles/2008/11/08/59723.html.

16. "Protection of Civilians Weekly Report, 18–24 June 2008," United Nations Office for the Coordination of Humanitarian Affairs, https://www.ochaopt.org/content/protection-civilians-weekly-report-18-24-june-2008.

17. Amir Buhbut and Uri Binder, "Gaza: IDF Force Acts to Blast 'Ticking Tunnel,'" NRG, November 4, 2008, from: https://www.makorrishon.co.il/nrg/online/1/ART1/807/233.html.

18. "Hamas Officially Announced: The Ceasefire with Israel Is Over," NRG, December 18, 2008, https://www.makorrishon.co.il/nrg/online/1/ART1/827/576.html.

19. Prime Minister's Office Announcement, December 28, 2008, pmo.gov.il.

20. According to official data of IDF. Palestinian health and human rights organizations reported the number of casualties was between 1,300 to 1,434 (including 709 terrorists).

21. Associated Press, "UN Chief: Hamas Rockets Attacks Are Appalling and Unacceptable," *Haaretz*, January 20, 2009, from: https://www.haaretz.com/1.5065287.

22. "Masha'al Calls the Palestinians for a Third Intifada against the Occupation," Al Jazeera, December 27, 2008, https://www.aljazeera.net/news/arabic/2008/12/27/.

23. TOI staff, "Mashaal Calls for Guerilla Warfare to Liberate West Bank and All Palestine," *Times of Israel*, December 15, 2008, https://www.timesofisrael.com/mashaal-calls-for-guerrilla-warfare-to-liberate-west-bank-and-all-palestine/.

24. "Address by President Mahmoud Abbas to the European Parliament in Strasbourg—France," WAFA News Agency, February 4, 2009, http://info.wafa.ps/ar_page.aspx?id=5898.

25. "Address by President Mahmoud Abbas to the European Parliament in Strasbourg—France."

26. "Hamas to Abbas: End Talks with Israel before Any Reconciliation," *Jerusalem Post*, https://www.jpost.com/Middle-East/Hamas-to-Abbas-End-talks-with-Israel.

27. "Analysts Say Abbas Went to Cairo to Save PA Legitimacy; Hamas Members Urge PLO Restructuring," *IMRA*, February 1, 2009, https://www.imra.org.il/story.php?id=42615.

28. Palestine Centre for Policy and Survey Research, December 3–5, 2008, pcpsr.org/sites/default/files/p30e.pdf: 9; https://www.pcpsr.org/en/node/222.

29. "Hamas Upbeat at Cairo on Ceasefire, Palestinian Unity—Rejects Halt to Arms Smuggling," *IMRA*, February 4, 2009, https://www.imra.org.il/story.php?id=42669.

30. "Palestinian PM Fayyad Steps Down," BBC News, March 7, 2009, http://news.bbc.co.uk/2/hi/middle_east/7929927.stm.

31. Adam Morrow and Khaled al-Omrani, "Palestinian Unity Talks Failing," *Electronic Intifada*, March 19, 2009, https://electronicintifada.net/content/palestinian-unity-talks-failing/8144.

32. Miftah, *Consequence of the Split on National and Social Interest*, http://www.miftah.org/Publications/Books/Factsheet_The_Impact_of_the_Political_Division_on_National_and_Social_Reconciliation_2019.pdf, 3–4.

Chapter 7. Cairo Dialogue, April 2011

1. "Hamas and Fatah Agree to Form Caretaker Government," *Guardian*, April 27, 2011, https://www.theguardian.com/world/2011/apr/27/hamas-fatah-agree-government-deal.

2. Miftah, "Fateh-Hamas Reconciliation Efforts," July 17, 2017, http://www.miftah.org/Display.cfm?DocId=23330&CategoryId=4.

3. "PCHR Condemns Bloody Clashes in Rafah, 28 Persons Killed and at Least 100 Others Wounded," Palestinian Centre for Human Rights, August 15, 2009, https://www.pchrgaza.org/en/?p=2327.

4. "PCHR Condemns Police Assault on Wedding Party of al-Madhoun Clan in Beit Lahia," Palestinian Centre for Human Rights, July 15, 2009, https://www.pchrgaza.org/en/?p=2337; https://www.pchrgaza.org/en/?p=2334.

5. "Fatah: Mediation Failed, Hamas Won't Let Delegates Leave," *IMRA*, https://www.imra.org.il/story.php?id=44942, retrieved: April 10, 2002.

6. "PCHR Condemns Raid on Ramattan News Agency in Gaza, and Expresses Deep Concerns over Measures Taken by the Gaza Government to Prevent Commemoration of Late President Yasser Arafat's Death," Palestinian Centre for Human Rights, November 10, 2009, https://www.pchrgaza.org/en/?p=2306, retrieved: April 9, 2020.

7. Ethan Bronner, "Hamas Shifts from Rockets to Culture War," *New York Times*, July 23, 2009, https://www.nytimes.com/2009/07/24/world/middleeast/24gaza.html.

8. "PCHR Condemns Police's Prevention of Show in Gaza City," Palestinian Centre for Human Rights, April 25, 2010, https://www.pchrgaza.org/en/?p=2259.

9. "PCHR Condemns Unjustified Intervention into Public Freedoms and Prevention of Public and Private Meetings by Ministry of Interior in Gaza," Palestinian Centre for Human Rights, May, 25, 2010, https://www.pchrgaza.org/en/?p=2246.

10. "PCHR Calls Upon the Government in Ramallah to Investigate Death of Palestinian in GIS Custody in Nablus," Palestinian Centre for Human Rights, August 15, 2009, https://www.pchrgaza.org/en/?p=2331.

11. "3 Security Officers, 2 Members of the Izz al-Din al-Qassam Brigades and One Civilian Killed in Qalqilya," Palestinian Centre for Human Rights, May 31, 2009, https://www.pchrgaza.org/en/?p=2357; https://www.pchrgaza.org/en/?p=2352.

12. "Palestinian Security Officer and 2 Members of the Izz al-Din al-Qassam Brigades Killed in Qalqilya," Palestinian Centre for Human Rights, June 5, 2009, https://www.pchrgaza.org/en/?p=2350; "Three Palestinians Killed in Renewed Hamas-PA Clashes in Qalqilya," Ma'an News Agency, June 4, 2009, www.maannews.net/en/index.php?opr=ShowDetails&ID=38291.

13. Military Communique, "Official Hamas Statement on Clash with PA in Qalqilya," Qassam, May 31, 2009, http://www.alqassam.ps/english/?action=showsta&sid=1324.

14. Ali Waked, "PA: Hamas West Bank Terror Plot Exposed," Ynetnews, https://www.ynetnews.com/articles/0,7340,L-3728366,00.html.

15. "Hamas: No Unity without Release of All Hamas Prisoners in West Bank," Ma'an News Agency, June 26, 2009, www.maannews.net/en/index.php?opr=ShowDetails&ID=38825.

16. Avi Issacharoff, "PA: Arrested Hamas Activists Planned to Assassinate Abbas," *Haaretz*, July 3, 2009.

17. Salaah Jum'ah, "Hamas Rejects Proposal That Their Gunmen Join PA Forces in Gaza," *IMRA*, June 29, 2009, https://www.imra.org.il/story.php?id=44163.

18. "Hamas: Future of Dialogue Is Dependent on Terminating the Security Mission of US Officer Keith Dayton in the West Bank," *IMRA*, July 13, 2009, https://www.imra.org.il/story.php?id=44488.

19. "15,000 PA Forces Won't Return to Gaza Anytime Soon," Ma'an News Agency, July 18, 2009, www.maannews.net/eng/ViewDetails.aspx?ID=212715.

20. "PCHR Condemns Decision to Suspend Al Jazeera's Work in the West Bank," Palestinian Centre for Human Rights, July 16, 2009, https://www.pchrgaza.org/en/?p=2336.

21. "Al-Habash: Hamas Cannot Perpetuate Division, and the Palestinians Must Change This Reality," Ma'an News Agency, December 10, 2010, https://www.maannews.net/news/340807.html.

22. Khaled Abu Toameh, "Hamas, Fatah Set to Sign Reconciliation Accord by 2010," *Jerusalem Post*, September 9, 2009 from; https://www.jpost.com/Middle-East/Hamas-Fatah-set-to-reconcile-by-2010.

23. "Fatah Official Urges Hamas to End 'Incitement,'" *IMRA*, October 8, 2009, https://www.imra.org.il/story.php?id=45999.

24. "A Televised Speech by the President on the Latest Political Developments—Ramallah," WAFA News Agency, October 11, 2009, http://info.wafa.ps/ar_page.aspx?id=5898.

25. United Nations Fact Finding Mission on the Gaza Conflict. See: "Palestine Is an Occupied Land and Should Be Returned to the Palestinians," *IMRA*, https://www.imra.org.il/story.php?id=46046.

26. "Masha'al Claims 'Big Strides' in Palestinian Unity Talks," *Jerusalem Post*, January 3, 2010, https://www.jpost.com/Breaking-News/Mashaal-claims-big-strides-in-Palestinian-unity-talks.

27. "Hamas: Abbas No Longer Represents the Palestinians," IMEMC News, February 2, 2010, https://imemc.org/article/57839/; https://www.imra.org.il/story.php?id=47075.

28. United Nations, Division for Palestinian Rights, Chronological Review of Events Relating to the Question of Palestine, monthly media monitoring review, February 2010, https://www.un.org/unispal/document/auto-insert-200479/; "Shaath Met Hamas Seniors in Gaza," Ma'an News Agency, https://www.maannews.net/news/258976.html.

29. Saleh al-Naami, "Mahmoud al-Zahar: Salam Fayyad Must Allow the Resistance Movements to Operate Freely in the West Bank," *IMRA*, March 1, 2010, https://www.imra.org.il/story.php?id=47372.

30. "Hamas: Return to Talks a Betrayal of the Nation," *IMRA*, March 4, 2010, https://www.imra.org.il/story.php?id=47392.

31. "Shaath: There Is Very Little Difference between the Fatah and Hamas Programs and the Chances of Success of the Negotiations," Ma'an News Agency, https://www.maannews.net/news/285600.html.

32. "Hamas to Boycott West Bank Elections," Qassam, May 24, 2010, http://www.qassam.ps/news-2874-Hamas_to_boycott_W_Bank_elections.html.

33. "Al-Masri Leads a Leadership Delegation to the Sector to Complete the Reconciliation," Ma'an News Agency, June 1, 2010, https://www.maannews.net/news/317149.html.

34. "Egypt Bans Arab Delegation from Entering Gaza," Qassam, July 4, 2010, http://www.qassam.ps/news-3072-Egypt_bans_Arab_delegation_from_entering_Gaza.html.

35. "Barak-Fayyad Meeting Weakens Resistance," Qassam, July 5, 2010, http://www.qassam.ps/news-3086-Barak_Fayyad_meeting_weaken_resistance.html.

36. "Al-Khoudari Meets President Abbas and Telephones Masha'al," Ma'an News Agency, September 6, 2010, https://www.maannews.net/news/290732.html.

37. "Hamas, Fatah 'Closer than Ever' to Unity Deal,' Ma'an News Agency, September 25, 2010, https://www.maannews.net/news/317711.html.

38. "Palestinians Hand 20-Year Sentence to Hamas Fighter," Zee News, October 6, 2020, https://zeenews.india.com/news/world/palestinians-hand-20-year-sentence-to-hamas-fighter_659850.html.

39. "Hamas Focuses on Nation Building: Top Ideologue," December 18, 2010, http://www.qassam.ps/news-3928-Hamas_focus_on_nation_building_top_ideologue.html.

40. "President Mahmoud Abbas's Speech at a Festival Commemorating the Sixth Anniversary of the Martyrdom of President Yasser Arafat, Ramallah," WAFA News Agency, November 11, 2010, http://info.wafa.ps/ar_page.aspx?id=5990.

41. "Palestinian Reconciliation Is an Illusion," December 22, 2010, http://www.qassam.ps/news-3955-Palestinian_reconciliation_absurd_in_light_of_West_Bank_situation.html.

42. Palestine Centre for Policy and Survey Research, December 3–5, 2010, http://www.pcpsr.org/sites/default/files/p38e.pdf: 14–15.

43. Palestine Centre for Policy and Survey Research, March 11–13, 2011, http://www.pcpsr.org/sites/default/files/p39e.pdf: 6.

44. "Gazan Youth Issue Manifesto to Vent Their Anger with All Sides in the Conflict," *Guardian*, January 2, 2011, https://www.theguardian.com/world/2011/jan/02/free-gaza-youth-manifesto-palestinian.

45. United Nations, Division for Palestinian Rights, Chronological Review of Events Relating to the Question of Palestine, monthly media monitoring review, February 2011, https://www.un.org/unispal/document/auto-insert-196883/.

46. United Nations, Division for Palestinian Rights, Chronological Review of Events Relating to the Question of Palestine, monthly media monitoring review, February 2011, https://www.un.org/unispal/document/auto-insert-196883/.

47. "Facebook Campaign Demanding Removal of Abbas," February 13, 2011, http://www.qassam.ps/news-4166-Facebook_campaign_demanding_removal_of_Abbas.html; "Time to Establish New Situation," March 6, 2011, http://www.qassam.ps/news-4254-Time_to_establish_new_situation.html.

48. "PCHR Condemns Forceful Dispersal of Peaceful Assemblies in Gaza," Palestinian Centre for Human Rights, March 16, 2011, https://www.pchrgaza.org/en/?p=2151; "Haniyeh Calls on Abbas to Visit Gaza," March 16, 2011, http://www.qassam.ps/news-4296-Haniyya_calls_on_Abbas_to_visit_Gaza.html.

49. "Abbas Asked Egypt to Support Unity Initiative," Group 194, March 20, 2011, http://group194.net/english/article/21948.

50. "Fatah, Hamas Reach Agreement on All Issues of Difference," WAFA News Agency, April 27, 2011, http://english.wafa.ps/page.aspx?id=RhJP3ca15220433976aRhJP3c.

51. Agreement between Fatah and Hamas, Cairo, May 3, 2011. https://peacemaker.un.org/sites/peacemaker.un.org/files/OPt_AgreementFatahHamas2011.pdf.

Chapter 8. Doha Agreement, 2012

1. International Crisis Group, "Palestinian Reconciliation: Plus Ça Change . . . Middle East Report N°110—20 July 2011," https://www.refworld.org/pdfid/4e2d9e2b2.pdf, 23.

2. Palestine Centre for Policy and Survey Research, June 16–18, 2011, http://www.pcpsr.org/sites/default/files/p40e.pdf: 1–2.

3. Mahmoud Abbas, "The Long Overdue Palestinian State," *New York Times*, May 16, 2011, https://www.nytimes.com/2011/05/17/opinion/17abbas.html.

4. Mr. President's Speech to the Arab Follow-Up Committee (Doha), May 28, 2011, http://info.wafa.ps/ar_page.aspx?id=6041.

5. "Hamas Denounces Abbas's Statements," June 21, 2011, http://www.qassam.ps/news-4642-Hamas_Denounces_Abbass_Statements.html.

6. "Hamas Head Holds Unity Talks with Turkey Officials," June 22, 2011, http://www.qassam.ps/news-4653-Hamas_head_holds_unity_talks_with_Turkey_officials.html.

7. "Report: Fatah and Hamas to Delay Formation of Unity Government," *IMRA*, June 29, 2011, https://www.imra.org.il/story.php?id=52937.

8. Palestine Centre for Policy and Survey Research, September 15–17, 2011, http://www.pcpsr.org/sites/default/files/p41e.pdf.

9. "Palestinian Elections in October Only in the West Bank," July 27, 2011, https://www.imra.org.il/story.php?id=53258.

10. "President Abbas's Advisor Denies the Latter's Visit to Gaza before Next September," Al-Arab, August 16, 2011, https://www.alarab.com/Article/390871.

11. "Fatah: Reconciliation on Hold until September," *IMRA*, August 23, 2011, https://www.imra.org.il/story.php?id=53488.

12. Michele K. Esposito, "Update on Conflict and Diplomacy Source," *Journal of Palestine Studies* 41.2 (Winter 2012): 169.

13. "President Mahmoud Abbas's Speech on the Eve of His Departure to the United Nations in Ramallah," WAFA News Agency, September 16, 2011, http://info.wafa.ps/ar_page.aspx?id=6041.

14. "President Mahmoud Abbas's Speech on the Eve of His Departure to the United Nations in Ramallah."

15. "Hamas, Fatah Agree to No Rallies during UN Bid," September 20, 2011, http://www.qassam.ps/news-4929-Hamas_Fatah_agree_to_no_rallies_during_UN_bid.html.

16. "Fatah: No Agreement with Hamas to Prevent UN Bid Rallies," September 20, 2011, https://www.imra.org.il/story.php?id=53797.

17. "PCHR Condemns Preventing Displaying the Palestinian President's Speech at 'Gallery' Restaurant and Arresting the Director of the Restaurant by the GIS," Palestinian Centre for Human Rights, September 25, 2011, https://www.pchrgaza.org/en/?p=2064.

18. "Hamas: Move by Abbas Has No Substance—Should Be Going for All of Palestine," September 24, 2011, http://www.qassam.ps/news-4938-Hamas_Move_has_no_substance.html.

19. "Masha'al: No Alternative to Resistance," October 2, 2011, http://www.qassam.ps/news-4966-Mashaal_No_alternative_to_resistance.html.

20. "Stop Using the Reconciliation for Peace Talks with Israel," October 3, 2011, http://www.qassam.ps/news-4970-Stop_using_the_reconciliation_for_peace_talks_with_Israel.html.

21. "Abu Marzook: Abbas-Mishaal Meeting in Ten Days," November 15, 2011, http://www.qassam.ps/news-5102-Abu_Marzouk_Abbas_Mishaal_meeting_in_ten_days.html.

22. "Unpublished details—Mesha'al and Abbas Will Meet Face to Face for Half an Hour," Ma'an News Agency, November 24, 2011, https://www.maannews.net/news/439105.html.

23. "Abbas, Mesha'al Agree to Work as Partners," WAFA News Agency, November 24, 2011, http://english.wafa.ps/page.aspx?id=2cPYxVa17244812607a2cPYxV.

24. Michele K. Esposito, "Update on Conflict and Diplomacy Source," *Journal of Palestine Studies* 41.3 (Spring 2012): 181–182.

25. "Hamas: The Arrests by the Palestinian Authority Increased after Abbas met Masha'al in Cairo," Ma'an News Agency, December 21, 2011, https://www.maannews.net/news/444314.html.

26. Osama Hamdan, "Popular Resistance against the Occupation Comes with Cessation of Security Coordination with Israel," November 25, 2011,

Al-Quds Television; Izzat Rishq, "Popular Resistance Is No Substitute for Armed Resistance," November 27, 2011, http://www.qassam.ps/news-5131-The_popular_resistance_is_no_substitute_for_the_armed_resistance.html.

27. "Haniyeh Urges Abbas to Ignore US Demands," *IMRA*, November 26, 2011, https://www.imra.org.il/story.php?id=54582.

28. "Fatah and Hamas Affirm Their Commitment to Implement the Reconciliation Agreement," Ma'an News Agency, December 3, 2011, https://www.maannews.net/news/441920.html.

29. "Al-Ahmad Informs the Fatah Leadership in Nablus of the Efforts to Achieve Reconciliation," Ma'an News Agency, December 11, 2011, https://www.maannews.net/news/444308.html.

30. "Palestinian Factions Walk Out of Cairo Meeting," *IMRA*, December 20, 2011, https://www.imra.org.il/story.php?id=54945.

31. "Hamas: Factions Agree on 6 Reconciliation Steps in Cairo," American Task Force on Palestine, December 21, 2011, http://www.americantaskforce.org/daily_news_article/2011/12/21/1324443600.

32. "Hamas Says It Plans to Join Abbas's PLO," Reuters, December 22, 2011, https://uk.reuters.com/article/uk-palestinians-israel/hamas-says-it-plans-to-join-abbass-plo-idUKTRE7BL1T120111222.

33. Salah Juma, "Hamas and Fatah Both Made Mistakes," *IMRA*, December 24, 2011, https://www.imra.org.il/story.php?id=55011.

34. Saleh al-Na'ami, "National Unity Government Depends on Quartet Reply," *IMRA*, December 26, 2011, https://www.imra.org.il/story.php?id=55042.

35. "Israeli, Palestinian Officials to Meet in Amman," *Jerusalem Post*, January 1, 2012, from: https://www.jpost.com/Diplomacy-and-Politics/Israeli-Palestinian-officials-to-meet-in-Amman.

36. "Fatah and Hamas Resolving Issues over Passports and Detainees," WRP, January 6, 2012, https://wrp.org.uk/features/fatah-and-hamas-resolving-issues-over-passports-and-detainees/.

37. "PCHR Condemns Obstruction of Passage of Fatah Delegation at Beit Hanoun (Erez) Crossing," Palestinian Centre for Human Rights, January 8, 2012, https://www.pchrgaza.org/en/?p=2009.

38. "President Mahmoud Abbas's Speech during the Work of the Advisory Council of the Fatah Movement," WAFA News Agency, January 12, 2012, http://info.wafa.ps/ar_page.aspx?id=7369.

39. Ali Sawafta, "Palestinian Rivals Agree to Form Unity Government," Reuters, February 6, 2012, https://www.reuters.com/article/us-palestinians-government/palestinian-rivals-agree-to-form-unity-government-idUSTRE8150KU20120206.

40. "Senior Hamas Leader Slams Agreement with Fatah," Israel National News, February 14, 2012, http://www.israelnationalnews.com/News/News.aspx/152683.

41. Avi Issacharoff and Amos Harel, "Jenin Governor Has Fatal Heart Attack After Gunmen Raid His Home," *Haaretz*, May 2, 2012, https://www.haaretz.com/jenin-governor-dies-of-heart-attack-after-home-attacked-by-gunmen-1.5218811.

42. "The Text of the Official Agreement between Fatah and Hamas on May 20, 2012," WAFA News Agency, http://info.wafa.ps/ar_page.aspx?id=8715.

Chapter 9. Cairo Accord, 2013

1. "Haniyeh: We Will Not Allow the Return of Chaos—Minister of Interior. Article: There Is No Peace with Secularism," Ma'an News Agency, June 13, 2012, https://www.maannews.net/news/496557.html.

2. "Fatah: The black page split that exhausted our people and an exception that should go away," Ma'an News Agency, June 13, 2012, https://www.maannews.net/news/495476.html.

3. "Palestinian Reconciliation: Faltering Stations," Al Jazeera, July 11, 2012 from: https://www.aljazeera.net/news/reportsandinterviews/2012/7/11/%D8%A7%D9%84%D9%85%D8%B5%D8%A7%D9%84%D8%AD%D8%A9-%D8%A7%D9%84%D9%81%D9%84%D8%B3%D8%B7%D9%8A%D9%86%D9%8A%D8%A9-%D9%85%D8%AD%D8%B7%D8%A7%D8%AA-%D9%85%D8%AA%D8%B9%D8%AB%D8%B1%D8%A9.

4. "Fatah: Hamas's Decision to Suspend the Election Committee's Work Is a Suspension of Reconciliation," Ma'an News Agency, July 2, 2012, https://www.maannews.net/news/500652.html.

5. "Fatah Youth Movement: Al-Zahar's Allegation Is a Political Bankruptcy," Ma'an News Agency, July 3, 2012, https://www.maannews.net/news/500803.html.

6. "Abbas Thanks Saudi Arabia for $100M Grant," WAFA News Agency, July 15, 2012, http://english.wafa.ps/page.aspx?id=scHzQSa19290129804ascHzQS.

7. "Mr. President's Speech to Hebron Governorate Activities," WAFA News Agency, August 2, 2012, http://info.wafa.ps/ar_page.aspx?id=7369.

8. "Nunu Attacks Al-Ahmad's Statements and Demands the Speedy Opening of the Rafah Crossing in Both Directions," Ma'an News Agency, August 12, 2012, https://www.maannews.net/news/512082.html.

9. "Haniyeh: Morsi Won't Allow Siege on Gaza," July 14, 2012, http://www.qassam.ps/news-5920-Haniyeh_Morsi_Wont_Allow_Siege_on_Gaza.html.

10. "Hamas Delegation Visits Brotherhood Headquarters," *Egypt Independent*, August 28, 2012, https://www.egyptindependent.com/hamas-delegation-visits-brotherhood-headquarters/.

11. Reuters and Avi Issacharoff, "A Blow to the Palestinian Authority: Hamas Leader Accepts Iran Invitation to Attend Non-Aligned Summit," *Haaretz*, August 25, 2012, https://www.haaretz.com/hamas-leader-accepts-iran-invite-1.5290847.

12. "Haniyeh's Office: Iranian Vice President Confirms Haniyeh's Invitation to Attend the Non-Aligned Summit," Ma'an News Agency, August 28, 2012, https://www.maannews.net/news/515301.html retrieved.

13. Saleh al-Na'ami, "Hamas Seeks to Enter the World of Diplomacy," *Asharq al-Awsat*, September 5, 2012, https://web.archive.org/web/20121205170941/http://www.asharq-e.com/news.asp?section=1&id=30949.

14. "Abu Shahala: Fatah Still Adopts the Option of a Two-State Solution," Ma'an News Agency, September 15, 2012, https://www.maannews.net/news/520256.html.

15. "Qatar Ruler Uses Historic Gaza Visit to Call on Palestinian Factions to Unite," *Times of Israel*, October 23, 2012, https://www.timesofisrael.com/gaza-offers-qatari-ruler-heros-welcome/.

16. "Fayyad: Ready to Resign over Protests," Israel National News, September 6, 2012, http://www.israelnationalnews.com/News/News.aspx/159731.

17. Palestine Centre for Policy and Survey Research, September 13–15, 2012, http://www.pcpsr.org/sites/default/files/p45e.pdf.

18. "PCHR Calls Upon the Palestinian Authority to Release the Detainees on Hunger Strike in Its Prisons," Palestinian Centre for Human Rights, June 28, 2012, https://www.pchrgaza.org/en/?p=1933.

19. "PCHR Strongly Condemns the Use of Force against Peaceful Demonstrations in Ramallah," Palestinian Centre for Human Rights, July 2, 2012, https://www.pchrgaza.org/en/?p=1931.

20. "Palestinian Security Services Arrest Dozens of Hamas Members in the West Bank," Palestinian Centre for Human Rights, September 19, 2012, https://www.pchrgaza.org/en/?p=1904.

21. "PCHR Condemns Banning Mass Marriage Ceremony in Gaza," Palestinian Centre for Human Rights, August 31, 201, https://www.pchrgaza.org/en/?p=1910; "PCHR Condemns Security Services' Intervention to Stop Events Commemorating the Death of President Arafat," Palestinian Centre for Human Rights, November 13, 2012, https://www.pchrgaza.org/en/?p=1881.

22. TOI staff, "After Eight Days of Fighting, Ceasefire Is Put to the Test," *Times of Israel*, November 21, 2012, https://www.timesofisrael.com/several-casualties-in-explosion-in-central-tel-aviv/.

23. Report of the United Nations High Commissioner for Human Rights on the Implementation of Human Rights Council Resolutions S-9/1 and S-12/1, March 6, 2013, https://www.ohchr.org/Documents/HRBodies/HRCouncil/RegularSession/Session22/A.HRC.22.35.Add.1_AV.pdf.

24. "President Mahmoud Abbas's Speech before the Emergency Meeting of the Palestinian Leadership, Ramallah," WAFA News Agency, November 16, 2012, http://info.wafa.ps/ar_page.aspx?id=7369.

25. "Sha'ath Reveals the Leadership's Steps to Achieve Reconciliation," Ma'an News Agency, November 25, 2012, https://www.maannews.net/news/541959.html.

26. "Khaled Masha'al Visits Gaza for the First Time in 45 Years," *Al Bayan*, December 7, 2012, https://www.albayan.ae/one-world/arabs/2012-12-07-1.1780620.

27. "Masha'al: Free and Fair Elections Followed by Partnership and a Reconciliation Meeting Should Take Place Soon," Ma'an News Agency, December 9, 2012, https://www.maannews.net/news/546281.html.

28. "Al-Ahmad: Masha'al's Speech Is Very Positive and the President's Call to the Factions Was Postponed for Days," Ma'an News Agency, December 9, 2012, https://www.maannews.net/news/546087.html.

29. Noha Al-Badry, "Hamas Committed to Cairo for Reconciliation Talks," December 20, 2012, Ahram Online, http://english.ahram.org.eg/NewsContent/2/8/60981/World/Region/Hamas-committed-to-Cairo-for-reconciliation-talks.aspx.

30. "Haniyeh: Reconstruction, Breaking the Siege, and Achieving Reconciliation Are Our Priorities in the Next Phase," Ma'an News Agency, January 2, 2013, https://www.maannews.net/news/552859.html.

31. "Tens of Thousands Commemorate the Start of Fatah in Gaza," Ma'an News Agency, January 4, 2013, https://www.maannews.net/news/553347.html.

32. "Morsi to Meet Abbas, Meshaal in Cairo for Reconciliation Talks," Ahram Online, January 9, 2013, http://english.ahram.org.eg/NewsContent/2/8/62067/World/Region/Morsi-to-meet-Abbas,-Meshaal-in-Cairo-for-reconcil.aspx; Jodi Rudoren, "Abbas and Hamas Leader Meet at Egypt's Invitation," *New York Times*, January 9, 2013, https://www.nytimes.com/2013/01/10/world/middleeast/abbas-and-hamas-leader-meet-at-egypts-invitation.html.

33. "Al-Ahmad: Form a National Unity Government No Later than January 30," Ma'an News Agency, January 17, 2013, https://www.maannews.net/news/557036.html.

34. Khaled Abu Toameh, "Hamas, Fatah Agree to Implement Unity Agreements," *Jerusalem Post*, January 18, 2013, https://www.jpost.com/middle-east/hamas-fatah-agree-to-implement-unity-agreements.

35. Jodi Rudoren, "Abbas and Hamas Leader Meet at Egypt's Invitation," *New York Times*, January 9, 2013, https://www.nytimes.com/2013/01/10/world/middleeast/abbas-and-hamas-leader-meet-at-egypts-invitation.html.

36. "Hamas Prime Minister Prepares for Elections in Gaza," Ahram Online, January 24, 2013, http://english.ahram.org.eg/NewsContent/2/8/63177/World/Region/Hamas-prime-minister-prepares-for-elections-in-Gaz.aspx.

37. "Abu Shahala: Fatah Rejects Aziz Al-Dwaik's Calls for a Legislative Session," Ma'an News Agency, February 2, 2013, https://www.maannews.net/news/561378.html.

38. "Jordanian TV Interviews Khaled Masha'al Today," Jafra News, January 29, 2013, http://www.jfranews.com.jo/more-53271-3-%7Bclean_title%7D.

39. "Accord Evades Fatah, Hamas in Palestinian Unity Bid," *Egypt Independent*, February 9, 2013, https://www.egyptindependent.com/accord-evades-fatah-hamas-palestinian-unity-bid/.

40. "Palestinian Official: Cairo Meetings Have Not Met Expectations," *IMRA*, February 11, 2013, https://www.imra.org.il/story.php?id=60066.

41. Elad Benari, "PA Security Forces Arrest 25 Hamas Members," Israel National News, February 8, 2013, http://www.israelnationalnews.com/News/News.aspx/165022.

42. "Haniyeh: We started to see outside infiltration to stop the reconciliation and we are not afraid of the elections," Ma'an News Agency, February 22, 2013, https://www.maannews.net/news/567928.html.

43. "Qatari Emir Opens Fund for Jerusalem's Arab Identity," *Times of Israel*, March 26, 2013, https://www.timesofisrael.com/qatari-emir-opens-fund-for-jerusalems-arab-identity/.

44. Kifah Zaboun, "A Source for Asharq Al-Awsat: Abu Mazen Will Not Attend an Arab Summit Attended by Hamas," *Asharq al-Awsat*, March 30, 2013, https://archive.aawsat.com/details.asp?section=4&issueno=12541&article=722755#.XqV4XGgzZPY.

45. "US Backed Palestinian Prime Minister Salam Fayyad Resigns," *Guardian*, April 13, 2013, https://www.theguardian.com/world/2013/apr/14/palestinian-pm-salam-ayyad-resigns; Jack Khoury, "Haniyeh Heads to Doha for Talks That Could Spur Palestinian Reconciliation," *Haaretz*, April 19, 2013, https://www.haaretz.com/.premium-qataris-pushing-for-palestinian-peace-1.5238778.

46. Kifah Zaboun, "Abu Mazen Announces the Start of Consultations to Form a Consensus Government . . . and Hamas: We Are Not Run by Remote Control," *Asharq al-Awsat*, April 27, 2013, https://archive.aawsat.com/details.asp?section=4&issueno=12570&article=726405#.XqWBeWgzZPY.

47. "Fatah-Hamas Agree to Form Palestinian Unity Government," *IMRA*, May 15, 2013, https://www.imra.org.il/story.php?id=60987.

Chapter 10. Al-Shati Agreement, 2014

1. Al-Shati means "beach" in English. It is also the name of a refugee camp located north of Gaza.

2. Lara Friedman, "New Palestinian PM Rami Hamdallah: Resources/Background," Peace Now, June 5, 2013, http://archive.peacenow.org/entries/new_palestinian_pm_rami_hamdallah_resources_background.

3. "Gaza Factions Denounce Hamdallah Appointment," June 5, 2003, Al-Monitor, https://www.al-monitor.com/pulse/iw/contents/articles/opinion/2013/06/hamdallah-palestinian-authority-hamas.html.

4. "Haniyeh's Advisor: The New Government Is an Extension of the Fayyad Government's Mistake," Ma'an News Agency, June 3, 2013, https://www.maannews.net/news/601691.html.

5. "PA Security Arrest 7 Hamas Affiliates," June 5, 2013, http://www.qassam.ps/news-7083-PA_security_arrest_7_Hamas_affiliates.html, retrieved.

6. "New Palestinian Authority Cabinet Sworn In," *Palestine Chronicle*, June 7, 2013, http://www.palestinechronicle.com/new-palestinian-authority-cabinet-sworn-in/.

7. "Rami Hamdallah Resigned," Fager TV, June 20, 2013, https://alfajertv.com/news/77808.html; https://www.mobtada.com/details/76139.

8. "Ahmad Yusuf: We Are Not Afraid of Morsi's Fall," Ma'an News Agency, July 3, 2013, https://www.maannews.net/news/610872.html.

9. "Hamas Demands PA Stop Security Coordination with the Occupation," July 13, 2013, http://www.qassam.ps/news-7227-Hamas_demands_PA_to_stop_security_coordination_with_the_occupation.html.

10. "Hamas Rejects the Fatah Deadline and Denies Any Contacts Regarding Reconciliation," Ma'an News Agency, July 17 2013, https://www.maannews.net/news/614744.html.

11. "Hamas: America Marketed the Illusion of Power and Reconciliation Further under Negotiations," Ma'an News Agency, July 20, 2013, https://www.maannews.net/news/615418.html.

12. "PCHR Concerned over Closing Offices of al-Arabiya Channel and Ma'an News Agency in Gaza by Attorney-General's Decision," Palestine Centre for Human Rights, July 28, 2013, https://www.pchrgaza.org/en/?p=1764.

13. "Abbas Is Involved in a Conspiracy to Liquidate the Palestinian Cause," July 31, 2013, http://www.qassam.ps/news-7301-Hamdan_Abbas_is_involved_in_a_conspiracy_to_liquidate_the_Palestinian_cause.html.

14. "Security Forces Raid the Homes of Leaders from Fatah and Abu Shamalah, Warning of a Massive Campaign," Ma'an News Agency, August 9, 2013, https://www.maannews.net/news/619948.html.

15. "ISS Launches Summons and Arrest Campaign against Members of Fatah Movement in the Gaza Strip," Palestine Centre for Human Rights, August 13, 2013, https://www.pchrgaza.org/en/?p=1762.

16. "Fatah Says Hamas Not Ready for Reconciliation," WAFA News Agency, August 15, 2013, http://english.wafa.ps/page.aspx?id=nGdJi8a21876994458anGdJi8.

17. "Hamas Leader Calls for Escalating Resistance in the West Bank," October 10, 2013, http://www.qassam.ps/news-7575-Hamas_leader_calls_for_escalating_resistance_in_the_West_Bank.html.

18. "Abbas Issues Anti-Hamas Statement on Egypt's Sinai," Ahram Online, November 13, 2013, http://english.ahram.org.eg/NewsContent/1/64/86325/Egypt/Politics-/Abbas-issues-antiHamas-statement-on-Egypts-Sinai-.aspx.

19. "Informed Sources for Ma'an: Hamas Agrees to Form a National Unity Government," Ma'an News Agency, December 17, 2013, https://www.maannews.net/news/657697.html.

20. "PA Ready for Reconciliation with Hamas at Any Price," Group 194, December 21, 2013, http://group194.net/english/article/33480.

21. "Ministry of Interior to release 7 Fatah elements," Ma'an News Agency, January 8, 2014, https://www.maannews.net/news/663599.html; http://www.israelnationalnews.com/News/News.aspx/176092.

22. "Rawhi Ftooh Arrived Gaza," Ma'an News Agency, January 22, 2014, https://www.maannews.net/news/667417.html.

23. "Sha'ath: We Came to Solve Internal Fatah Problems and Are Optimistic about Reconciliation," Ma'an News Agency, February 9, 2014, https://www.maannews.net/news/671964.html.

24. "Fatah Accuses Hamas of Evading Reconciliation," A Sclerotic Goes to War, February 12, 2014, https://warsclerotic.com/2014/02/12/off-topic-fatah-accuses-hamas-of-evading-reconciliation/.

25. "Maqbul: There Is No Reconciliation with Hamas and the Choice of Abu Mazen's Thorny Deputy," Ma'an News Agency, February 18, 2014, https://www.maannews.net/news/674439.html.

26. "Hamas Questions the Egyptian Sponsorship of the Reconciliation File," Ma'an News Agency, March 5, 2014, https://www.maannews.net/news/678875.html.

27. "Fatah: Hamas Bans Abbas Support Festival in Gaza," *Al Tahrir*, March 16, 2004, https://altahrir.wordpress.com/2014/03/16/fatah-hamas-bans-abbas-support-festival-in-gaza/.

28. "President Mahmoud Abbas's speech to the thirteenth session of the Revolutionary Council of Fatah," WAFA News Agency, March 12, 2014, http://info.wafa.ps/ar_page.aspx?id=9206.

29. "Hamas: We Are Not Aware of Any Upcoming Visit by the Fatah Delegation to Gaza," Ma'an News Agency, April 2, 2014, https://www.maannews.net/news/686939.html; "After Netanyahu's Decision, Hamas Calls for Unleashing Resistance in the West Bank," Ma'an News Agency, April 9, 2014, https://www.maannews.net/news/688756.html.

30. "The Palestinian Reconciliation Agreement 'Al-Shati' 2014," Al Araby, October 11, 2015, https://www.alaraby.co.uk/encyclopedia/2015/10/11/%D8%A7%D8%AA%D9%81%D8%A7%D9%82-%D8%A7%D9%84%D9%85%D8%B5%D8%A7%D9%84%D8%AD%D8%A9-%D8%A7%D9%84%D9%81%D9%84%D8%B3%D8%B7%D9%8A%D9%86%D9%8A%D8%A9-%D8%A7%D9%84%D8%B4%D8%A7%D8%B7%D8%A6-2014, retrieved: May 1, 2020.

31. "Senior Hamas Official Arrives in Gaza for Reconciliation Talks," IMEMC News, April 21, 2014, https://imemc.org/article/67601/.

32. TOI staff, "Hamas and Fatah Agree to Unity Government in Historic Deal," *Times of Israel*, April 23, 2014, https://www.timesofisrael.com/hamas-and-fatah-agree-to-form-unity-government-in-historic-deal/.

33. Adnan Abu Amer, "Hamas Optimistic That Palestinian Reconciliation Will Stand," Al-Monitor, April 24, 2014, https://www.al-monitor.com/

pulse/originals/2014/04/palestine-reconciliation-hamas-hopes-end-isolation.html.

34. "Statement Issued by a Meeting of the Palestine Liberation Organization Delegation, with Hamas to End the Division and Implement the National Reconciliation Agreement 4/23/2014," WAFA News Agency, http://info.wafa.ps/ar_page.aspx?id=9281.

Chapter 11. Cairo Agreement, October 2017

1. Herb Keinon, "Israel Cancels Planned Peace Talks Meeting after Fatah-Hamas Unity Deal Announced," *Jerusalem Post*, April 24, 2014, https://www.jpost.com/Diplomacy-and-Politics/Israel-cancels-planned-peace-talks-meeting-after-Fatah-Hamas-unity-deal-announced-350203.

2. "Chemistry between Abu Mazen and Masha'al . . . and Physics between Azzam al-Ahmad and Haniyeh," Ma'an News Agency May 5, 2014, https://www.maannews.net/news/695062.html.

3. Palestine Centre for Policy and Survey Research, June 3–5, 2014, http://www.pcpsr.org/sites/default/files/p52e.pdf.

4. "Abu 'Ita: Government Formation Consultations Will End before the Five-Week Deadline," Ma'an News Agency, May 10, 2014, https://www.maannews.net/news/696248.html.

5. "Al-Ahmad: The Rafah Crossing Was Opened Immediately after the Formation of the Unity Government," Ma'an News Agency, May 14, 2014, https://www.maannews.net/news/697213.html.

6. "Haniyeh: We Are on the Cusp of Forming a Unity Government," May 14, 2014 from: http://www.qassam.ps/news-8406-Hanneya_We_are_on_the_cusp_of_forming_a_unity_government.html.

7. Jodi Rudoren and Isabel Kershner, "With Hope for Unity, Abbas Swears In a New Palestinian Government," *New York Times*, June 2, 2014, https://www.nytimes.com/2014/06/03/world/middleeast/abbas-swears-in-a-new-palestinian-government.html.

8. "Haniyeh: We will cooperate with the government to overcome all obstacles," Ma'an News Agency, June 2, 2014, https://www.maannews.net/news/701706.html.

9. "Haniyeh: The Emir of Qatar Pledged to Support the Unity Government and to Pay the Salaries of Its Employees," Ma'an News Agency, June 5, 2014, https://www.maannews.net/news/702623.html.

10. "Hamas: Security Forces Arrest 16 Young People in the West Bank," Ma'an News Agency, June 8, 2014, https://www.maannews.net/news/703090.html.

11. "Thumbnails of Key Ministers in Palestinian Cabinet," Al Arabiya, June 3, 2014, https://english.alarabiya.net/en/perspective/profiles/2014/06/03/Thumbnails-of-Key-Ministers-in-Palestinian-Cabinet.html.

12. "A Vicious Circle Speeds Up Again," *Economist*, July 5, 2014, https://www.economist.com/middle-east-and-africa/2014/07/05/a-vicious-circle-speeds-up-again; https://www.terrorism-info.org.il//Data/articles/Art_20659/H2_093_14_1527671630.pdf.

13. Barak Ravid, "Abbas Condemns Kidnapping of Israeli Teens, Death of Palestinian Youth," *Haaretz*, June 16, 2014, https://www.haaretz.com/.premium-abbas-condemns-kidnapping-1.5252048.

14. "Palestinian Resistance: Israeli Threats Will Not Scare Us," June 17, 2014, http://www.qassam.ps/news-8527-Palestinian_Resistance_Israeli_threats_will_not_scare_us.html.

15. "Masha'al: We Cannot Deny or Confirm the Kidnapping of Settlers," June 25, 2014, http://www.qassam.ps/news-8558-Mashaal_We_cannot_deny_or_confirm_the_kidnapping_of_settlers.html.

16. "Bodies of Three Missing Israeli Teenagers Found in West Bank," *Guardian*, June 30, 2014, https://www.theguardian.com/world/2014/jun/30/bodies-missing-israeli-teenagers-found-west-bank.

17. Chaim Levinson and Nir Hasson, "Six Jews Were Arrested on Suspicion of Murdering Palestinian Youth Muhammad Abu Khdeir," *Haaretz*, July 6, 2014, https://www.haaretz.co.il/news/politics/1.2368211.

18. Statement by PM Netanyahu, Israel Ministry of Foreign Affairs, July 8, 2014, https://mfa.gov.il/MFA/PressRoom/2014/Pages/Statement-by-PM-Netanyahu-8-July-2014.aspx.

19. Udi Dekel, "Operation Protective Edge: Strategic and Tactical Asymmetry," in *The Lessons of Operation Protective Edge*, ed. Anat Kurz and Shlomo Brom (Tel Aviv: INSS, 2014), 15.

20. "Behind the Headlines: Israel Accepts Egyptian Ceasefire," Israel Ministry of Foreign Affairs, August 26, 2014, https://mfa.gov.il/MFA/ForeignPolicy/Issues/Pages/Israel-accepts-Egyptian-ceasefire-26-Aug-2014.aspx.

21. Khaled Abu Toameh, "Abbas, Masha'al, Emir of Qatar Hold 'Positive' Talks in Doha, Palestinians Report," *Jerusalem Post*, August 21, 2014, https://www.jpost.com/arab-israeli-conflict/abbas-mashaal-emir-of-qatar-hold-positive-talks-in-doha-palestinians-report-371864.

22. "Hamas: PA Should Pave the Way for Opening Gaza Borders," Middle East Monitor, September 1, 2014, https://www.middleeastmonitor.com/20140901-hamas-pa-should-pave-the-way-for-opening-gaza-borders/.

23. "Abbas Threatens to End Hamas Unity Deal," Al Jazeera, September 8, 2014, https://www.aljazeera.com/news/asia/2014/09/abbas-warns-he-may-end-unity-deal-with-hamas-20149794312283293.html.

24. "Hamas Invites the Prime Minister to Visit Gaza and Shoulder His Responsibilities," Ma'an News Agency, September 7, 2014, https://www.maannews.net/news/726051.html.

25. "Hamas Begins Paying Gaza Workers Backdated Wages," *Times of Israel*, September 11, 2014, https://www.timesofisrael.com/hamas-begins-paying-workers-backdated-wages/.

26. "Hamdallah: An International Third Party to Pay Gaza Employees' Salaries," Palestinian Information Center, September 27, 2014, https://english.palinfo.com/news/2014/9/27/Hamdallah--An-international-third-party-to-pay-Gaza-employees%E2%80%99-salaries/.

27. "Factions Welcome the Government's Visit to Gaza and Calls to Assume Its Responsibilities," Ma'an News Agency, October 9, 2014, https://www.maannews.net/news/732224.html.

28. "Hamas Blasts PA for Failing to Begin Gaza Reconstruction," Marsad, October 19, 2014, https://www.marsad.ps/en/2014/10/19/hamas-blasts-pa-for-failing-to-begin-gaza-reconstruction/?doing_wp_cron=1588838232.3001289367675781250000.

29. Palestine Centre for Policy and Survey Research, December 13–15, 2014, http://www.pcpsr.org/sites/default/files/poll-54-Dec2014-English%20new.pdf, 2.

30. "Fatah: The Unity Government Remains until the Elections," Ma'an News Agency, November 30, 2014, https://www.maannews.net/news/743733.html.

31. "Masha'al: Reconciliation Is Stalled and Not Broken with Fatah and We Do Not Seek War," Ma'an News Agency, December 15, 2014, https://www.maannews.net/news/747306.html.

32. "Resheq: PA-Arab Draft Resolution Is against National Consensus," December 24, 2014, http://www.qassam.ps/news-8973-Resheq_PA_Arab_draft_resolution_is_against_national_consensus.html; "Report: Doha Puts Its Support for Hamas on Hold," *Jerusalem Post*, December 26, 2014, https://www.jpost.com/middle-east/report-doha-puts-its-support-for-hamas-on-hold-385838.

33. "Hamas: The PA Uses Gaza Reconstruction Funds for Other Purposes," Palestinian Information Center, January 6, 2015, https://english.palinfo.com/print/2015/1/6/Hamas--The-PA-uses-Gaza-reconstruction-funds-for-other-purposes.

34. "Hamas Officials Reactivate Separate Parliament in Gaza," Marsad, January 14, 2015, https://www.marsad.ps/en/2015/01/14/hamas-officials-reactivate-separate-parliament-in-gaza/.

35. "Hamas: We Will Give the Consensus Gov't a Chance," *IMRA*, January 17, 2015, https://www.imra.org.il/story.php?id=66096.

36. "Majdalani: The Delegation of the Organization Entertains Ideas to Solve the Issues of Crossings, Construction and Employees," Ma'an News Agency, February 4, 2015, https://www.maannews.net/news/758887.html.

37. "Palestinian Security Services Launch Arrest Campaign against Hamas Member in the West Bank," Palestinian Centre for Human Rights, March 9, 2015, https://www.pchrgaza.org/en/?p=1536.

38. "PA Prime Minister Hamdallah Receives Cool Welcome in Gaza," Middle East Eye, March 25, 2015, https://www.middleeasteye.net/news/pa-prime-minister-hamdallah-receives-cool-welcome-gaza.

39. Elhanan Miller, "Historic PA Visit to Gaza Failed after Hamas Confined Ministers," *Times of Israel*, April 22, 2015, https://www.timesofisrael.com/historic-visit-to-gaza-fails-after-hamas-confines-ministers-to-hotel/; https://www.maannews.net/news/773513.html.

40. "Hamas Accuses Fatah of Launching a Smear Campaign against It," Ma'an News Agency, April 25, 2015, https://www.maannews.net/news/774174.html; "Haniyeh: We Look Forward to Saudi Intervention to End the Division," May 1, 2015, http://www.qassam.ps/news-9385-Haniyeh_We_look_forward_to_Saudi_intervention_to_end_the_division.html.

41. "Haniyeh: We Look Forward to Saudi Intervention to End the Division," May 1, 2015 from: http://www.qassam.ps/news-9385-Haniyeh_We_look_forward_to_Saudi_intervention_to_end_the_division.html.

42. "Palestinian Unity Government 'to Resign over Gaza Row,'" BBC, June 17, 2015, https://www.bbc.com/news/world-middle-east-33160184.

43. "Abbas Tells French PM 'No Place for Hamas' in New Government," *Times of Israel*, June 21, 2015, https://www.timesofisrael.com/abbas-tells-french-fm-no-place-for-hamas-in-new-government/.

44. "Hamas: Fatah's Call to Form a Government Maneuvering Media," Ma'an News Agency, July 28, 2015, https://www.maannews.net/news/788495.html.

45. "Hamas Ready to Hand Over Control of Rafah Crossing," Middle East Monitor, December 10, 2015, https://www.middleeastmonitor.com/20151210-hamas-ready-to-hand-over-control-of-rafah-crossing/.

46. "Abu Zuhri: Fatah Will Fail to Restore Gaza," Ma'an News Agency, March 5, 2016, https://www.maannews.net/news/832784.html.

47. "Hamas Leaders Meet with Abbas in Qatar, Present 'Complete Vision' for Reconciliation," *Israel Behind the News*, October 30, 2016, https://israelbehindthenews.com/hamas-leaders-meet-abbas-qatar-present-complete-vision-reconciliation/15253/.

48. "Haniyeh Returns to Gaza after 5 Month Tour," Palestinian Information Center, January 27, 2017, https://english.palinfo.com/news/2017/01/27/Haneyya-returns-to-Gaza-after-5-month-tour.

49. "Sinwar in His First Statement: Going on the Path of Sheikh Ahmed Yassin," Ma'an News Agency, March, 22, 2017, https://www.maannews.net/news/898855.html.

50. Hani al-Masri, "Gaza, Where after the Understandings of 'Hamas'—Dahlan?" Ma'an News Agency, June 21, 2017, https://www.maannews.net/articles/912007.html; Mustafa Lidawi, "Dahlan and Sinwar's Understanding Is Need and Necessity," Ma'an News Agency, July 8, 2017, https://www.maannews.net/articles/913704.html.

51. "The Goals and Significance of Hamas's New Political Document," Meir Amit Intelligence and Terrorism Information Center, May 8, 2017, https://www.terrorism-info.org.il//Data/articles/Art_21201/E_093_17_956569418.pdf.

52. "Scores of Former Hamas Prisoners Say Their Salaries Withheld," Ynet news, June 5, 2017, https://www.ynetnews.com/articles/0,7340,L-4971474,00.html.

53. "Palestinian Authority Censors at Least 11 News Websites," Committee to Protect Journalists, June 21, 2017, https://cpj.org/2017/06/palestinian-authority-censors-at-least-11-news-web.php.

54. Dov Lieber, "Abbas Said to Cut Salaries of 37 Hamas Lawmakers," *Times of Israel*, July 9, 2017, https://www.timesofisrael.com/abbas-said-to-cut-salaries-of-37-hamas-lawmakers/; https://www.pchrgaza.org/en/?p=9228.

55. Yolande Knell, "Hamas Says It Is Ready to Hold First Elections since 2006," BBC, September 17, 2017, https://www.bbc.com/news/world-middle-east-41297016.

56. "Sinwar: We Will Make Stunning Concessions, and I Will Break the Neck of Everyone Who Does Not Want Reconciliation," Ma'an News Agency, September 27, 2017, https://www.maannews.net/news/923914.html.

57. Kifah Zaboun, "Fatah, Hamas Leaders to Discuss Unresolved Issues in Cairo," *Asharq al-Awsat*, October 4, 2017, https://english.aawsat.com//home/article/1042106/fatah-hamas-leaders-discuss-unresolved-issues-cairo.

58. Patrick Strickland, "Will Hamas Give Up Arms for Palestinian Reconciliation?," Al Jazeera, October 9, 2017, https://www.aljazeera.com/indepth/features/2017/10/hamas-give-arms-palestinian-reconciliation-171008123019895.html.

59. "Palestinian Factions Hamas and Fatah End Split on Gaza," BBC, October 12, 2017, https://www.bbc.com/news/world-middle-east-41591450, or https://www.bbc.com/news/world-middle-east-41591450.

60. Elior Levi and Ro'i Kais, "A Historic Agreement: Hamas and Fatah Signed Reconciliation," Ynetnews, October 12, 2017, https://www.ynet.co.il/articles/0,7340,L-5027566,00.html.

61. Khaled Abu Toameh, "Abbas Refuses Reconciliation until Hamas Cedes Control of Gaza—PA Ex-minister," *Times of Israel*, February 16, 2018, https://www.timesofisrael.com/abbas-refuses-reconciliation-until-hamas-cedes-control-of-gaza-pa-ex-minister/.

62. "Al-Ahmad: Without Enabling the Government, We Will Not Move to Another Square," Ma'an News Agency, November 23, 2017, https://www.maannews.net/news/930489.html; "Sinwar: Hamas Will Not Return to the Rule and Administration of the Gaza Strip," Ma'an News Agency, December 20, 2017, https://www.maannews.net/news/933837.html.

Conclusion

1. Mahmoud Abbas, "The Long Overdue Palestinian State," *New York Times*, May 16, 2011, https://www.nytimes.com/2011/05/17/opinion/17abbas.html.

Bibliography

Abdul-Dayyem, Mariam, and Efrat Ben-Ze'ev. "The Shahid as a Palestinian Icon: Negotiating Meanings." *British Journal of Middle Eastern Studies* (2019): 1–19.

Abu Amer, Adnan. "Hamas Optimistic That Palestinian Reconciliation Will Stand." Al-Monitor, April 24, 2014. https://www.al-monitor.com/pulse/originals/2014/04/palestine-reconciliation-hamas-hopes-end-isolation.html.

Abu Taha, Hisham, and Mohammed Mar'i. "Palestinian OK Unity Govt." *Arab News*, March 18, 2007. https://www.arabnews.com/node/296042.

Abu Toameh, Khaled. "Abbas, Masha'al, Emir of Qatar Hold 'Positive' Talks in Doha, Palestinians Report." *Jerusalem Post*, August 21, 2014. https://www.jpost.com/arab-israeli-conflict/abbas-mashaal-emir-of-qatar-hold-positive-talks-in-doha-palestinians-report-371864.

Abu Toameh, Khaled. "Abbas Refuses Reconciliation until Hamas Cedes Control of Gaza—PA Ex-minister." *Times of Israel*, February 16, 2018. https://www.timesofisrael.com/abbas-refuses-reconciliation-until-hamas-cedes-control-of-gaza-pa-ex-minister/.

Abu Toameh, Khaled. "Hamas, Fatah Agree to Implement Unity Agreements." *Jerusalem Post*, January 18, 2013 from: https://www.jpost.com/middle-east/hamas-fatah-agree-to-implement-unity-agreements.

Abu Toameh, Khaled. "Hamas, Fatah Set to Sign Reconciliation Accord by 2010." *Jerusalem Post*, September 9, 2009. https://www.jpost.com/Middle-East/Hamas-Fatah-set-to-reconcile-by-2010.

Alami, Musa. "Lessons from Palestine." *Middle East Journal* 3.4 (October 1949): 373–405.

Al-Badry, Noha. "Hamas Committed to Cairo for Reconciliation Talks." Ahram Online, December 20, 2012. http://english.ahram.org.eg/NewsContent/2/8/60981/World/Region/Hamas-committed-to-Cairo-for-reconciliation-talks.aspx.

Al-Ayyam newspaper. October 22, 2000; November 2, 2000; April 22, 2002.

Alfredson, Tanya, and Azeta Cungu. "Negotiation Theory and Practice: A Review of the Literature." In *Rome, Italy: Food and Agriculture Organization of the*

United Nations, 2008. http://www.fao.org/docs/up/easypol/555/4-5_negotiation_background_paper_179en. pdf

Al-Hayat newspaper. May 11, 2006.

Al-Hayat Al-Jadeeda newspaper. October 2, 29, 2000; November 8, 13, 2000; March 30, 2001; September 18, 2003.

Allen, Lori. "Getting by the Occupation: How Violence Became Normal during the Second Palestinian Intifada." *Cultural Anthropology* 23.3 (2008): 453–487.

Al-Mughrabi, Nidal. "Abbas Declares State of Emergency." Reuters, June 14, 2007. https://uk.reuters.com/article/uk-palestinians/abbas-declares-state-of-emergency-idUKMAC32084020070614?src=061407_1507_TOPSTORY_crisis_in_gaza.

Alon, Ilai, and Jeanne M. Brett. "Perceptions of Time and Their Impact on Negotiations in the Arabic-Speaking Islamic World." *Negotiation Journal* 23.1 (2007): 55–73.

Al-Quds. October 1, 2000; November 10, 2000; February 12, 2001; January 7, 2002; April 23, 2002; May 2, 2002; May 16, 2003.

Al-Ukaz. June 16, 2007.

Al-Watan (Saudi). September 1, 2007.

Amended Palestinian National Charter (1968). English: http://ecf.org.il/media_items/677.

Arad, Uzi. "The Process of Arrangements from Oslo to the Present: A Historical View and a Strategic Perspective." In *Negotiations with the Palestinians: Deadlock or a Window of Opportunity?* Ramat-Gan: Begin-Sadat Center for Research, Bar-Ilan University, 2014.

Aristotle. *Nicomachean Ethics*, book II. http://classics.mit.edu/Aristotle/nicomachaen.2.ii.html.

Asharq al-Awsat. August 18, 2005.

Associated Press. "UN Chief: Hamas Rockets Attacks are Appalling and Unacceptable." *Haaretz*, January 20, 2009. https://www.haaretz.com/1.5065287.

Axelrod, Robert. *The Evolution of Cooperation*. New York: Basic Books, 1984.

Baroud, Ramzi. "The Mecca Agreement between Hamas and Fatah: What Should We Expect?" *Global Research*, February 17, 2007.

Bar-Tal, Daniel, and Dikla Antebi. "Beliefs about Negative Intentions of the World: A Study of the Israeli Siege Mentality." *Political Psychology* (1992): 633–645.

Bar-Tal, Daniel, Lily Chernyak-Hai, Noa Schori, and Ayelet Gundar. "A Sense of Self-Perceived Collective Victimhood in Intractable Conflicts." *International Review of the Red Cross* 91.874 (2009): 229–258.

Baumgarten, Helga. "The Three Faces/Phases of Palestinian Nationalism, 1948–2005." *Journal of Palestine Studies* 34.4 (2005): 25–48.

Blaydes, Lisa, and James Lo. "One Man, One Vote, One Time? A Model of Democratization in the Middle East." *Journal of Theoretical Politics* 24.1 (2012): 110–146.

Blum, Gabriella. "The Fog of Victory." *European Journal of International Law* 24.1 (2013): 391–421.

Bourdieu, Pierre. "The Attitude of the Algerian Peasant toward Time." In *Mediterranean Countrymen: Essays in the Social Anthropology of the Mediterranean*, edited by Julian Pitt-Rivers, 55–72. Paris: Mouton, 1963.

Bronner, Ethan. "Hamas Shifts from Rockets to Culture War." *New York Times*, July 23, 2009. https://www.nytimes.com/2009/07/24/world/middleeast/24gaza.html.

Buhbut, Amir, and Uri Binder. "Gaza: IDF Force Acts to Blast 'Ticking Tunnel.' " NRG, November 4, 2008. https://www.makorrishon.co.il/nrg/online/1/ART1/807/233.html.

Burns, John. *Leadership*. New York: Harper and Row, 1978.

Byman, Daniel. "The Decision to Begin Talks with Terrorists: Lessons for Policymakers." *Studies in Conflict and Terrorism* 29.5 (2006): 403–414.

Chorev, Harel, and Yvette Shumacher. "The Road to Operation Protective Edge: Gaps in Strategic Perception." *Israel Journal of Foreign Affairs* 8.3 (2014): 9–24.

Churchill, Winston. "An Address to the House of Commons" (13 May 1940). In *Blood, Toil, Tears and Sweat: The Speeches*, edited by David Cannadine. London: Penguin, 1989.

Dekel, Udi. "Operation Protective Edge: Strategic and Tactical Asymmetry." In *The Lessons of Operation Protective Edge*, edited by Anat Kurz and Shlomo Brom, 13–20. Tel Aviv: INSS, 2014.

Dekel, Udi, and Emma Petrack. "The Israeli-Palestinian Political Process: A Return to the Process Approach." *Strategic Assessment* 19.4 (2017): 29–42.

Deutsch, Morton. "Trust and Suspicion." *Journal of Conflict Resolution* 2.4 (1958): 265–279.

Dunya al-Watan. March 23, 2007. https://www.alwatanvoice.com/arabic/index.html.

El-Khoday, Taghreed, and Isabel Kershner. "Palestinian Interior Minister Resigns Monday, Unable to Control Factions." The Tech, May 15, 2007. https://thetech.com/2007/05/15/long5-v127-n26.

Erekat, Saeb. "Imam Ali Bin Abi Taleb and Negotiation." *Journal of Peace Research* (2015): 1–160.

Erlich, Reese. "One Man, One Vote, One Time." Common Dreams Organization, February 14, 2011. www.commondreams.org/views/2011/02/14/one-man-one-vote-one-time.

Esposito, Michele K. "16 May–15 August 2008." *Journal of Palestine Studies* 38.1 (Autumn 2008): 190–210.

Esposito, Michele K. "16 November 2006–15 February 2007." *Journal of Palestine Studies* 36.3 (Spring 2007): 132–160.

Esposito, Michele K. "Quarterly Update on Conflict and Diplomacy: 16 May 2007–15 August 2007." *Journal of Palestine Studies* 37.1 (Autumn 2007): 142–171.

Esposito, Michele K. "Update on Conflict and Diplomacy Source." *Journal of Palestine Studies* 41.3 (Spring 2012): 169–204.

Esposito, Michele K. "Update on Conflict and Diplomacy Source." *Journal of Palestine Studies* 41.2 (Winter 2012): 153–189.

Etzioni, Amitai. "Minorities and the National Ethos." *Politics* 229 (2009): 100–110.

"Excavations of the Israel Antiquities Authority." February 6, 2007. http://www.antiquities.org.il/Article_heb.aspx?sec_id=25&subj_id=240&id=1181&hist=1.

Fields, Karen E. "The Elementary Forms of Religious Life," 1995. https://www.academia.edu/14655183/The_Elementary_Forms_of_Religious_Life.

Filiu, Jean-Pierre. *Gaza: A History*. Oxford: Oxford University Press, 2014.

Fisher, Roger, Elizabeth Kopelman, and Andrea Kupfer Schneider. *Beyond Machiavelli: Tools for Coping with Conflict*. New York: Penguin, 1996.

Fisher, Roger, William L. Ury, and Bruce Patton. *Getting to Yes: Negotiating Agreement without Giving In*. New York: Penguin, 2011.

Franks, Tommy. "The Meaning of Victory: A Conversation with General Franks." *National Interest* 86 (2006): 8–11.

Friedman, Lara. "New Palestinian PM Rami Hamdallah: Resources/Background." Peace Now, June 5, 2013, http://archive.peacenow.org/entries/new_palestinian_pm_rami_hamdallah_resources_background.

Galinsky, Adam D., Michael Schaerer, and Joe C. Magee. "The Four Horsemen of Power at the Bargaining Table." *Journal of Business and Industrial Marketing* (2017): 606–611.

Gelber, Yoav. "The Project That Lost Its Train: Gaza Exit after the 1967 War." Dunya al-Watan, June 2, 2016. https://www.alwatanvoice.com/arabic/index.html.

Ghanim, Honaida. "Poetics of Disaster: Nationalism, Gender, and Social Change among Palestinian Poets in Israel after Nakba." *International Journal of Politics, Culture, and Society* 22.1 (2009): 23–39.

Gleis, Joshua L., and Benedetta Berti. *Hezbollah and Hamas: A Comparative Study*. Baltimore: Johns Hopkins University Press, 2012.

Grois, Arnon, and Roni Shaked. *PA Textbooks: The Reference to Jews, Israel and Peace* (2017). https://www.terrorism-info.org.il/app/uploads/2017/12/H_259_17.pdf.

Hakham, David. "And the Country Is Full of Hamas." Haifa University, 2006.

Hasan, Suheib. "Between 1996 to 2009: A Scene Repeated." Palestine Dialogue Network, July 2005. https://www.paldf.net/forum/showthread.php?t=435398.

Halbwachs, Maurice. *On Collective Memory*. Chicago: University of Chicago Press, 1992.

"Hamas and Fatah Agree to Form Caretaker Government." *Guardian*, April 27, 2011. https://www.theguardian.com/world/2011/apr/27/hamas-fatah-agree-government-deal.

Hammami, Rema, and Salim Tamari. "The Second Uprising: End or New Beginning?" *Journal of Palestine Studies* 30.2 (Winter 2001): 5–25.

Hitman, Gadi. "The West and the Middle East: Liberal Nationalism, Instrumental Nationalism." *Cultural and Religious Studies* 4.3 (2016): 161–174.

Human Rights Watch. *Internal Fight: Palestinian Abuses in Gaza and the West Bank*. July 29, 2008, https://www.hrw.org/report/2008/07/29/internal-fight/palestinian-abuses-gaza-and-west-bank.

Ibahis, Hasan, and Wael Sa'ad, eds. *The Security Developments in the Palestinian Authority, 2006–2007*. Beirut: Zaytoona Centre for Research, 2008.

Iklé, Fred Charles, and Nathan Leites. "Political Negotiation as a Process of Modifying Utilities." *Journal of Conflict Resolution* 6.1 (1962): 19–28.

Issachroff, Avi, and Amos Harel. "Fatah to Israel: Let Us Get Arms to Fight Hamas." *Haaretz*, June 7, 2007. https://www.haaretz.com/1.4824399.

Jacoby, Tami A. "A Theory of Victimhood: Politics, Conflict and the Construction of Victim-Based Identity." *Millennium* 43.2 (2015): 511–530.

Jasini, Alba, Ellen Delvaux, and Batja Mesquita. "Collective Victimhood and Ingroup Identity Jointly Shape Intergroup Relations, Even in a Non-violent Conflict: The Case of the Belgians." *Psychologica Belgica* 57.3 (2017): 98–114.

Jum'ah, Salaah. "Hamas Rejects Proposal Their Gunmen Join PA Forces in Gaza." *IMRA*, June 29, 2009. https://www.imra.org.il/story.php?id=44163.

Kanfani, Nu'man. "As If There Is No Occupation." *Middle East Report Online* (2011). https://merip.org/2011/09/as-if-there-is-no-occupation/.

Khalidi, Rashid I. "Observations on the Right of Return." *Journal of Palestine Studies* 21.2 (1992): 29–40.

Khoury, Elias. "Rethinking the Nakba." *Critical Inquiry* 38.2 (2012): 250–266.

Khuri, Fuad I. "The Etiquette of Bargaining in the Middle East 1." *American Anthropologist* 70.4 (1968): 698–706.

Kilduff, Martin, and Daniel J. Brass. "Organizational Social Network Research: Core Ideas and Key Debates." *Academy of Management Annals* 4.1 (2010): 317–357.

Knell, Yolande. "Hamas Says It Is Ready to Hold First Elections since 2006." BBC, September 17, 2017. https://www.bbc.com/news/world-middle-east-41297016.

Lauer, Robert H. *Temporal Man: The Meaning and Uses of Social Time*. New York: Praeger, 1981.

Leech, Phillip, "Re-reading the Myth of Fayyadism: A Critical Analysis of the Palestinian Authority's Reform and State Building Agenda, 2008–2011."

Research Paper (2012). https://www.dohainstitute.org/en/lists/ACRPS-PDF-DocumentLibrary/Rereading_the_Myth.pdf (dohainstitute.org).

Levi, Elior, and Ro'i Kais. "A Historic Agreement: Hamas and Fatah Signed Reconciliation." Ynetnews, October 12, 2017. https://www.ynet.co.il/articles/0,7340,L-5027566,00.html.

Levinson, Chaim, and Nir Hasson. "Six Jews Were Arrested on Suspicion of Murdering Palestinian Youth Muhammad Abu Khdeir." *Haaretz*, July 6, 2014. https://www.haaretz.co.il/news/politics/1.2368211.

Lewin, Eyal. "The Importance of National Ethos in Military Victories." *Social Sciences* 5.3 (2016): 45, 1–16.

Lieber, Dov. "Abbas Said to Cut Salaries of 37 Hamas Lawmakers. *Times of Israel*, July 9, 2017. https://www.timesofisrael.com/abbas-said-to-cut-salaries-of-37-hamas-lawmakers/.

Lieutenant Colonel M. "Operation Inferno—Battle of Jordan's East Bank, March 1968." *Ma'arachot* 293 (March 1984): 18–32.

Maannews.com Archive. 2007–2017.

Mackinnon, Mark. "Abbas's Choice for New PM Angers Hamas." *Globe and Mail*, June 16, 2007. https://www.theglobeandmail.com/news/world/abbass-choice-for-new-pm-angers-hamas/article1087105/.

Malki, Riad. "The Palestinian Elections: Beyond Hamas and Fatah." *Journal of Democracy* 17.3 (July 2006): 131–137.

Maniou, Theodora A., Irene Photiou, and Elena Ketteni. "Mediating Patriotism and Triumph through the National Press: Newspaper Content and Journalistic Perceptions." *International Journal of Social Science Studies* 4 (2016): 65–75.

Masalha, Nur. "Remembering the Palestinian Nakba: Commemoration, Oral History and Narratives of Memory." *Holy Land Studies* 7.2 (2008): 123–156.

"Masha'al Calls the Palestinians for a Third Intifada against the Occupation." Al Jazeera, December 27, 2008. https://www.aljazeera.net/news/arabic/2008/12/27/.

Mecca accord. February 2007. https://web.archive.org/web/20080212122709/http://www.jmcc.org/documents/meccaagree.htm.

Merriam-Webster Dictionary. Springfield, MA: Merriam-Webster, 1994.

Michael, Kobi, and Omer Dostri. "The Process of Political Establishment of Sub-state Actors: Hamas' Conduct between Sovereignty and the Continuation of Violence." *Journal of Interdisciplinary Middle Eastern Studies* 3 (2018): 1–34.

Miftah. *Consequence of the Split on the National and Social Interest*. http://www.miftah.org/Publications/Books/Factsheet_The_Impact_of_the_Political_Division_on_National_and_Social_Reconciliation_2019.pdf.

Military Communique. "Official Hamas Statement on Clash with PA in Qalqilya." May 31, 2009. from: http://www.alqassam.ps/english/?action=showsta&sid=1324.

Military Wing of Hamas website, 2010–2017. https://he.alqassam.ps/.

Miller, Elhanan. "Historic PA Visit to Gaza Failed after Hamas Confined Ministers." *Times of Israel*, April 22, 2015. https://www.timesofisrael.com/historic-visit-to-gaza-fails-after-hamas-confines-ministers-to-hotel/.

Mintzberg, Henry. "Patterns in Strategy Formation." *Management Science* 24.9 (1978): 934–948.

Moghadam, Assaf. "Palestinian Suicide Terrorism in the Second Intifada: Motivations and Organizational Aspects." *Studies in Conflict and Terrorism* 26.2 (2003): 65–92.

Morrow, Adam, and Khaled al-Omrani. "Palestinian unity talks failing." *Electronic Intifada*, March 19, 2009. https://electronicintifada.net/content/palestinian-unity-talks-failing/8144.

Nasr, Islam. "Political Detention Is a Crime." September 2005. https://www.paldf.net/forum/showthread.php?t=300624.

National Palestinian Covenant, July 1968. Al Jazeera. https://www.aljazeera.net/specialfiles/pages/25de66cd-075b-4c8e-9bc3-ddf5ef253676.

"New Hamas Puts Terror on Hold for Shot at Polls." *Daily Telegraph*, January 15, 2006.

Noor, Masi, Johanna Ray Vollhardt, Silvia Mari, and Arie Nadler. "The Social Psychology of Collective Victimhood." *European Journal of Social Psychology* 47.2 (2017): 121–134.

Nüsse, Andrea. *Muslim Palestine: The Ideology of Hamas*. Abingdon: Routledge, 2012.

Office for the Coordination of Humanitarian Affairs (OCHA). Archives from September 2008 to the present. https://www.ochaopt.org.

Office for the Coordination of Humanitarian Affairs (OCHA). Protection of Civilians Weekly Report, 18–24 June 2008. https://www.ochaopt.org/content/protection-civilians-weekly-report-18-24-june-2008.

O'Hara, Kieron. "A General Definition of Trust." Working paper, University of Southampton, Southampton, Great Britain, 2012.

Palestine Centre for Policy and Survey Research. March 13–15, 2008. https://www.pcpsr.org/en/node/226.

Palestine Documents for the Year 2007. Zaytoona Centre for Research, Beirut, 2009.

Palestinian Centre for Human Rights. Archive 2007–2018.

"Palestinian PM Fayyad Steps Down." BBC, March 7, 2009. http://news.bbc.co.uk/2/hi/middle_east/7929927.stm.

Paq, Anne. "Mr. Bush's Trip to Ramallah." *Electronic Intifada*, January 16, 2008. https://electronicintifada.net/content/mr-bushs-trip-ramallah/7304.

Podeh, Elie. *Chances for Peace: Missed Opportunities in the Arab-Israeli Conflict*. Austin: University of Texas Press, 2015.

Pressman, Jeremy. "The Second Intifada: Background and Causes of the Israeli-Palestinian Conflict." *Journal of Conflict Studies* 23.2 (2003): 114–139.

"Preventive Security Apparatus Abuses the Leaders of Hamas and Exposes Them to Ghosts during the Investigation." Palestinian Centre for Information. https://web.archive.org/web/20150619175541/https://www.palinfo.com/site/pic/newsdetails.aspx?ItemId=8766.

"Proposal for Creating Suitable Conditions for Ending the Conflict." *Palestine-Israel Journal.* https://pij.org/articles/988/proposal-for-creating-suitable-conditions-for-ending-the-conflict.

Rabbani, Mouin. "A Hamas Perspective on the Movement's Evolving Role: An Interview with Khalid Mishal: Part II." *Journal of Palestine Studies* 37.4 (Summer 2008): 59–81.

Rashid, Hamid. "What Is the PLO?" *Journal of Palestine Studies* 4.4 (1975): 90–109.

Rieker, Pernille, and Ole Jacob Sending, eds. *Inter-cultural Dialogue in International Crisis.* Oslo: Norwegian Institute of International Affairs, 2012.

Rivera, Lauren A. "Ivies, Extracurriculars, and Exclusion: Elite Employers' Use of Educational Credentials." *Research in Social Stratification and Mobility* 29.1 (2011): 71–90.

Robinson, Glenn E. "Hamas as Social Movement." In *Islamic Activism: a Social Movement Theory Approach*, edited by Quintan Wiktorowicz, Charles Tilly, and Mark A. Tessler, 112–139. Bloomington: Indiana University Press, 2004.

Rosenberg, Rochelle L. "Why Camp David II Failed: A Negotiation Theory Perspective." *Harvard Negotiation Law Review* (2012): 1–13.

Ross, Dennis. "The Middle East Predicament." *Foreign Affairs* (2005): 61–74.

Roy, Sara. *Hamas and Civil Society in Gaza: Engaging the Islamist Social Sector.* Vol. 50. Princeton: Princeton University Press, 2013.

Rudoren, Jodi. "Abbas and Hamas Leader Meet at Egypt's Invitation." *New York Times*, January 9, 2013. https://www.nytimes.com/2013/01/10/world/middleeast/abbas-and-hamas-leader-meet-at-egypts-invitation.html.

Rudoren, Jodi, and Isabel Kershner. "With Hope for Unity, Abbas Swears In a New Palestinian Government." *New York Times*, June 2, 2014. https://www.nytimes.com/2014/06/03/world/middleeast/abbas-swears-in-a-new-palestinian-government.html.

Sa'adeh, Elias. "How 1,500 Teachers, Palestinian Teachers Were Dismissed after the Hamas-Fatah Split." Arab Reporters for Investigative Journalism, May 14, 2013.

Safi, Ahmad S. *Assessment of the Environmental Impact of the War on Gaza Using a Participatory Method* (Arabic). Ramallah: Development Work Centre, 2015. http://www.pengon.org/uploads/articles/3.pdf.

Sahdra, Baljinder, and Michael Ross. "Group Identification and Historical Memory." *Personality and Social Psychology Bulletin* 33.3 (2007): 384–395.

Sawafta, Ali. "Palestinian Rivals Agree to Form Unity Government." Reuters, February 6, 2012. https://www.reuters.com/article/us-palestinians-government/palestinian-rivals-agree-to-form-unity-government-idUSTRE8150KU20120206.

Sayigh, Yezid. "Reconstructing the Paradox: The Arab Nationalist Movement, Armed Struggle, and Palestine, 1951–1966." *Middle East Journal* 45.4 (1991): 608–629.

Schachet, Carol. "Gaza Drowns in Blood because of the Conflict between Fatah and Hamas Movements." Grassroots International, June 14, 2007. https://grassrootsonline.org/blog/newsbloggaza-drowns-blood-because-conflict-between-fatah-and-hamas-movements/.

Schori-Eyal, Noa, Yechiel Klar, and Yarden Ben-Ami. "Perpetual Ingroup Victimhood as a Distorted Lens: Effects on Attribution and Categorization." *European Journal of Social Psychology* 47.2 (2017): 180–194.

Sebenius, James K. "BATNAs in Negotiation: Common Errors and Three Kinds of 'No.'" *Negotiation Journal* 33.2 (2017): 89–99.

Segev, Tom. "The June 1967 War and the Palestinian Refugee Problem." *Journal of Palestine Studies* 36.3 (2007): 6–22.

Sha'aban, Salah al-Din. "Abu Mazen Met Khaled Masha'al after They Both Met Egyptian President." *Asharq al-Awsat*, January 10, 2013. https://archive.aawsat.com/details.asp?section=4&issueno=12462&article=712511&feature=#.XnkOu6gzZPY.

Shaked, Roni. "Religious War in Gaza." Ynetnews. https://www.ynetnews.com/articles/0,7340,L-3360655,00.html.

Shamir, Eitan, and Edo Hecht. "Gaza 2014: Israel's Attrition vs. Hamas' Exhaustion." *Parameters* 44.4 (2014): 81–90.

Sharabi, Hisham. Palestine and Israel: The Lethal Dilemma. New York: Pegasus, 1969.

"The Sharem Summit Is Closed: Sharon and Abu Mazen Announce the Cessation of Violence." *Globes*, February 8, 2005.

Shilling, Chris, and Philip A. Mellor. "Durkheim, Morality and Modernity: Collective Effervescence, Homo Duplex and the Sources of Moral Action." *British Journal of Sociology* (1998): 193–209.

Shin, Jihae, and Katherine L. Milkman. "How Backup Plans Can Harm Goal Pursuit: The Unexpected Downside of Being Prepared for Failure." *Organizational Behavior and Human Decision Processes* 135 (2016): 1–9.

Silverstein, Richard. "Meshal Accepts Israel as 'Reality' and 'Matter of Fact,' Concedes Right of Palestinian State to Recognize It." *Tikun Olam* (blog), January 11, 2007. https://www.richardsilverstein.com/2007/01/11/meshal-accepts-israel-as-reality-and-matter-of-fact-concedes-right-of-palestinian-state-to-recognize-it/.

Simanovsky, Natalia. "The Fayyad Plan: Implications for the State of Israel." *Palestine-Israel Journal* 17.12 (2012). http://www.pij.org/details.php?id=1317.

Staub, Ervin, and Daniel Bar-Tal. "Genocide, Mass Killing and Intractable Conflict: Roots, Evolution, Prevention and Reconciliation." In *Oxford Handbook of Political Psychology*, edited by D. O. Sears, L. Huddy, and R. Jervis, 714–731. New York: Oxford University Press, 2003.

Stepp, John R., Kevin M. Sweeney, and Robert L. Johnson. "Interest-Based Negotiation: An Engine-Driving Change." *Journal for Quality and Participation* (1998): 36–43.

Strickland, Patrick. "Will Hamas Give Up Arms for Palestinian Reconciliation?" Al Jazeera, October 9, 2017. https://www.aljazeera.com/indepth/features/2017/10/hamas-give-arms-palestinian-reconciliation-171008123019895.html.

Sudam, Mohamed. "Fatah and Hamas Sign Reconciliation Deal." Reuters, March 23, 2008. https://uk.reuters.com/article/uk-palestinians-yemen-deal/fatah-and-hamas-sign-reconciliation-deal-idUKL23831120080323.

"Teen Killed in Mass Hamas Rally Near Rafah." *Jerusalem Post*, July 31, 2007. https://www.jpost.com/Middle-East/Teen-killed-in-mass-pro-Hamas-rally-near-Rafah.

Terrorist Suicide Bombers during the Israeli-Palestinian Conflict (September 2000–December 2005), Intelligence and Terrorism Information Centre, January 2006. https://www.mfa.gov.il/mfa/foreignpolicy/terrorism/palestinian/pages/victims%20of%20palestinian%20violence%20and%20terrorism%20sinc.aspx.

"Text of the Official Agreement between Fatah and Hamas on May 20, 2012." WAFA News Agency. http://info.wafa.ps/ar_page.aspx?id=8715.

TOI staff. "Hamas and Fatah Agree to Unity Government in Historic Deal." *Times of Israel*, April 23, 2014. https://www.timesofisrael.com/hamas-and-fatah-agree-to-form-unity-government-in-historic-deal/.

TOI staff. "Mashaal Calls for Guerilla Warfare to 'Liberate West Bank' and 'All Palestine.'" *Times of Israel*, December 15, 2018. https://www.timesofisrael.com/mashaal-calls-for-guerrilla-warfare-to-liberate-west-bank-and-all-palestine/.

Turki, Fawaz. "To Be a Palestinian." *Journal of Palestine Studies* 3.3 (1974): 3–17.

United Nations, Division for Palestinian Rights. Chronological Review of Events Relating to the Question of Palestine, December 2006. https://www.un.org/unispal/document/auto-insert-195339/.

United Nations, Division for Palestinian Rights. Chronological Review of Events Relating to the Question of Palestine." Monthly media monitoring review, July 2007. https://unispal.un.org/DPA/DPR/unispal.nsf/0/9F83B1413FFAF52E8525737600688B9B.

United Nations Human Rights Council. *Report of the United Nations High Commissioner for Human Rights on the Implementation of Human Rights Council Resolutions S-9/1 and S-12/1*. March 6, 2013. https://www.ohchr.org/Documents/HRBodies/HRCouncil/RegularSession/Session22/A.HRC.22.35.Add.1_AV.pdf.

von Neumann, John. "A Certain Zero-Sum Two-Person Game Equivalent to the Optimal Assignment Problem." *Contributions to the Theory of Games* 2.0 (1953): 5–12.

Waked, Ali. "PA: Hamas West Bank Terror Plot Exposed." Ynetnews, June 9, 2009. https://www.ynetnews.com/articles/0,7340,L-3728366,00.html.

Westervelt, Eric. "Hamas-Fatah Rift Deepens, Threatens Peace Efforts." NPR, December 18, 2008. https://www.npr.org/templates/story/story.php?storyId=98449470.

Wishakh, Ghassan, and Mohammad Al-Qudra. *Al-Tahwalat al-Mawdayya fi al-Qad'ia ba'ad Oslo* (2016) (Substantive Transformation in the Palestinian Question). Palestinian Information Center. https://www.palinfo.com/Uploads/Models/Media/book/2017/war/war.pdf.

Yaffe, Aharon. "The Arabs in the West Bank and Gaza Strip: Ten Years of Terror." *Nativ* 119 (November 2007): 32–36.

"Yemen Initiative to Resume the Dialogue and End the Palestinian Separation." WAFA News Agency, August 5, 2007. http://www.wafainfo.ps/ar_page.aspx?id=4920.

Zaboun, Kifah. "Abu Mazen Announces the Start of Consultations to Form a Consensus Government . . . and Hamas: We Do Not Manage the Remote Control." *Asharq al-Awsat*, April 27, 2013. https://archive.aawsat.com/details.asp?section=4&issueno=12570&article=726405#.XqWBeWgzZPY.

Zaboun, Kifah. "Fatah, Hamas Leaders to Discuss Unresolved Issues in Cairo." *Asharq al-Awsat*, October 4, 2017. https://english.aawsat.com//home/article/1042106/fatah-hamas-leaders-discuss-unresolved-issues-cairo.

Zaboun, Kifah. "A Source for *Asharq al-Awsat*: Abu Mazen Will Not Attend an Arab Summit Attended by Hamas." *Asharq al-Awsat*, March 30, 2013. https://archive.aawsat.com/details.asp?section=4&issueno=12541&article=722755#.XqV4XGgzZPY.

Zanotti, Jim. *Israel and Hamas: Conflict in Gaza (2008–2009)*. Darby, PA: Diane, 2010.

Zuebi, May. "Three Power Government." Al Jazeera, July 10, 2007. https://www.aljazeera.net/specialfiles/pages/89b5fa41-7567-4d64-82b3-84a346b40944.

Zuhur, Sherifa. "Gaza, Israel, Hamas and the Lost Calm of Operation Cast Lead." *Middle East Policy* 16.1 (2009): 40–50.

Zweiri, Mahjoob. "The Hamas Victory: Shifting Sands or Major Earthquake." *Third World Quarterly* 27.4 (May 2006): 675–687.

Index

www.ingramcontent.com/pod-product-compliance
Lightning Source LLC
LaVergne TN
LVHW040157080826
844660LV00001B/14

* 9 7 8 1 4 3 8 4 8 7 0 3 8 *